Psychological Approaches to Child Abuse

Edited by Neil Frude

ROWMAN AND LITTLEFIELD
TOTOWA, NEW JERSEY

© Neil Frude 1981
First published in the United States of America, 1981, by
Rowman and Littlefield, 81 Adams Drive, Totowa, New Jersey 07512.

Library of Congress Cataloging in Publication Data

Main entry under title:
Psychological approaches to child abuse.

    1. Child abuse—Psychological aspects—Addresses,
essays, lectures.   2. Child abuse—Prevention—
Addresses, essays, lectures.   I. Frude, Neil.
HV715.P79   362.7′044   80 – 21371

ISBN 0 – 8476 – 6925 – 4

Printed in Great Britain

CONTENTS

Authors

Neil Frude, Lecturer in Clinical Psychology, University College, Cardiff.

Mary Main, Professor of Psychology, University of California, Berkeley, California.

Hilary Graham, Lecturer in Health Policy, Department of Applied Social Studies, University of Bradford.

Alison Goss, Research worker, Department of Psychology, University College, Cardiff.

John and Elizabeth Newson, Directors, Child Development Research Unit, University of Nottingham.

Kevin Browne, Research Officer, Department of Human Biology and Health, University of Surrey.

Robert Parr, Research worker, Bradford College.

Clare Hyman, Senior Lecturer, Department of Human Biology and Health, University of Surrey.

Theodore Gaensbauer, David Mrazek, and *Robert Harmon*, M.D. Department of Psychiatry, University of Colorado Medical Center, Denver, Colorado.

Carolyn Okell Jones, Lecturer, Post-experience Courses Unit, The Open University.

Arnon Bentovim, Consultant Psychiatrist, Department of Psychological Medicine, The Hospital for Sick Children, Great Ormond Street, London.

Judy Hutchings, Senior Clinical Psychologist, Child Department, Llanfairfechan Psychiatric Hospital, Wales.

William Reavley, Principal Clinical Psychologist, Graylingwell Hospital, Chichester.

Gary Griffiths, Social worker, West Sussex County Council.

Mia Kellmer Pringle, Director, National Children's Bureau, London.

Introduction

1 A psychological perspective on child abuse

Neil Frude

Although there is a long history of concern about cruelty to children and physical injury inflicted by parents (Radbill, 1969, has provided an interesting historical account), the present high level of concern may be traced to the 1940s, when Caffey (1946) and Silverman (1953) reported X-ray evidence of a number of apparently similar cases of repeated skeletal lesion. These were often associated also with subdural haematoma, so that there appeared to be a 'syndrome', and it soon became clear that this syndrome was associated with trauma and with parental attacks upon the child.

In 1962 Kempe and his colleagues published a paper in the Journal of the American Medical Association entitled 'The Battered Child Syndrome' (Kempe et al., 1962) which included paediatric, psychiatric and radiological evidence and which also considered relevant aspects of the law. In presenting this as a comprehensive description of the syndrome an important transformation had taken place. What had originally been a series of observations of patterns of physical symptoms had now broken the 'tissue barrier' and included psychological and sociological factors too.

There followed an explosion of interest in the syndrome by paediatricians and psychiatrists and, a little later, by social workers, sociologists and psychologists, and the result has been wide-ranging developments in treatment, policy and education. These most welcome attentions to the physical cruelty inflicted by some parents upon their children have been very productive and there is now a noticeable spread of concern to other forms of mistreatment, some of them less dramatic but more widespread and of great importance to those involved in the well-being, care and development of children. Thus new attention is being given to sexual abuse, 'psychological abuse', physical discipline and more general parental mishandling. Questions arise as to how similar or different these are to injurious assault, both in their antecedents and in their longer-term effects on the child. If there is a definite 'syndrome' then it should follow that a rather circumspect analysis is possible. If, on the other hand, injurious attacks are in fact just an extreme of disciplining, parental mishandling or an impaired parent-child relationship then we might be led to call into question the syndrome quality of 'the battered child syndrome'.

Observation and research often leads in medicine to the identification of syndromes and 'disease entities' and this, in turn, sometimes leads to the discovery of a single pathogen responsible for all cases. On the other hand, it sometimes becomes apparent that a formerly recognized syndrome is not real and that continued use of that unitary concept would obscure a clear view of the phenomena to be explained. Thus diseases occasionally disappear from the medical dictionary. Nosology, the classification of diseases, is more volatile in psychiatry than in other branches of medicine, and syndrome identification in the social sciences has not generally been successful or useful. Attempts to consider 'criminal behaviour', for example, or 'marital disharmony' as disease-like entities in terms of their antecedents or effects have often led to totally inadequate formulations.

The uselessness of the syndrome approach depends on the uniformity of the phenomenon and on the tightness in the clustering of different elements. The assumption of the syndrome identity does, however, critically affect the premises of research, the type of explanation attempted and the approach to treatment and change. Because of its special intermediate status with regard to medicine and social science there is cause, then, to examine carefully the characterization of child abuse as a syndrome. Whether or not there is a cluster of physical and psychological factors associated with child abuse is an empirical question, and a question which may be answered with reference to the enormous amount of research which has been generated in recent years and which has been well reviewed elsewhere (Parke & Collmer, 1975; see also the extensive annotated bibliography by Kalisch, 1978).

The evidence for clustering has been disappointing to those who have taken the syndrome position, for it seems that injury deliberately inflicted on children by their parents is of many types, and that the personality of the parents themselves, their social background, the circumstances in which the attack takes place and the age and personality of the child involved all vary prodigiously. Long-bone fractures, subdural haematomas and severe bruising may be common physical symptoms of child abuse but fractured skulls, burns, stab wounds, and the effects of poisoning and attempted drowning are also found and clearly cannot be excluded from the 'diagnosis' of child abuse. It is also generally the case that precisely the same symptoms occur as a result of accidental trauma. With regard to non-physical aspects there seems to be even less uniformity. Sometimes the child has been previously well-cared for, sometimes great deal to tell us about the nature of abuse. Mary Main has shown how the interactive styles in certain non-abusive relationships seem to have much in common with cases in which there actually has been abuse, and the next three chapters all examine aspects of behaviour and reactions in general population samples which parallel factors known to operate in many abusive incidents. The themes are anger and punishment.

Hilary Graham describes mothers' first experiences of parenthood and shows that experiences of anger and aggression are common. The majority of mothers report feelings of anger and these seem to be largely associated, for mothers of very young babies, with the baby's crying and with their own tiredness. Significantly, most of the women felt that their understanding of, and empathy for, mothers who batter their babies had been increased through their own experiences of baby-care.

Neil Frude and Alison Goss survey mothers with children some years older than those in Graham's study and find that, while there is enormous variation in parenting experiences, anger is by no means an unusual reaction or a rare occurrence. Reconstructions of crisis incidents in parenting bring out many of the features, both of the mothers' attitudes and reactions and of the child's behaviour, which appear to be very similar to those encountered in case reports on abuse. Of particular interest are the numerous and varied strategies which mothers report of their own attempts to deal with their anger in a non-destructive way.

John and Elizabeth Newson examine current attitudes and practices in the area of parental discipline. Stressing that corporal punishment needs to be understood as a communication from the parent to the child they describe the use of threats and punishments by parents of seven and 11-year-old children. There are relationships between the use of corporal punishment, cultural and sub-cultural background, and the sex of the child but the overall level of physical discipline is high. Evidence suggests that children's attitudes and behaviour are affected by such actions, and not in the way which parents would wish. Against such a background of culturally tolerated or approved physical discipline, the Newsons suggest, it is hardly surprising that we also have a high incidence of extreme and injurious assault.

One of the most interesting aspects of the extensive abuse literature is the variety of approaches which have been brought to bear on analysis and treatment. As an important social problem child abuse has occupied the attention of sociologists, psychoanalysts, paediatricians and lawyers, to name only a few. Relatively little has so far been written from the perspective of behavioural biology, however, and Kevin Browne and Robert Parr demonstrate in their chapter how an ethological approach may make a contribution. Their careful statements about the likely relevance of animal studies and their critical examination of attachment theory and the experimental and clinical work on 'bonding' suggest that a consideration of the biology of the abusive relationship and the abusive incident will add much to our understanding, and they make useful suggestions about how work on 'normal' mother-child interaction may be employed in the special 'applied' case of abusive relationships.

Clare Hyman provides a 'worked example' of such an approach. In a controlled study of interaction in abuse and non-abuse mother-infant dyads, she was able to isolate a number of features which seemed to characterize relationships in abusing families. Abused children tend to show more distress on reunion with the mother, for example, and less vocalization, and abusing mothers seem anxiously preoccupied with the child and yet respond less to the infant's initiatives. The behaviour patterns of abused children, Hyman notes, seem rather similar to those found in other studies among certain sub-groups of non-abused infants. Considering the likely antecedents of the mothers' behaviour Hyman suggests that biological and personality factors may have so far been under-emphasized. If this is the case then certain implications for treatment and management follow and the prognosis may not be an optimistic one. In other sections of her chapter Hyman presents evidence regarding demographic factors contributing to abuse and the results of psychometric studies examining the intellectual and personality traits of abusing parents.

Theodore Gaensbauer, David Mrazek and Robert Harmon have also been conducting observational studies with abused and neglected infants and their conclusions are again based on comparisons with baseline data obtained from a large sample of non-abused children. Those who have been abused show fewer pleasurable responses during play, they express anger more frequently and they seem less distressed at the mother leaving the room. As in Hyman's study a lack of sensitive interaction and reciprocity is found between mother and child. The authors point to the marked variability in the reactions of the abused children and, on the basis of their behavioural observations, they devise a number of categories within which it seems useful to characterize the individual abused children – they may be 'retarded', 'depressed', 'affectively labile' or 'angry'. Clinical impressions further suggest that such patterns may well be associated with particular styles of maternal behaviour and the authors stress the need for analysis to be focused principally on styles of interaction between mother and child.

The now considerable literature on violence towards children is examined by Neil Frude, using a model of the aggression incident. Most abuse consists of specific acts of aggression, although these may well take place in the context of longer-term mistreatment. By considering how the antecedents, both situational and psychological, may precipitate such actions it may well be possible to increase our understanding of the nature of abuse and then to formulate suggestions for treatment and prevention. Particular emphasis is given to the judgements which parents make of the child's actions and of the lack of inhibitions which might otherwise restrain the adult's behaviour and prevent anger from becoming expressed as injurious aggression. Attention is drawn to the marked variability of cases and to the many alternative options which, in principle, may underlie successful intervention.

Carolyn Okell Jones examines the research evidence concerning the after-effects of abuse on children, drawing attention to the relatively little concern which has so far been given to this and illustrating some of the methodological difficulties which such follow-up studies present. It is not surprising, therefore, that there are wide-ranging estimates of the degree of residual organic and psychological damage. Neurological effects may result from the direct effects of head trauma but it is often difficult to disentangle the effects of such damage from those of wider environmental origin. A major problem in interpreting what is essentially correlational data is that of identifying cause and effect, and some of the behavioural and personality characteristics of abused children could well have pre-dated the injurious attack and have played a part in its provocation. This is a familiar problem and has already been illustrated by the rather different conclusions which Main, Gaensbauer, Mrazek and Harmon and Hyman draw from their data concerning the parent-child interaction styles of abused children and their parents.

Even if the aetiology of some deficits and developmental delays remains problematic there is every reason for their accurate assessment, for they may markedly affect the clinical picture and should play a vital part in decisions regarding the management of the family. The assessment of psychological functioning, in particular, demands great skill and the psychologist must constantly bear in mind, from the abused child's perspective, the social psychological nature of the testing situation. Research evidence relating to larger populations has a good deal to add to our knowledge of the after-effects of abuse, but clinical practice must avoid generalizing to the individual case. Problems are wide-ranging and occur in varying combinations. There is no composite picture of *the* abused child.

Arnon Bentovim considers some of the practical difficulties and considerations involved in dealing with the family in which abuse has taken place. The parents may well be suspicious, defensive and uncooperative and considerable skill and sensitivity is needed in circumventing the problems if the best interests of the family as a whole are to be met. On the one hand the crisis situation and the longer term involvement need to be dealt with with firmness and control while on the other there is the need for sympathetic handling. The often considerable stresses placed on the individual professional and on the team need to be anticipated and worked through. In reviewing a variety of treatment settings and modalities attention is drawn to the range of interventions which may be available and some of the factors affecting the decision-making processes involving the degree of separation between the parents and the abused child are discussed.

The behavioural approach to the treatment and prevention of child abuse is one which a number of psychologists have recently explored and Judy Hutchings examines the techniques which have been employed within this framework. She points out that most of the therapists in this field adopt the position that physical abuse is not different in kind from the more common difficulties in parenting and that teaching parents to handle their children in more effective ways can do much to reduce the incidence of crisis points at which assault is most likely to take place. Treatment may be focused on the acquisition of management skills, particularly those concerned with disciplining, or on desensitizing the parent to particularly annoying aspects of the child's behaviour, but self-help skills may be developed in order to enable the parent to deal with stress and with aggressive impulses. Several such aspects can be introduced into an effective multi-modal programme.

The need for adequate baseline assessment, contracting with the parents, and monitoring of therapeutic progress and outcome is stressed. Many of the behavioural techniques are relatively easy to learn and easy to apply and personnel from a number of disciplines may employ such methods. Behavioural programmes typically deal with a broad range of parent-child problems in such cases and are aimed not just at reducing the risk of physical attack but at providing for the general improvement of relationships within the family.

The theme of training social workers and nurses to use behavioural techniques is taken up in the chapter by William Reavley and Gary Griffiths. The authors describe the training experience of a social worker and provide guidelines for selection, training and monitoring. They provide a case example illustrating aspects of contracting and the implementation of the multimodal approach. Social workers with abusing clients often feel the need for a more formal therapeutic element in their work and Reavley and Griffiths describe a highly

14

practical way in which this can be achieved.

In the chapters by Mia Kellmer Pringle the prediction and prevention of abuse are examined and recommendations are made regarding the ways in which policy and professional practice can reduce the incidence of the problem. A greater vigilance is required and for this to be effectively managed there is need for greater awareness of the problem and its antecedents by those professionals who may come into contact with potentially violent situations, and for greater manpower. The salutary case of Maria Colwell again provides a number of lessons. While it is true that not all cases are alike it is also true that a number of predictive factors have been isolated and check lists of common characteristics of abusive parents and abused children are reproduced from the available research literature.

Preventive measures involve both the management of previously abused or 'high risk' cases and also wider societal changes aimed at reducing the levels of those 'background factors', such as low parenting skill and general attitudes towards the physical treatment of children, which provide a context in which abuse can too easily result. In returning children to parents who have mistreated them extreme caution is required, and if certain rigid criteria are not met then a 'divorce' between parents and children must be considered. Freedom from risk of further injury is not a sufficient condition for return; the parents must be able to provide adequately for the child's overall care and development. The need for comprehensive assessment and developmental checks for children is stressed, and suggestions for the practical implementation of such screening are made. The task of prevention is a multidisciplinary one, involving social, health and educational professionals, but not only should professionals be involved, for all of us have a role to play in working towards a substantial reduction of the mistreatment of children.

Together, these contributions to our understanding of the nature of abuse and suggestions for its remedy add up to a considerable and varied development of evidence and thinking. In particular they suggest a number of changes in policy and demonstrate ways in which the psychologist, as a member of the inter-disciplinary team, can make a greater contribution than is sometimes now realized, to analysis and treatment. Direct involvement with abusive families is only one aspect of the work and the potential for preventive effort is vast. The translation of the theory, the empirical knowledge and the techniques and skills described in this volume into effective practice is a vital challenge which some have already begun to tackle and which others will certainly take up as researchers, educationalists, advisors to policy-makers and clinicians.

Introduction

REFERENCES

Caffey, J. (1946) 'Multiple fractures in the long-bones of children suffering from chronic subdural haematoma'. *American Journal of Roentgenology*, *56*, pp. 163–73.

Goldstein, A.P. (1978) 'Introduction'. In: A.P. Goldstein, (Ed.) *Prescriptions for Child Mental Health and Education*. Pergamon, New York.

Kalisch, B.J. (1978) *Child Abuse and Neglect: An Annotated Bibliography*. Greenwood, Westport, Connecticut.

Kempe, C.H., Silverman, F., Steele, B., Droegmueller, W., and Silver, H. (1962) 'The battered child syndrome'. *Journal of the American Medical Association*, *181*, pp. 17–24.

Kempe, R. and Kempe, C.H. (1978) *Child Abuse*. Fontana/Open Books, London.

Parke, R.D. and Collmer, C.W. (1975) 'Child abuse: an interdisciplinary analysis'. In: E.M. Hetherington (Ed.) *Review of Child Development Research. Vol. V*, University of Chicago Press.

Radbill, S.X. (1968) 'A history of child abuse and infanticide'. In: R.E. Helfer and C.H. Kempe (Eds.) *The Battered Child*, University of Chicago Press.

Silverman, F.N. (1953) 'The roentgen manifestations of unrecognized skeletal trauma in infants'. *American Journal of Roentgenology, Radium Therapy and Nuclear Medicine*, *69*, pp. 413–27.

Parenting Styles and Parent Anger

2 Abusive and rejecting infants

Mary Main

This chapter is based largely on observational studies of infants and toddlers. It has three principal themes. The first is that, even within the first year of life, rejection, aggression and avoidance can become so mutual within an infant-mother dyad that it becomes almost as accurate to say that the infant rejects the mother as that the mother rejects the infant. The second is that infants *tend* to repeat in new relationships the patterns of interaction which they have established in primary relationships. Thus, a mother-rejecting infant is likely to reject new persons who attempt to initiate interaction or caregiving. In addition, abused toddlers observed in daycare centres assault their peers, harass their caregivers, and avoid both in response to friendly overtures.

The third theme, however, provides ground for optimism. Though relationships inevitably affect relationships, so that a rejected infant initially rejects others, infants *can* form very different kinds of relationships with different persons when extensive experience is provided. Thus the same infant who seems rejecting, cold and aggressive towards its mother may nonetheless form a close and affectionate relationship with its father. I shall end by suggesting that therapeutic daycare should be provided for the battered child.

Angry and rejecting behaviour in the first two years of life: Normal samples.

Both parents and researchers suggest that the abused child can be a 'difficult' child —(Friedrich & Boriskin, 1976; Martin, 1976), and according to one brief report some have even become the target of abuse in several different environments (Milowe & Lourie, 1964). If the abused child really is difficult in terms of its behaviour, it would be of considerable interest to understand the cause of this, since difficult behaviour can only enhance the likelihood of further abuse and rejection. At present, however, it is not clear whether the abused child (1) has been 'difficult' – uncuddly, or unresponsive, or given to excessive crying – from the beginning of life, or (2) *becomes* difficult because of events in its early life (neonatal illness, maternal illness, separation from the parents), or (3) *becomes* difficult because of the experience of physical abuse itself. In many cases these factors may act in combination (for a discussion of these factors see Galdston, 1965; Kempe & Kempe, 1978; Lynch, 1976; Morse, Sahler & Friedman, 1970; Parke & Collmer, 1975; Smith & Hanson, 1975).

I shall describe several recently completed studies of 'difficult' behaviour in children in the first two years of life – studies of anger, avoidance, and rejection. These children and their mothers did not experience illness, birth complication, or separation in the neonatal period – nor have I been able to produce evidence that, as newborns, they were difficult. Neither were they battered. Yet the children in these entirely normal samples showed a behavioural syndrome which, as I shall show in a later section, appears also in battered infants. Thus the study of their history is relevant.

In this section I shall show the broad range of individual differences in angry and rejecting behaviour among normal infants, the correlations in maternal behaviour, and the relationships between what might be called a dyadic (infant-mother) syndrome of anger, avoidance and rejection and the infant's response to persons *other* than the mother in the second year of life. The infants studied in these samples were medically normal infants of white middle-class parents who had obtained an average of two years college education. Parents were contacted from birth records, or with the cooperation of pediatricians or daycare centres. The studies involved only intact families (both parents living at home). In each (except the daycare) study infants were excluded if the mother worked full-time. About 80% of parents contacted agreed to participate.

The development of angry behaviour in the first year of life.

In a study of the development of infant-mother attachment in the first year of life, Ainsworth and her colleagues made a series of home visits (about four hours per visit, about every three weeks) to 26 infant-mother pairs in Baltimore, Maryland. During these visits observers made notes on infant and maternal behaviour, stressing social (especially attachment) behaviours. Following the visit, these notes were dictated and transcribed (see Ainsworth, Blehar, Waters & Wall, 1978, for a summery of some of the data analyses).

For her honours thesis conducted at the University of California at Berkeley, Sharon Slaton (assisted by several student coders) conducted an extensive analysis of infant anger and 'angry behaviour' as recorded in the Ainsworth narratives. An episode was identified as involving anger if any of a large variety of 'anger words' (e.g., 'angry', 'enraged', 'cross', 'slaps', 'scowls') was used in its description. Only delimitable occurrences (i.e., 'he slapped her', but not, 'he often slaps her') were coded – for these, the stimulus or objective could also be identified in most cases (Main, Slaton & Ainsworth, 1979). In addition, an examination of all episodes led to a reliable ranking of infants for 'the extent to which anger appears to direct the infant's mood and activities' between nine and 12 months. So far as we know this is the first study of angry behaviour in infancy based on direct observation.

There were only a few recorded episodes of angry behaviour in the first and second quarters of the first year (three, on average, in each quarter), but by the fourth quarter of the year there were a substantial number of episodes (12, on average) over the ten hours of waking observation. Some stability was established between the third and fourth quarter of the year, and between the third and fourth quarters definite stability for number of episodes was established ($r = .56$). The study of the Ainsworth records points first, however, to the tremendous range of individual difference. Over the year as a whole, each infant was observed for a total of about 40 waking hours. During the year's observation, one infant exhibited not a single episode of angry behaviour – another exhibited 111 episodes. In the ten hours of observation made in the fourth quarter one infant was credited with 65 anger episodes, another with 50, while another exhibited two and another none.

What has this to do with the study of the 'difficult' infant? Although there must be some difference between mothers' experiences of an infant who has six bouts of angry behaviour per hour and an infant who has none, examination of the records suggested that it would be a mistake to equate a simple count of episodes with the extent to which the infant is experienced by the mother as negative or difficult. For many infants bouts of angry behaviour would consist, for example, merely in brief petulant protests at not being served food immediately, angry and seemingly self-addressed ('swearing') noises connected to unsuccessful efforts to climb the stairs, or scowls during tugs-of-war with a sibling. The infant who had 50 episodes during the fourth quarter mostly had episodes of this type. She did not once strike or threaten to strike her mother. But in the case of another infant slapping the mother suddenly and seeming inexplicably constituted six out of eight total episodes.

It seems to me that three aspects of infant anger and angry behaviour are of special interest to the concept of the angry, negative or 'difficult' baby. These are (1) the overall rating for the extent to which anger seems to direct the infant's mood and activities (2) the number of episodes which actually involve striking or threatening to strike the mother, and (3) the percentage of episodes of angry behaviour whose occurence seems inexplicable. In studying each of these aspects we were concerned only with behaviour in the fourth quarter. This is because there was a considerable amount of relevant data for this period and because only at this age could we feel comfortable in regarding the infant's striking the mother as directed or intentional and feel justified in speaking of an episode as 'inexplicable'. In the case of younger babies the stimulus antecedents of an episode might well be merely unascertainable.

Let us begin by considering the four infants who received the highest ratings for the extent to which their mood and activities seemed directed by anger. The rater (Sharon Slaton, 'blind' at that time to all other assessments of these infants) felt that these four belonged together as a group because their anger had a 'raggedy' or anxious quality. Three out of these four babies threw tantrums in which all control appeared to be lost. One rocked back and forth in a mild rage, momentarily giving the observer the impression that this was the only available means of expression of feeling. At other times, however, this infant would slap at his mother, but without apparent effect and with no discernible stimulus ('Now the baby slaps at mother's leg. He is barking in a breathing-like manner for a moment. Now he slaps at mother's legs again'.) Another baby violently fought the mother during feeding, and gave inexplicable 'blood-curdling screams' from the crib. He too sometimes struck at the mother without explanation: 'He goes to mother and slaps at her feet'. The third baby seemed even more openly aggressive in the home situation, sometimes tearing at the mother's dress or (when punished) pounding the chair she generally sat in. This baby also struck the mother suddenly and inexplicably: 'Baby now goes over to mother and starts slapping at her and he laughs'. The fourth baby contrasted with the others in that an immediate stimulus could be found for all his episodes of angry behaviour. Many were due to maternal inter- ference: 'Now baby gets angry with mother and kicks his legs at her. Mother waves her hands at the baby, threatening him . . . Mother yells to the baby, "Don't touch me!".'

All of these babies were clearly attached to their mothers. In the home situation they pursued them, crying in distress when mother merely moved from living room to kitchen. Seen at the end of the year in a laboratory situation involving separation and reunion in an unfamiliar environment, however (the Ainsworth Strange Situation, see Ainsworth et al, 1978), their behaviour was most surprising. This situation commonly arouses attachment behaviour, but these other- wise clearly attached babies exhibited no attachment. It commonly arouses anger, but these otherwise angry babies showed no anger. These four babies, identified as a single group by Slaton on the basis of anxious and deep anger, were also classified together as a single group on the basis of their 'Strange Situation' behaviour. In this environment these otherwise anxiously angry and proximity-seeking babies were uniform in showing only affectless rejection of the mother. In contrast to the other infants seen in this situation, these infants did not cry on being left by their mothers, either when they were left alone or when they were left in the company of a stranger. In contrast to most infants, who seek the mother on reunion and demand to be held, these infants turned away from the mother. If picked up they indicated a wish to be put down, and they actively turned away from and ignored the mother if she further sought their attention. Their avoidance of the mother on reunion was extreme – it seemed to appear as an alternative to distress and anger.

In their attacks on the mother observed in the home situation, and in the cool and affectless rejection of the mother shown in the stress situation, these infants could certainly be described as difficult, unpleasant and even rejecting. But could they be identified as having been difficult from the beginning? A search for early identification of a 'difficult infant' syndrome proved futile. Only one of these four infants had an exceptional number of 'anger' episodes in the first quarter. Records made by Ainsworth and her colleagues showed that these infants as a group cried no more than others during the early months of life (see Ainsworth et al., 1978). Finally, all but one responded to holding by actively sinking in or cuddling into the adult's body within the first two weeks of life – the other seemed passive when held, until the fourth week when he too became cuddly. Thus in the early months they did not cry outstandingly and neither did they seem more angry than other infants or fail to respond positively to holding.

This analysis having failed, we turned to other ratings and records made regarding the mothers, again independently collected. This information showed that the *mothers* of these infants strongly resembled one another. During the first quarter of the first year, *every one* of them displayed a strong aversion to physical contact with the infant – to holding it, touching it, or being touched by it. The rating was based upon observed acts of withdrawal or physical rejection, or upon what the mother said about her feelings about physical contact in general (one mother said it always made her anxious) or about contact with this particular baby. These mothers were also markedly emotionally inexpressive, rigid, and compulsive. When their babies showed angry behaviour during the first half of the first year of life, these mothers, in contrast to most, responded extremely slowly or not at all. Finally, by the end of the year, rejection of the infant was openly expressed. Some wished they had never decided to have a baby. Codings undertaken in another context showed that three out of these four mothers actively rejected bids for physical contact in the fourth quarter, for example by saying 'Don't touch me!'.

The description of this small group of dyads should make clear the strong similarity which can develop between mothers and infants even by the end of the first year of life. The avoidance of the mother which the infant shows in the mildly stressful laboratory situation is shown by mother to infant in the home at the beginning of the year. The angry, avoidant and inexpressive infant is a member of a dyad in which the mother is also angry, and avoidant and affectless.

I have described this set of dyads as a group simply because the congruency in behaviour of mother and infant at home and in laboratory separation and reunion studies is so striking. I should add, however, that the statements made regarding this small group can be re-stated as (in some cases, extremely) significant correlations involving the entire Ainsworth sample. Thus ratings of the mother's aversion to contact in the first three months of life, her emotional inexpressiveness, and her failure to respond to episodes of angry behaviour are significantly positively correlated with the number of instances of the infant striking its mother or threatening to strike her in the fourth quarter, with the infant's rated anger in the fourth quarter, and with the degree to which the infant avoids the mother (looking away, turning away, moving away and ignoring) in the Strange Situation (Main, Slaton & Ainsworth, 1979).

Anger, avoidance and active disobedience in the second year of life.

I shall begin by describing an interview with the mother of a 20 month old infant named Sara. The mother was one of 38 interviewed just prior to a video-taped play session conducted in Berkeley. The interview asked in part for a description of the child, and the interviewer's notes were rated later for the degree to which the mother found the child troublesome, and the degree to which the child was described as angry. This child was described as the angriest and most troublesome in our sample.

Sara's mother reported that it was impossible to leave her without being subjected to extreme temper tantrums, including screaming at night when the mother attempted to leave her with a sitter. In addition, however, Sara sometimes attempted to run away. She was described as extremely difficult and angry, and the entire interview was permeated with the mother's concern for disciplining and controlling Sara. She said that at times she wished to kill her, and that she spanked her very severely.

Just following the interview, Sara and her mother were video-taped in a toy-filled playroom. A detailed narrative description was made of this tape from repeated viewings. The followings are excerpts from the first three minutes:

> Mother is sitting erect, but leaning forward. Her posture suggests that she is angry or else giving warning. Her back is stiff as she leans forward, and her elbows are held out from her side. The set of her head is very determined . . . She seems to be trying to see exactly what Sara is doing . . . Sara is looking directly at the fan, and suddenly slaps her hand down very hard on the table . . . Sara stands up. She has a smile on her face for the first time. It is a peculiar smile. Her upper lip is restricted or pulled down and her eyes are squinting. She picks up the toy broom and reaches up and knocks down the mobile of birds which hangs from the ceiling. Immediately the mother says 'No'. Mother leans forward. Sara backs up as mother leans forward. . .
>
> Now Sara takes the broom over towards the fan and crashes it onto the fan covering. Mother says in a heavy, ominous voice, 'No, Sara'. Sara moves over toward the mother, but as she is looking back toward the fan rather than toward the mother she is approaching . . . It almost looks as though the broom is about to hit the mother. Mother is saying, 'No, Sara, we do not do that'. She says, 'No, no' again. She says 'No, absolutely not', but through all this she does not look at Sara. She continues writing, her face absolutely blank. Sara has backed up close to her now. She looks at the fan. She looks around as though she is going to look in the mother's direction, and as she does so mother looks down more firmly at her paper. Sara has got the beginnings of an odd little smile again . . . (within three seconds) . . . she again hits down hard with the broom this time on the box.

In the remainder of the free play session, Sara behaved similarly. Our codings from video-tape showed that she stood second highest in the sample for the proportion of mother's commands and prohibitions to which she responded with *active* disobedience (Main, Londerville and Townsend, 1979) – defined as responding to a command with active opposition rather than simply failing to respond, as when the child, called to come, moves even further away from the mother. Sara also engaged in more angry hitting of toys and other objects in the room than any other child in the sample, and she exhibited some odd behaviours (e.g., anxious echoing of parts of her mother's sentences).

When free to approach on her own, that is when approaching *spontaneously* rather than in response to an invitation, Sara seemed friendly although relatively affectless. During the home visit she came

25

and stood with her hand on the visitor's knee and played with her keys. During the office interview a thunderstorm took place and a bolt of lightning struck very near the building. The event was frightening even for the adults present, and Sara, though equidistant between both, dashed whimpering to the unfamiliar interviewer rather than to her mother.

During the video-taped play session, however, Sara (as all infants in the sample) was invited to play a game of ball with a friendly and relatively unfamiliar adult playmate. The game took place in the mother's presence. Throughout the game, the adult playmate is assigned the task of engaging the child in play and interaction. A micro-analysis of Sara's behaviour during this game of ball (George and Main, in press) was most enlightening. The most striking aspect of the session was Sara's physical avoidance of the playmate's efforts to initiate interaction. Pressed to interact, she avoided social interaction by turning away, moving away, looking away, and actively ignoring. Those interactional responses which did occur were never immediate. They were hesitant, and her movements were ambivalent. She used side-steps rather than approaching the playmate *en face*, and her approaches were followed by immediate back-stepping away from the playmate. Once she gradually encircled the playmate and approached her finally from behind, but she turned her face away as she reached the point of closest proximity. During part of the 'game' she simply turned her back to the playmate. In addition, like the abused infants described by Gaensbauer and his colleagues (Chapter 8) this infant had little affect expression. While most infants enjoyed the game of ball, this infant showed no pleasure. Interestingly, however, in the midst of it she suddenly attempted to hit her mother.

From the above it is clear that Sara strongly resembled the infants described in the Ainsworth sample. Seen in the Ainsworth Strange Situation, she behaved exactly as the four infants described earlier. Although her reported attachment to her mother was extreme and anxious, and although she was clearly normally an angry and aggressive infant, in the stressful laboratory separation session she showed neither anger nor attachment. Throughout each reunion she avoided her mother, moving away and steadfastly ignoring the mother's efforts to gain her attention. Avoidance is scored on a seven-point scale (see Ainsworth et al., 1978), and Sara in fact received the highest scores within the sample.

The ratings of the mother made from repeated viewing of the video-tapes of the play session showed the same syndrome of behaviours uncovered in the mothers of aggressive-avoidant infants in the Ainsworth sample. The mother was outstanding in the sample for lack of affect expression and apparent anger, and she showed an outstanding aversion to physical contact with Sara.

Here again, although I have simply presented a case study, it is a case which represents the pattern found within the entire (38 dyad) sample. In the sample as a whole the dyadic syndrome described earlier was again uncovered (Main, 1973; Main, Tomasini & Tolan, 1979; Main, Londerville & Townsend, 1979). The infant's affectless avoidance of the mother on reunion in the laboratory situation was again strongly related to the mother's apparent aversion to (avoidance of) contact with the infant, her apparent anger toward the infant, and her lack of affect expression. The infant's attacks and threats of attack upon the mother were also related to this syndrome of maternal behaviours within this sample, and again to the infant's affectless avoidance of the mother in the laboratory.

In this study, however, new information was gained through the use of adults who attempted to interact with the infant. Infants who avoided their mothers tended to fail to approach the adult playmate when she first invited them to participate in a game of ball, and then over the next 20 minutes they tended to actively avoid her. The infants seen in this study were also seen with a Bayley (developmental) examiner, who recorded her impression of the personal interaction between herself and the infant. Infants who avoided their mothers in the Strange Situation failed to engage in personal or joyful interaction with the examiner, although some cooperated with her in an impersonal manner.

This suggests that avoidance of the mother on reunion may serve as a marker not only of anger toward the mother, but of difficulties in other relationships. In a separate study of toddlers (one to two years old) in daycare we found indications that this was accurate (Blanchard and Main, 1979). First, infants who avoided their mothers (or fathers) on the reunions we observed at the care centre also avoided them (and to almost exactly the same degree) in the laboratory. This of course provides 'field' validation for the laboratory studies. Secondly, avoidance on reunion in the care centre *or* in the laboratory was negatively related to 'social-emotional adjustment' with peers and caregivers as observed in the daycare centre. A recent further study of the case records (N = 10) shows that avoidance of the parent on reunion is positively correlated with avoidance of the caregivers as they seek interaction, and is also positively correlated with aggression toward the caregivers. With peers, no such relationship emerges.

An observational study of battered toddlers in the daycare setting

The findings reported above may be summarized as follows:
 1. A syndrome of avoidance, anger and affectless rejection toward

27

the mother has been identified in some infants studied in white middle-class samples.

2. We have failed to find evidence that infants who would develop this syndrome by the end of the first year of life differed from others at the beginning of the year in crying, excessive anger or rage reaction, or in failure to respond positively to holding.

3. This syndrome is found associated with the mother's aversion to physical contact with the infant from the earliest months of infant life, and with the mother's emotional inexpressiveness and anger.

4. Infants who are members of such dyads seem to avoid persons attempting to initiate new relationships by their second year. Preliminary results suggest they also avoid and aggress against daycare caregivers.

The way the mother behaves toward the infant would seem, then, to be implicated in the development of this syndrome of infant behaviour. But *why* the mother behaves in this way toward a particular infant is, of course, an entirely separate question. It may reflect her normal way of responding to infants, or only to infants of a particular sex, or only to infants who seem active. It may reflect her current feelings about her spouse, or a stress temporarily imposed upon her. It is manifestly the case that it is easier to be insensitive to some infants than to others (George & Main, 1979; see also Osofsky, 1976).

Reflecting upon this syndrome, Carol George (a graduate student in psychology at Berkeley) suggested that a study of abused toddlers in daycare should be undertaken. While not every abused toddler experiences continual parental rejection, it seems reasonable to suppose that many experience extremes of rejection in their daily interactions with the parent (see Burgess and Conger, 1978, and Gaensbauer, Mrazek & Harmon, Chapter 8 of this volume, for supportive evidence). The abused toddler should then exhibit the syndrome which we had identified in the relatively mildly rejected infants seen in normal samples.

A positive finding in this case would be of considerable import to those interested in child abuse prevention. While not every abused child becomes an abusing parent, parents who abuse their children have, by their own report and that of other investigators, commonly experienced abuse within their own childhoods (see Spinetta & Rigler, 1972, for a summary of almost two dozen corroborative studies; see also Green, 1976, and DeLozier, 1978). In itself this suggests a cycle, and one which must somehow be broken. George and I reasoned that if we found strong aggression and avoidance in abused children in infancy as expected, then efforts to prevent child abuse should begin by providing abused infants with alternative models of caregiving (and perhaps peer) interaction.

The abused children in our study were observed in special daycare centres in the San Francisco Bay Area which had been set up for their care and protection. From these centres we obtained four girls and six boys for observation – all between the ages of one and three – and all physically battered (trauma ranged from severe bruises to burns and. skull fractures). Neglect cases and sexual abuse cases were excluded. The behaviour of these children was compared with that of ten control children observed in (separate) centres for 'families undergoing stress' in the neighbouring areas. The controls were matched with the abused children for age, sex and race, and as closely matched as possible for parental marital status and education, parental occupation and the adult(s) predominantly caring for the child during the course of the study. (Finding subjects so closely matched to the target subjects occupied one year of the study).

Observations of the child's social behaviour were made over the course of four half-hour visits to the centres and these were recorded in detailed narrative form. Since the target and control children resided in separate centres, and the physical condition of some of the abused children was obvious, it was not possible for the observers to be kept blind to the child's study status. Four of the five observers were, however, blind to our specific hypotheses.

Since the results of this study have been reported elsewhere (George & Main, 1979), I shall only summarize them here. (Unless otherwise stated, all results reported are statistically significant: two-tailed t-tests for matched pairs, and Fisher's exact tests were employed.) In keeping with the descriptions of relatively 'rejected' children given earlier, I shall begin by considering aggressive behaviour.

1. A simple count was made of physical assault upon peers and caregivers. The abused toddlers physically assaulted their peers (hitting, kicking and slapping, etc.) more than twice as often as the control children assaulted them – in fact, they physically assaulted their peers more than twice per hour. *Only* the abused infants *ever* assaulted or threatened to assault caregivers, but actual assault was infrequent even in this group. It was only when assault and threat to assault were combined into a single category that the abused infants were found to be more physically aggressive toward their caregivers than were the controls. (Five of the abused children, but none of the control children, assaulted or threatened to assault caregivers).

2. We also examined aggressive behaviour following a schema provided by Margaret Manning and her colleagues at Edinburgh (Manning, Heron & Marshall, 1979) for use with nursery school children. The schema organizes aggressive behaviour (non-verbal or

29

verbal) by apparent intention and categories include 'teasing', 'specific hostility' (generally, instrumental or retaliatory aggression, as when a toy is grabbed back by its owner) and 'harassment'. Harassment is a special category of aggressive behaviour which seemingly has the sole intent of causing discomfiture to the victim. It often appears inexplicably and 'out of context'.

The abused infants were not statistically significantly more aggressive toward peers than were the control children, following this schema (all categories inclusive). The mean difference was, however, large. On average the abused children were aggressive towards peers 6.5 times per hour, while the controls averaged 3.8 times per hour.

The abused toddlers were far more aggressive towards their caregivers than the control children. The greatest (although still not statistically significant) difference was found in the category of aggressive acts identified as 'harassment'. Seven of the abused toddlers but only two of the control toddlers harassed their caregivers. (For the abused group, harassment of caregivers occurred an average of twice per hour. For the control group harassment of caregivers occurred an average of 0.2 times per hour. An example of harassment of caregivers in the abused group: suddenly running at the caregiver and spitting on her.)

Consider now approach, avoidance and approach-avoidance behaviour – three mutually exclusive categories in our system. Approach is defined here simply as locomotor approach (walking, creeping or crawling toward the 'target' person), and avoidance as locomotor avoidance (creeping away, pulling away, walking away, etc.). An instance of approach-avoidance was said to occur if (1) movements of approach and avoidance occurred in very rapid sequence – as, 'she moves towards him, but immediately veers away', or (2) movements of approach and avoidance occurred simultaneously, as, 'she approaches but with head and gaze averted'. (This latter specific form of approach-avoidance, in which the head moves in opposition to the body, struck most observers as odd and indicative of strong conflict).

Since our previous studies had shown failure to approach and active avoidance in rejected children precisely at the moment when they were pressed to interaction, we paid special attention to the proportion of friendly overtures by peers and caregivers to which the children responded with approach, avoidance, or approach-avoidance. (Note: there were no significant differences in the number of friendly overtures made to the abused versus the control children). This analysis produced the following conclusions:

1. There were no differences in the number of *spontaneous* approaches (approaches not preceded by friendly overtures) which

the abused versus the control children made to peers. Nor was there a difference in the number of spontaneous approaches made to caregivers.

2. When we considered the proportion of friendly overtures to which a child responded by approaching, we found no differences between the groups in response to peer overtures. But the abused children responded to caregiver overtures by approaching only half as frequently as the control children.

3. We also considered orientation during approach in response to friendly overtures. The usual orientation for approach in response to invitation is of course a direct one (*en face* orientation). But, when the abused children *did* approach peers or caregivers in response to invitations, they were more likely than the control children to approach them indirectly; that is, they were more likely than the control children to approach both peers and caregivers to the side, to the rear, or by turning about and back-stepping.

4. The abused children were also more likely to respond to friendly overtures from peers and from caregivers by moving away from them, i.e., with avoidance.

5. They were also more likely to respond to peers and caregivers with approach-avoidance movements. In fact, *all ten* of the abused children but *none* of the control children responded to the friendly overtures of peers with rapidly sequential or simultaneous movements of approach and avoidance.

We did not have an opportunity to observe this group of infants with their parents. The syndrome exhibited by these children is however that exhibited by relatively (maternally) rejected children in normal samples, with their mothers and with persons attempting to establish new relationships. Above, I have reported that such children tend to avoid their mothers in the reunion episodes of laboratory separation-reunion situations. If the syndrome is in fact on a single continuum, then abused children, like maternally rejected children, would be expected to avoid their parents.

Gaensbauer, Mrazek & Harmon (Chapter 8) have begun to conduct separation studies with parents of abused and/or neglected infants. An apparently substantial percentage of infants in their sample pay no attention to the mother or explicitly avoid interactions with her following brief laboratory separations. Lewis and Schaeffer (1979) observed reunions between abused and/or neglected infants and their mothers in a daycare centre in which controls were also present. They found the abused/neglected children less likely to approach their mothers and more likely to avoid proximity, making them 'most similar to (Ainsworth's) insecurely-attached, mother-avoidant children'.

31

What data there are, then, appear corroborative. Abused infants do behave like maternally rejected infants observed in normal samples. This set of studies provides the first affirmation based on controlled observation that abused children really are relatively 'difficult' children to handle. The set of studies taken as a whole further suggests that relationships formed with primary caregivers affect relationships with others. If this is the case then, given the reported inter-generational continuity in child abuse (cited earlier), early intervention in the simple form of providing the abused child with supplementary caregiving figures would be in order. But can infants really form very different kinds of relationships with different persons? It is possible that infants who are or will be abused form the same kinds of relationships with all persons (aggressive, avoidant and rejecting relationships), from parents through caregivers. If this is the case then there would be little hope for the effectiveness of early intervention.

Infants form different relationships with different persons

Above I have reported that rejected and abused babies are abusive and rejecting toward others, and moreover, that they are avoidant in situations in which approach is expected. These data already imply a pattern, and this in itself should imply stability and consistency. The 'marker' behaviour for this pattern of dyadic rejection (and rejection of others outside of the dyad) is the infant's avoidance of the parent on reunion in the laboratory or daycare centre. It may be worth noting here that stability of scores for this 'marker' behaviour is high. Three independent investigations have been conducted using the Ainsworth Strange Situation with white middle-class samples of mothers and infants. These samples have been seen in Maryland, New York and Minnesota. Scores for avoidance of the mother summed over the two reunion episodes of the Strange Situation have been shown to be stable over a two-week period, r (N$=$26) $=$ .66, (Ainsworth et al., 1978), and also over a six-month period, r (N$=$50) $=$ .62 (Waters, 1978). Connell (1976) has also found the behaviour to be stable. Although stability of this kind is to be expected simply because avoidance in this situation is an indicator of a pattern which is itself stable (Main, 1979a; Main, 1979b), it even further raises the suspicion of stability of temperament in the 'rejecting' infant. This, again, would not have hopeful indications for breaking the abused-abusing cycle.

Studies which I have been conducting recently at the University of California at Berkeley with Donna Weston (Main and Weston, 1979) lead to the conclusion that infants can form very different kinds of relationships with father and with mother, and that a great deal more is known about an infant's likely response to new persons (and its likelihood of showing signs of disturbance) when we assess its relationships to *both* mother and father. The results reported here are based on our first analyses of only about 30 triads. The full sample is not yet collected, nor are our data completely analyzed. There seems little likelihood, however, of a major reversal in the overall pattern to be described.

In these studies we have been seeing infants with mother and with father in the Ainsworth Strange Situation (with one parent at 12 months and with the other at 18 months). In addition, one week before each infant is seen with a given parent it is seen in a free play session and in a 'Clown Session' with a given parent. In the Clown Session an adult actor goes through a structured set of activities designed at first to arouse slight apprehension (the clown stands in the doorway silently, wearing a mask), then amusement (with mask removed, the clown plays a flirtatious game of 'peek-a-boo' with the infant, then somersaults), and then to establish a positive relationship with the infant (the clown offers his or her hands, talks gently to attract attention, and engages the infant in a game of ball). Finally, being told that he or she must leave the room, the clown protests that he does not want to leave, and begins a realistic cry which lasts a full 50 seconds. (Details of the cry and of the control condition for assessment of infant response to the cry are reported in Main, Weston & Wakeling, 1979).

We find that whereas in our sample, as in others, infant avoidance of the mother is stable over a long time period (to date we have seen 25 mothers and infants at both 12 and 20 months), there is *no* relationship between an infant's avoidance of its mother at 12 and its father at 18 months. Thus, the relationship with the father cannot be predicted from the relationship with the mother. The same infant who is affectless and avoidant with its mother in the Strange Situation at 12 *and* at 20 months may cling ardently to its father at 18 months, and show in every way a joyful response to reunion with him.

Moreover, in this sample as in those reported earlier, avoidance of the mother seems highly associated with maternal rejection as assessed in separate situations (in this case, in the Clown Session). Avoidance of the father also seems predictable from the Clown Session – specifically, this seems to be related to the father's emotional unresponsiveness. Thus avoidance of the father, as avoidance of the mother, seems likely to be an index of some kind of parental rejection. Even if we only knew that infants could behave entirely differently with the two parents in the Strange Situation, we would be in a position to realize that Strange Situation behaviour reflects relation-

33

ships rather than child characteristics or immutable child temperament. However, the most important item of information for those concerned with the effect of relationships upon relationships, or with the abused child, is whether such differences in relationship make a difference to the infant's social and emotional behaviour and development. For this reason we are conducting a close analysis of the infant's behaviour in the 12-month Clown Session.

First, consider the extent to which the infant seems able to form some kind of friendly or positive relationship to the clown, or to take pleasure in participating with the clown in the game of ball. Infants who avoid both parents show, as we would expect, almost no interest in the clown – indeed, they actively avoid the clown throughout the session. Infants who show little or no avoidance with both parents (those who seem secure with both parents) tend to respond to the clown extremely positively, i.e., they show high relatedness. Infants who avoid one parent but are not avoidant with the second parent fall between the extremes – positive, although not joyful.

This same pattern seems to hold when we consider the extent to which the infant shows 'concerned attention' to the crying of the Clown at the end of the session, by attending to the Clown with a sorrowful expression, or even offering the ball as though to cheer him or her. Not one of the infants who was strongly avoidant of both parents in the Strange Situation showed 'concerned attention' to the crying of the adult actor. Every one of the infants who seemed secure and non-avoidant with both parents showed at least some indications of concern, and indeed the mean on the 10-point 'concerned attention' scale is 7.5 for this group of infants. The mean for infants secure with one parent but avoidant with the other is 3.7.

The preliminary analyses reported above seem already to make the point that even one relationship which is not rejecting affects positively relationships with others. Still greater argument for the preventive effects of one secure relationship is found in the data regarding disturbance. Close review of the video-tapes for the Clown Session (conducted by Loretta Townsend) permits us to assess the degree to which an infant shows signs of disturbance in any of many forms such as stereotypes, sudden and inappropriate changes in affect, odd posture and movement, and odd vocalizations. Disturbance shown across the session is rated on a four-point scale from slight to extreme disturbance. *Five* of the six infants who strongly avoided both parents in the Strange Situation showed signs of disturbance in the Clown Session, and the mean for the group was 1.5. Infants secure and non-avoidant with *either* one or both parents showed virtually *no* disturbance. Thus, providing the infant has one non-rejecting relationship, we may expect some positive response to the adult, some concerned attention to the distress of the adult, and no signs of disturbance.

Conclusions

I shall not summarize again the findings reported in this chapter, but rather conclude with what I see as the practical application of the work reported. This is that therapeutic daycare should be provided for the battered child.

It seems surprising that, at least within the United States, there exist very few therapeutic daycare programmes for the battered child (George & Main, in press), where 'therapeutic' means no more than a programme in which caregivers are urged to pay special attention to the child's social relations and development. This is all the more surprising given the millions of dollars which are spent in the service of detection and prevention of child abuse, and in therapy for the parents themselves. (It is disheartening to note that, during the course of our own observations of abused children in the Bay Area, one of the two special centres at which our observations were made was closed for lack of funding. It was our impression that the children placed in this centre had made very positive gains in social relationships during the course of their attendance).

In trying to understand why such programmes have not developed, I have only been able to conclude that to date there has been insufficient understanding of the effects of *relationships* upon relationships in early life. Thus, those concerned with child abuse may concern themselves with the prevention of physical abuse only, and fail to realize the likely effects of the extreme parental rejection which may continue even in the absence of abuse itself. Placing the behaviour of the abused child on a continuum with that of relatively rejected infants in normal samples may be helpful in that we can then see that the same syndrome may develop even when *physical* abuse is absent. 'Saving' an abused child from further physical *abuse* may not be sufficient to break a cycle which essentially represents a problem in relationships.

In a recent report concerning a study of abused and/or neglected children in daycare, Lewis and Schaeffer (1979) have come to similar conclusions. They too urge that daycare should be provided for the abused child. Their conclusions are based in large part on finding virtually no differences between abused/neglected children and control children in play with peers. This suggests to them that the peer interaction system is left open for the formation of positive relationships, despite the child's unfortunate experience with the parents.

Since in our own study we found abused children both more

35

aggressive and more avoidant with peers than were control children (George & Main, 1979), there appears to be some contradiction in results. There are, however, differences in methodology and target behaviours which may account for the apparent contradiction. Lewis and Schaeffer focused almost exclusively upon positive play behaviour, they used a different observational method (ten-second time sampling), and they included neglected as well as battered children as targets. Whatever the differences between our studies, the finding of some positive response to peers in abused/neglected children is heartening, and it can only serve to reinforce the position presented here.

Although relationships affect relationships, infants and young children are flexible. Even where one relationship has been unfortunate, another may compensate and keep the infant from fully developing the abusive, avoidant and rejecting social interaction pattern here described. Caregivers who would work with abused children should, however, be warned of this pattern. They should be warned that they may be greeted with rejection and avoidance, and that they must respond to this with a steady affection rather than, however naturally, responding with diminished interest in the child. If they are able to do this, and to remain available over a long period, then the preliminary results from the studies conducted with Weston and Wakeling at Berkeley provide foundation for optimism. Alternative models of relationship will then have been provided for the battered child.

Acknowledgements
  The research on which this chapter is based was generously supported by the Institute of Human Development at Berkeley, by Biomedical Research Support Grants 1–444036–32024 and 1–444036–32025, and by the William T. Grant Foundation. I am grateful to Carol George and Judith Solomon for their earlier readings of this manuscript, and to Jackie Stadtman for her irreplaceable assistance as coordinator of the Social Development Project at the University of California, Berkeley.

REFERENCES
Ainsworth, M.D.S., Blehar, M.C., Waters, E., and Wall, S. (1978) *Patterns of Attachment: A Psychological Study of the Strange Situation*. Hillsdale, N.J.: Lawrence Erlbaum Associates.
Blanchard, M., and Main, M. (1979) 'Avoidance of the attachment figure and social-emotional adjustment in daycare infants'. *Developmental Psychology*. 15, pp. 445–6.
Burgess, R.L., and Conger, R.D. (1978) 'Family interaction in abusive, neglectful and normal families'. *Child Development, 49*, pp. 1163–73.
Connell, D.B. (1976) *Individual differences in attachment: An investigation into stability, implications, and relationships to structure of early language development.* Unpublished doctoral dissertation, Syracuse University.
DeLozier, P. (1978) *An application of attachment theory to the study of child abuse.* Unpublished doctoral dissertation, California School of Professional Psychology, Los Angeles.

Friedrich, W.N. and Boriskin, J.A. (1976) 'The role of the child in abuse: A review of the literature'. *American Journal of Orthopsychiatry, 46*, pp. 580–90.

Galdston, R. (1965) 'Observations on children who have been physically abused and their parents'. *American Journal of Psychiatry, 122*, pp. 440–43.

George, C. and Main, M. (1979) 'Social interactions of young abused children: Approach, avoidance and aggression'. *Child Development, 50*, pp. 306–18.

George, C. and Main, M. (in press) 'The social interaction patterns of abused children with caregivers and peers'. In T. Field, S. Goldberg, D. Stern and A. Sostek (Eds.), *High-risk Infants and Children: Adult and Peer Interactions.* Academic Press, New York.

Green, A.H. (1976) 'A psychodynamic approach to the study and treatment of child-abusing parents'. *American Academy of Child Psychiatry, 15*, 414–29.

Kempe, R.S. and Kempe, C.H. (1978) *Child abuse.* Fontana/Open Books, London.

Lewis, M. and Schaeffer, S. (1979) 'Peer behaviour and mother-infant interaction in maltreated children'. M. Lewis and L. Rosenblum (Eds.), *The Uncommon Child: The Genesis of Behaviour, Vol. III.* New York: Plenum.

Lynch, M. (1976) 'Risk factors in the child: A study of abused children and their siblings'. In H.P. Martin (Ed.), *The Abused child: A Multidisciplinary Approach to Developmental Issues and Treatment.* Ballinger, Cambridge, Mass.

Main, M. (1973) *Exploration, play and level of cognitive functioning as related to child-mother attachment.* Unpublished doctoral dissertation, Johns Hopkins University.

Main, M. (1979) 'The "ultimate" causation for some infant attachment phenomena: Further answers, further phenomena, and further questions'. Unpublished paper.

Main, M. (1979) 'Avoidance in the service of proximity'. In K. Immelmann, G. Barlow, M. Main and L. Petrinovitch (Eds.), *Behavioural Development: The Bielefeld Interdisciplinary Project.* New York: Cambridge University Press.

Main, M., Londerville, S., and Townsend, L. (1979) 'Compliance and aggression in toddlerhood: precursors and correlates'. Unpublished paper.

Main, M., Slaton, S. and Ainsworth, M.D.A. (1979) 'The development of angry behaviour in the first year of life'. Unpublished paper.

Main, M., Tomasini, L. & Tolan, W. (1979) 'Differences among mothers of infants judged to differ in security'. *Developmental Psychology.* 15, pp. 472–473.

Main, M. and Weston, D. (1979) 'The quality of the relationship to mother and to father in infancy: differences and influences'. Unpublished paper.

Main, M., Weston, D. and Wakeling, S. (1979) 'Concerned attention to the crying of an adult actor in infancy'. Paper given at the bi-ennial meeting of the Society for Research in Child Development, San Francisco, March.

Manning, M., Heron, J. and Marshall, T. (1979) 'Styles of hostility and social interactions at nursery, at school, and at home. An extended study of children'. In L. Hersov and M. Berger (Eds.), *Aggression and Anti-Social Behaviour in Childhood and Adolescence.* Pergamon, Oxford.

Martin, H.P. (1976) 'Which children get abused: High risk factors in the child'. In H.P. Martin (Ed.), *The Abused Child: A Multidisciplinary Approach to Developmental Issues and Treatment.* Cambridge: Ballinger.

Milowe, I.D. and Lourie, R.S. (1964) 'The child's role in the battered child syndrome'. *Journal of Paediatrics, 65*, pp. 1079–81.

Morse, W., Sahler, O.J., and Friedman, S.B. (1970) 'A three-year follow-up of abused and neglected children'. *American Journal of Diseases of Children, 120*, pp. 439–46.

Osofsky, J. (1976) 'Neonatal characteristics and mother-infant interaction in two observational studies'. *Child Development, 47*, pp. 1138–47.

Parke, R.D. and Collmer, C. W. (1965) 'Child abuse: an interdisciplinary analysis'. In E.M. Hetherington (Ed.), *Review of Child Development Research, Vol. 5.* Chicago: University of Chicago Press.

Smith, S.M. and Hanson, R. (1975) 'Interpersonal relationships and child-rearing practices in 214 parents of battered children'. *British Journal of Psychiatry, 127*, pp. 513–25.

Spinetta, J.J. and Rigler, D. (1972) 'The child-abusing parent: A psychological review'. *Psychological Bulletin, 77*, pp. 296–304.

Waters, E. (1978) 'The reliability and stability of individual differences in infant-mother attachment'. *Child Development, 49*, pp. 483–94.

3   Mothers' Accounts of Anger and Aggression Towards their Babies

Hilary Graham

This chapter describes a study of women's experiences of early motherhood, carried out in a northern town during 1970 and 1977.* The study was based on a stratified sample of 120 women, of whom half were expecting their first baby and half were expecting their second baby. Each mother was interviewed three times in her own home: during pregnancy, at one month after birth and at five months after birth. It is the material collected at the one month interview which is considered here. The material refers to the attitudes and experiences of an ostensibly non-violent group of mothers whose behaviour towards their children had not attracted the attention of outside agencies. However, as this chapter reveals, feelings of anger and aggression were frequently reported, and further, were reported in situations which were ubiquitous in the early weeks after birth. Feelings of anger typically arose in situations where the mother was chronically tired and was unable to placate her crying baby.

On the basis of these findings, this chapter argues for a sociological perspective on child abuse which takes account of the context, and particularly the constraints, of contemporary motherhood. Put at its simplest, it argues that child abuse can not be seen simply as a reflection of individual pathology, but rather as a response to social and psychological pressures which are woven into the fabric of mothers' lives.

This argument is advanced in four sections. The first section introduces some of the relevant literature on non-accidental injury, while the remaining sections consider material arising from the

* The material for this chapter is taken from a collaborative study carried out with Lorna McKee at the Institute of Social and Economic Research, University of York. The study was directed by Professor Laurie Taylor and was financed by the Health Education Council. The original study was based on a sample of 200 mothers; the questions on anger and aggression, however, were asked only of a sub-sample of 120. A full report of the study is available in H. Graham and L. McKee 'The First Months of Motherhood: A report on a Health Education Council Project', 1979, University of York.

survey. The second section gives an overview of the quantitative data, the third section focuses on the accounts the respondents gave of their experiences of anger and the final section describes their attitudes to the 'baby batterers' who physically injure their children.

Current research on child abuse

Recent studies have drawn attention to the role of social factors in the genesis of child abuse. Two insights, in particular, have greatly increased our understanding of its social aetiology. Research has demonstrated firstly, that the nature of the emotional bond between parent and child has a profound effect upon the child's vulnerability to non-accidental injury and secondly, that parental violence is typically triggered off by an emotional or domestic crisis.

On the first point, studies have uncovered a range of maternal and infant characteristics which increase the likelihood of abuse. The relation between these characteristics and child abuse is generally regarded as an indirect one, with their influence mediated through their impact upon the emotional bond between mother and baby in the early weeks after birth. A deficit in bonding is thus seen as an important underlying factor in battering, with characteristics associated with 'good' bonding serving to protect the baby and characteristics associated with 'poor' bonding increasing its vulnerability to abuse.

However, problems in bonding do not necessarily and inevitably express themselves in child abuse. Instead, the eruption of violence is seen to depend on a catalyst. The catalyst, it has been argued (Kempe, 1971) is a precipitating crisis, an 'immediate feeling of frenzy'. This, he suggests, is often associated with a crisis of confidence in the mother:

> The dynamics of the *immediate* outbursts towards the child are often related to the very quality of mothering being brought into question by the child's behaviour . . . The bashing often relates to the immediate feeling of frenzy about the inability to stop the crying, but other triggers exist, including soiling or rejection of feedings. (Kempe, op. cit., p.28).

It is the nature of these precipitating crises that we wish to discuss in this chapter. However, rather than tracing the origins of the crisis back through the process of bonding and through the net of predisposing factors in the mother and baby, we locate the causes of the crisis in the mother's immediate social environment. Thus, instead of seeing the crisis, and the resulting outburst of anger, as a manifestation of the psychological pressures which plague certain women, we suggest that it can be seen as an expression of the social and material pressures which all mothers face in the course of their daily lives.

Motherhood Study: quantitative data on the mother's anger.

In our interviews we did not include direct questions on physical abuse. Instead, we asked a range of questions about feelings towards the baby and its behaviour. We interviewed 111 mothers one month after the birth and asked, for example, whether they had experienced difficult times with the baby, whether they had ever felt unsure what to do, if they had ever felt angry with the baby and if they had ever felt like crying. In addition, we asked about attitudes to baby battering ('now that you've a small baby to care for, do you find it easier to understand why some women can harm their babies?').

The answers to these questions are revealing. Only 35% of the respondents interviewed at one month felt that there had been no particularly bad periods since their baby was born, 61% admitted that there had been times when they felt angry with their baby and 66% stated that there had been times when they felt like crying. In addition, 81% of the mothers felt that the experience of having a young baby to cope with had made them more sympathetic to baby batterers. Because these statistics were all collected at the one-month stage they reflect women's experiences within the first four to six weeks after birth.

Of these various statistics, it is the respondents' replies to the question on anger which provide us with the most accurate measure of the incidence of the emotions presumably associated with child abuse. The exact breakdown of responses to this question is as follows: no anger reported – 29%; anger towards baby reported – 61%; anger towards older child or husband reported – 10%. This last figure of 10% probably underestimates the incidence of anger towards other family members, since the way the question was phrased clearly centred on the baby.

Focussing on the respondents who reported feelings of anger towards their baby, the survey suggests that certain groups of mothers and babies are more likely to be involved in anger incidents. In general, our findings confirm the associations identified in the studies of child abuse discussed in the previous section. In particular, they underline the importance of the factors associated with 'poor bonding' in increasing the likelihood of anger. For example, the baby's low birth weight, its admission to the special care baby unit and its reported poor health and susceptibility to crying during the early weeks of life were all associated with higher rates of reported anger. Although the numbers involved are small, babies born under

41

six pounds were more likely to be victims of anger than those born at a weight of over six pounds (75% versus 60%), and babies with reported minor illnesses were more likely to be victims of anger than babies with no reported illnesses (69% versus 58%).

Similarly, maternal factors associated with bonding problems were related to higher incidences of anger. Thus, mothers who planned their pregnancies were less likely to report feelings of anger than those whose pregnancies lacked formal planning (57% versus 67%). There were in fact 68 mothers who stated that their pregnancy was planned, and of these 39 admitted to anger. Of the 43 mothers whose pregnancy was not actively planned, 29 admitted to anger. Almost all mothers (98 out of the sample) reported tiredness in the first month, so it it is difficult to get an accurate estimate of the relationship between tiredness and vulnerability to anger. Whereas six out of the 12 mothers (50%) who did *not* report tiredness had felt angry, 62% of the majority who *did* report tiredness reported feelings of anger. There was no clear association between reported depression and anger.

A relationship was also found between anger and both mothers' assessments of the amount their baby cried and their reactions to their baby crying, the latter being particularly marked. While 49 of the 67 mothers (73%) who found the baby's crying upsetting also reported feelings of anger, only 17 of the 38 (45%) who did not get upset by the crying reported feelings of anger. The impact of the mother's tiredness and the baby's crying emerges again when we consider the qualitative material in the next section, where these two issues appear as the motifs around which women's personal accounts of anger are constructed.

Before considering these accounts, we will briefly mention some of the more surprising associations which emerged from our data. The sex of the baby and the parity, feeding practices and social class of the mother all appeared to influence the mother's susceptibility to anger. For example, anger was more frequently reported among mothers of girls (70%) than among mothers of boys (53%), and among first-time mothers (39 out of 57; 68%) than among second-time mothers (29 out of 54; 54%). Twenty-six of the 36 breast feeders (72%) and 39 of the 71 bottle feeders (55%) also reported anger. Data on socio-economic class suggest that mothers in social class three are less likely to feel anger towards the baby than mothers in either the lower or higher social classes. Nineteen of the 31 mothers in social classes one and two, 35 of the 60 mothers in social classes three, and 10 of the 15 mothers in social classes 4 and 5 reported anger. This pattern is more marked if we consider mothers' occupations. Although the numbers are small, those formerly employed as secretaries, clerical workers and shop assistants report a lower incidence of anger (27 out of 50; 56%) than those in professional occupations (nurses, teachers, etc.: 20 out of 27; 75%) and those formerly employed as factory workers (8 out of 11; 73%). We can not, as yet, explain this interesting class pattern, nor the relationship between anger and the baby's sex. However, the qualitative material considered in the section below provides us with some hints as to why first-time mothers and breast feeders were more vulnerable to feelings of anger.

Motherhood Study: mothers' accounts of anger.

Running through women's accounts of their feelings of anger are two themes. The first, and more universal theme, relates to the baby's crying and the impact it has on the mother and other members of the family; the second relates to the mother's level of tiredness and its impact on her capacity to cope with the baby's crying. It is these two experiences which appear to provide the nexus from which the precipitating crisis arises. However, although anger was invariably set against a background of persistent crying and chronic tiredness, anger was not the only and inevitable outcome of such experiences. Instead, it appears as one of a number of responses to a stressful situation which the mother feels unable to control. In looking at women's experiences of crying and tiredness, we indicate some of these alternative responses. However, since most of our data deal with these experiences in the context of anger, our main concern in this chapter is to trace the way in which anger develops and is dealt with in the early weeks after birth.

The crying of the baby was a recurrent motif in women's accounts of anger. In particular, anger was talked about in the context of persistent crying which the mother was unable to control or escape from. Persistent, uncontrollable and inescapable crying appears to be more of a problem for certain groups of mothers: the first-time mothers, the breast feeders and those with housing, marital and financial difficulties. On the basis of our data we do not know whether the problems these mothers faced reflected real differences in the behaviour of their babies or whether their problems with crying reflected a greater sensitivity and a lower level of resistance to prolonged crying episodes. However, what is clear from our data is that prolonged and uncontrollable crying in the baby brought out in the mother the gamut of emotions which our survey suggests are intrinsic to the experience of pregnancy, childbirth and early motherhood: namely responsibility and uncertainty. In the context of crying, these emotions were expressed in terms of the mother's feeling of responsibility and of wanting to know the cause of the crying and

43

to eliminate it, together with her feeling of uncertainty about both cause and cure. These feelings come across in the following accounts, given in response to the question 'does your baby's crying ever upset you?'

> You get really upset because you think 'what on earth is the matter? Why is she crying? Haven't I done something right? She's utterly dependent on you and it's you she wants when she cries.

> The thing that really upsets me with this screaming business at night is you really don't know what it is, and you can't do anything to console them. It upsets me. When she wasn't getting any better I felt terrible. I thought if anything happens to her it's my fault because I haven't done anything.

Another mother touched on similar emotions in answering the question 'have you ever felt like crying?'

> I've felt like screaming, which I have done, when you just don't know what to do with them for the best. I mean he's crying, you've fed him, you've done everything possible. He still just cries and you just don't know what to do with him. I think that is awful. I think maybe I've taken it out on Alan more, you know, slammed all the doors in the house and say 'Oh I don't know what's wrong with him, you have a go.' I think it's that that's the worst, when you just don't know what is wrong with him, just screaming and carrying on for no reason.

Such screaming and carrying on could have particularly deleterious consequences for breast feeders:

Mother:　When I first came home, you know, and she started (screaming), I just didn't know what to do. She was screaming her head off and I'd just fed her and changed her nappy and done everything that I knew I had to do. And you feel absolutely panic-stricken, you don't know what to do next.

Interviewer: Have you found yourself getting tense?

Mother:　Yes, really tense. And you know there's this thing you should relax when you're breast feeding and I think I got to the stage where I was trying so hard to relax when I was making myself more tense than ever.

Women's feelings of tiredness frequently reinforced their exasperation with the baby's crying, and made it more difficult for them to reconcile their feelings of responsibility for the child and the uncertainty about what to do. In the sample as a whole, 88% of the mothers reported feeling tired at one month, and 70% felt they were not getting enough sleep. And as we have already noted, mothers who reported tiredness were more likely to report feelings of anger towards their baby. The way tiredness is woven into women's experiences both of their baby crying and their feelings of anger is illustrated in the following accounts, elicited in response to the question 'have you ever felt angry with your baby?'

> I was really tired – normally I can wake, feed him and go back – but this night I just couldn't wake up. And he was crying and I'd fed him and he still wasn't settling – this was when I was breast feeding and he wasn't getting enough . . . (She goes downstairs and makes a bottle while he continues to scream) I changed him and fed him the bottle and he still wouldn't go back. And I went to get another nappy cos he'd wet again. And I just went and sat down with my head in the airing cupboard and I just started to cry 'Oh for God's sake, shut up!' That was just that night. It was just being tired. If I can get my sleep, I can cope with it.

> Oh yea. I've been near it. Not hitting him but shouting at him. I shouted at him t'other night, he was getting all upset. I'm more tired than anything. If I could get a bit more sleep I don't think I'd be so irritable.

> Only once. I never thought I would get angry with children. I was past myself one night and I was really shouting at her. I felt sorry afterwards but I really did get cross with her. I'd been up that night, half past two I fed her, ten to seven I was still there. I was past myself that night.

These accounts illustrate not only the situations which precipitated the mothers' anger, but also the way in which their emotions were expressed. The first mother describes how she put her head in the linen cupboard and cried, and the second and third how they shouted at their babies. Although we have limited material on the mothers' responses to crying, these accounts appear typical of two rather different reactions. Some mothers, when faced with a crying baby who they felt unable to placate, reported how they got upset themselves – for example, through sympathizing with the baby or becoming overcome by a sense of personal failure. They noted how, in such situations, they tended to end up crying themselves. Other mothers coped with their feelings of exasperation differently and became angry with the baby. They were unlikely to empathize with the infant, tending instead to see the crying as the baby's fault. In some instances this blaming extended further, and the baby was seen

45

as directly and deliberately manipulating the mother through its behaviour. Several studies have suggested that a characteristic of abusive parents is their ignorance of or disregard for the age-appropriate abilities of the baby. They thus tend to expect too much of their baby (Kempe, 1971). Mothers in our sample saw babies as capable of 'trying it on', with the aim of getting the parent's attention and comfort. For example, two mothers gave these accounts of their six week old babies:

Interviewer: How long would you leave him (to cry) before you pick him up?

Mother: Well it depends on the cry. I don't know if he's trying it on, because I've heard they can even at this stage. Of course, I've learnt now that he was trying it on.

Interviewer: Do you ever find yourself angry with him?

Mother: There's times when I could, you know, shake him, but I wouldn't. But there's times when he won't shut up and Andrew's at it, and you know there's nothing wrong with him, that he's crying just to be picked up. And at times you could just pick him up and shake him.

As this last comment illustrates, other members of the family often play a crucial role in the development, and the expression, of anger. The toddler invariably exacerbated the situation, and as mentioned earlier, appears, for some mothers, to be the target of her irritation. For example, this mother makes a distinction between the legitimate crying of the baby and the illegitimate crying of her elder daughter:

I don't get angry with babies because they have to cry for attention. They have to cry for everything. Whereas Tracey she knows how to moan now and she knows how to cry for naughtiness, for no reason. Like at meal times, she won't eat and you say 'eat some food' and she just cries. There's no reason to cry because we haven't touched her. With Paul, I'd never dream of hitting him.

The husband's role is more complex. Like the toddler, he sometimes features in mothers' accounts as someone who reinforces the tensions they are already feeling. For example, some women noted how their husband's reactions to the baby's crying could fuel their own anger:

I can't get annoyed with her yet. But he has. He really – two nights he got really nasty. And that annoyed me more than anything, him getting annoyed.

In discussing her husband's reactions, another mother brought out how the presence of other family members can intensify her feelings of responsibility and uncertainty:

Well I get angry because Tim gets impatient. He thinks *why* is she crying? Well, *I* obviously don't know. I know she's not hungry. She's not this, she's not that, I don't know what she is. And he'll be saying to me 'well, what's wrong with her?' I keep saying 'well it may be this, it may be that' and he goes on 'It's no good saying what she *may* have, what is it?' This is when I get angry – not angry with her but angry because I think 'Oh God, I can't do anything and I've just got to let her cry!'

Other husbands had a more positive role to play, defusing their wife's anger and taking some of the pressures from her. In fact, for some mothers the husband was clearly a vital safety valve – as one mother put it 'Peter says "if you ever feel like clobbering him, let me take over" '. Other accounts suggest that the husband played a similar supportive role at times of crisis:

Just one particular night when he cried from three o'clock in the afternoon and it went on until ten'ish when he had another feed. And then he didn't settle. And I could have thrown him out of the window, quite honestly. And I did put him down and I left and my husband picked him up, and he shut up for him. Immediately. And went to sleep.

One time I put him down after a night feed, and I sort of felt that he knew I had to be up six or seven next morning (to go to work) but out of sheer devilment kept me up from three till five in the early hours. He had been fed and everything and was just lying in the cot . . . and all the time he was just wittering on that in the end I got out of bed and thumped the side of the cot and said 'shut up'. Andy shot out of bed and said 'what have you done, what have you done, I'll take over'. I said I just banged the side of the cot, but that sort of woke him up, the thought of me hitting him, and he sort of got up then and helped me.

Although we did not ask or collect data directly on battering, some respondents, including some of those quoted here, clearly got quite close to physical abuse. What is striking about the accounts in which imminent or actual abuse is reported is that the mothers rarely see their actions as instances of battering. They characteristically make a distinction between the way they express anger towards their baby and the way 'baby batterers' channel their aggression. For example, mothers made a distinction between *types* of aggression: between

47

verbal and physical aggression ('I'd shout at him but I wouldn't hit him') and between spontaneous and premeditated aggression (between an involuntary smack and a deliberate burn). Others made a distinction between *degrees* of aggression, between mild and severe aggression (a shake and a beating). In classifying abusive behaviour in this way mothers tended to see their own behaviour as the more acceptable of the alternatives. This tendency is illustrated by two mothers, replying to the question 'now that you've a young baby to care for, do you find it easier to understand why some women harm their babies?'

> I suppose some people are (batterers who hurt their children). I couldn't have hit him or anything like that. I mean I know I was picking him up a bit roughly and shouting at him but I think I could control myself that far.

> I can understand them getting angry and that and smacking a baby but I can't understand people who put them in hot water or fires, and cigarettes and things. You know you can smack a child, fair enough, you can get angry and you'll smack them. But when people deliberately go and run a hot bath or something – now to me that is sheer cruelty.

However, although mothers made a distinction between their behaviour and battering, they nonetheless felt guilty about those occasions when they deviated from their image of the ideal mother:

> If after the three o'clock morning feed he had one of those gemmy times when he wouldn't settle, I'd get irritable with him and I felt dreadful about it. I said to Stan 'I'm a bad mother', you know, because I was picking him up and shouting at him and frightening him more. I felt awful about it.

> One night I was past myself with it (being up and down with the baby), and I remember I shook him. And I thought 'oh I'm a battering mother' and I cried my eyes out after that. But I never hurt him or anything.

So far we have been looking at mothers' accounts of anger up until the moment at which anger was noted or expressed. We have looked at the exacerbatory factors and the types of emotional responses these gave rise to. What we have yet to consider is the strategies women developed for coping with these emotions. We have already indicated that the husband was part of the coping strategy of some mothers, a safety net in the event of emergencies. The role of the husband in such circumstances highlights the principle around which these strategies were constructed: namely, to get something or someone between oneself and one's baby. Thus, for example, some women called in friends, neighbours and parents to temporarily take over the care of the baby. For others, the radio and television served a similar function. For others, their only resort was to that of physical distance – going to another room, out into the garden or down the road.

> You know, I've always thought that women who hit their babies are terrible, cruel and all this. But some days, you know, if I'd been that way inclined I could have hit him. But I didn't. I just used to put him down and keep hold of myself. Put him down and go out of the room. Go away from him as far as possible, just so I couldn't hear him.

> I just didn't know what was wrong with him when he was yelling and I left him and I turned the radio on full blast and shoved him out somewhere so I couldn't hear. 'Cos I felt so tensed up that I thought, 'just leave him and cool down a bit'.

In looking at women's personal accounts of their baby's crying and their own responses, we have made a number of points which we feel are relevant to an understanding of non-accidental injury. Before summarizing these, we wish to consider one other dimension to child abuse, namely mothers' attitudes to parents who injure their children.

Motherhood Survey: women's attitudes to baby batterers

In view of the summary given above, it is not surprising to find that the mothers in our sample were overwhelmingly sympathetic to women who harm their babies. As mentioned earlier, 81% felt their personal experiences of baby care had softened their attitudes to 'baby battering'. This liberal stance reflected a widespread appreciation of the stresses and tensions that a young baby can produce. If we were to paraphrase the comments mothers made, it would be in the dictum 'there but for the grace of God, go I'.

> You know you can imagine somebody when you're changing his nappy and he's screaming and his legs are kicking and you can't get his nappy fastened up or anything like that. I can imagine how some women get carried away and give them a good slap . . . I don't think you can criticize anyone who does that unless you've had one of your own. They can be very, very trying.

Others elaborated this theme by noting specific factors which protected them from reaching 'battering point'.

I can understand quite easily. I mean I'm not intelligent by a long shot, but I can understand them not reasoning with themselves. You know, I can sort of sit down and reason with myself. But I can understand these people whose IQ is low or (who are) alone or whose accommodation is poor. I can really understand.

I do understand, yeh. I feel sorry for them because I know there's times when you feel as if you could, you know. Especially with nervous people or if you've had a lot of late nights or bad nights. I say it's understandable. They might feel right sorry afterwards, they must do, but you can understand it.

As these quotes suggest, mothers often compared their own favourable circumstances with those endured by other women. In doing so, they point to the important fact that some mothers face problems which not only make baby-care more stressful but which also limit the availability of key strategies by which she might be able to defuse her anger. Thus, for example, it is the single mother who, although facing additional demands on her physical and emotional resources, lacks the safety valve of a supporting husband. Similarly, a mother in poor accommodation faces more practical problems in coping with her baby (and is thus more prone to feelings of anger) and also lacks a possible escape route from the tensions that are created:

Yes, I think I can understand that in a way. I can see how if you're feeling down and your baby's crying and you're in a small flat or something and you can't get it out in the garden or anything, it must really get you down. I mean, I'm lucky having a nice garden at the back, you know, she doesn't get on top of you there.

Many mothers, like this one, took a sympathetic stand on baby battering. They cited a range of factors – poor housing, poor health in mother and baby, depression, lack of support – which they felt explained and even exonerated the mother's behaviour. However, a small proportion of mothers – 12% – took a more critical stand, expressing little or no sympathy for baby battering. While acknowledging that housing and health factors made the task more difficult for some women, they saw the issue as basically one of self-control. Interestingly, the comments of these disapproving mothers capture the essence both of the sample's experiences of anger and of their responses to it. For this reason, we conclude this section with the pithy answers of two mothers who remained unsympathetic to baby batterers:

You've just got to control yourself. I sort of find I'm shouting at them to relieve my feelings. Especially at her (her older child), because I say 'I'll hit you in a minute'. It's a good job we can control ourselves. You know you've really got to control yourself and it's really hard.

There'll be times when I think if I don't put her in the pram, I'll strangle her. But I mean you don't, it's just a point you get to.

Conclusions

Our material on anger and on attitudes to child abuse differs from many of the studies of non-accidental injury in that the sample was a 'normal' one of non-battering parents. Interesting insights can nevertheless be drawn from the experiences of those 'normal' mothers. In particular, our survey draws attention to the prevalence of anger in the early weeks after birth and to the widespread sympathy for parents who find themselves unable to contain their aggression. In looking at the factors associated with feelings of anger and the sympathy which these feelings awakened, we drew attention to the following points:
1. That anger, and the gamut of emotions associated with it, typically surfaced in situations where the mother was coping with her baby's persistent crying and her own chronic tiredness.
2. That in such situations, women's feelings of responsibility and uncertainty were accentuated to the point of crisis.
3. That anger directed towards the baby was one response to these feelings, but as an alternative a mother might direct anger towards others or towards herself.
4. That other family members and material circumstances played a key role in dissipating or intensifying the mothers' anger.
5. That mothers employed strategies to resolve or block their feelings of anger. These strategies hinged around intervention: introducing a barrier, either real or symbolic, between mother and baby.
6. That where anger escaped there was a tendency to define baby battering in such a way that her own behaviour lay outside its boundaries. Her behaviour nonetheless evoked considerable guilt.

Taken together, these points underline the need for a reformulation of the 'problem' of battering. In the light of these results, I suggest that the central question is not why a minority of parents batter their children, but why and how the majority of parents manage to survive the early months after birth without resorting to physical abuse.

REFERENCE
Kempe, C.H. (1971) 'Paediatric Implications of the Battered Baby Syndrome', *Archives of Disease in Childhood, 46,* pp. 28–37.

51

4 Maternal Anger and the Young Child

Neil Frude and Alison Goss

The overall impact of being a parent differs markedly from family to family and parent to parent. For some, parenthood brings intense joy and a sense of fulfilment but for others it may be a nightmare. Parents differ in their circumstances, their personalities and their initial attitudes to children, and children themselves vary widely in their health and behaviour. If some abuse reflects extremes of characteristics which vary within a 'normal', non-injuring, population then we might expect to be able to learn something of the antecedents of abuse, and perhaps even more about means of prevention, by studying appropriate aspects of the lives and interactions of such a non-injuring group.

A postal questionnaire was sent at the end of 1977 to a sample of mothers with a child between 18 months and four years old. Names and addresses were taken from hospital birth records in Cardiff, Wales and the return of 111 suitably completed forms represented a response rate of close to 50%. Questions focussed on mothers' difficulties in handling the child, styles of discipline and ways of dealing with feelings of anger.

The size and nature of the survey did not allow the definitive estimation of general population parameters for any of the variables which were examined but it did enable us to indicate estimates of at least minimal rates for certain of the difficulties and reactions which had been experienced. We were also able to examine relationships between variables within the questionnaire and between mothers' responses and data taken from the hospital records. Analysis of replies to open-ended questions provided information about particular problems and anxieties and enabled us to at least make a start in building up an inventory of those difficulties and of strategies which had been evolved for dealing with them.

There was no doubt that this group of mothers had been faced with a very wide range of situations. Some found it very easy and pleasurable whereas for one or two it had all been something of a nightmare, and several others had certainly had major troubles at some point along the way. The mothers were invited, after completing the questionnaire, to write freely about their experiences as parents, and the full range of reactions became clearly evident through their accounts.

There are days when Sophie screams for most of the day. If we go out shopping or visiting she usually has a tantrum. It can be very embarrassing. I keep calm mostly, there is no point in smacking her, it just makes things worse. Sophie's Daddy now does permanent night work so he is always at home in the day to help me cope. She gets us both down together but it is much easier that way. We have learned to be extra patient with Sophie.

What with my son's frequent illnesses, hospitalization and unsuccessful night breast-feeding, I found that this child has really dragged me down and got me down. Obviously I would never part with him, and love him very much, but from birth to 18 months I found it traumatic to say the least. I contemplated suicide and because of the pressure of my son and other things became very depressed. Despite more and more tranquillizers I became more suicidal and was finally put under a psychiatrist.

I have a bad temper and a tendency to be impatient, but a great deal of the time I feel so physically ill that I just feel that I cannot cope as I should. I am afraid that when this is the case I am too quick in what I do and say towards what the children are doing.

These illustrations of some of the more extreme negative experiences provide a sharp contrast with the following accounts.

We live in a large house, and as Sarah is the only child and granddaughter I am always free to go out with my husband and life for me hasn't changed much. Also, throughout the summer months, when Mam and Dad go to the caravan for the weekend, Sarah loves to go with them.

My son William, you might find it hard to believe, has been perfect since born. I have not had one night up with him, not known he's had a tooth through until I happened to look. Of course, he's a little devil, like all boys.

The thing is, we had to wait so long for our baby, plus two miscarriages on the way, that we were thrilled with him and love him very much, and that is all I can say.

Mothers' difficulties.

One fifth (20%) of the mothers claimed that the child had been more difficult to cope with than they had anticipated and for the same proportion (22%) there had been times during which problems with the child made them feel that they couldn't cope with him or her any longer. These difficulties included toilet-training and eating problems, but there were also many bedtime and sleeping difficulties, for example in getting the child to go to bed or with persistent night-time crying or screaming. One woman reported that she became 'physically and mentally exhausted' as a result of her little boy's 'persistent screaming for no reason, or for a reason I cannot understand' and the mother of a two-and-a-half year old claimed that she had 'rarely had a decent night's sleep since the birth'.

The questionnaire asked 'In what ways does your child get on your nerves?' and the free responses to this question provided a wide-ranging inventory of annoying behaviours. It is possible to classify these in various ways. Some, for example, are associated with care activities (not eating, not standing still while being dressed), some involve specific defiant gestures, and so forth. One way of attempting to characterize the various situations in the final comprehensive list as succinctly as possible involves a process of identifying a limited number of elements or themes, and when such an analysis was carried out three such elements became apparent in the list.

Some annoying situations could be seen primarily as *irritants* (involving, for example, crying, screaming, whining or eating messily), some involved *transgressions* (acts of defiance, lying, swearing) and some seemed primarily to involve *costs* for the mother, usually of time or effort (for example the child interfering when she was trying to work, or frequently wetting). All of the examples given by mothers seemed to include at least one of these elements and many contained more than one. If a child being dressed by a busy mother continues to wriggle after having repeatedly been told to stand still, then that situation may be seen by the mother as irritating, costly in terms of time and effort, and one in which the child is being deliberately naughty, or transgressing.

Almost all of the respondents (96%) reported that there had been days when 'everything got on top' of them, making them noticeably less patient with the child and several factors were identified as likely to contribute to this feeling. These included isolation in the house, housework, marital disharmony and worries, either about the children or about money. The two factors which seemed most strongly to influence mood in this way, however, were tiredness and symptoms associated with the menstrual cycle. Two-thirds of the women recognized that the monthly cycle affected their tolerance towards the child.

Reactions.

In several questions mothers were asked about their reactions during times of special difficulty with the child. In one of these they were asked how they coped with persistent crying or 'grizzling'. The free responses to this question were generally found to be easily codable into one of four categories.

One-fifth of the responses were coded into each of the three categories *punishment* (which included smacking, shouting, scream-ing, threats and 'sending to bed'), *ignoring*, and *comfort* (which included cuddling, giving attention, 'loving' and giving a dummy). Rather more mothers (one-third) gave a response coded as *distraction* as their first or only mentioned reaction. In order to distract crying children various mothers reported that they played with them, sang to them, took them for walks or sat them in front of a television set. A small number (5%) mentioned that they would typically try to find out the reason for the crying, and a slightly larger proportion gave some indication that they differentiated between types of crying and that their reaction would depend on their overall interpretation.

Many of the women reported that they would first try one technique to inhibit crying and then if that didn't work they would progress to another, but there was no easily discernible consensual 'hierarchy' of responses. Dealing with a crying child was clearly a fairly regular event for many of these women and it seemed that most had evolved strategies to deal with it, but there were a few exceptions to this. In one report a mother stated 'Any child's crying goes through me, it upsets me, and I just want to cry myself'.

A large proportion of the mothers expressed some anxiety over the adequacy of their control over the child and it was clear that the maintenance of discipline was highly valued in this population. Only 10% disagreed with the statement that 'too many children are allowed to do just as they like, and some strong discipline would do them good'. Physical punishment methods were much used. Only 4% said that they 'never' smacked the child, and 50% did this either 'very often' or 'fairly often'.

There were, however, worries about punishment being too extreme or erratic. Over one-third (38%) admitted that they sometimes punished the child for things which at other times they would have ignored, and one-quarter (26%) said they found themselves punishing the child in ways that they believed to be wrong. Most often these involved shouting or smacking too hard, but others mentioned giving undeserved punishments when feeling especially tired or irritable or over-reacting in public to embarrassing incidents. One woman regretted telling her three-year old daughter that she didn't like her which, she said, upset the little girl very much. Two mothers regretted giving the child a hard shaking and several mentioned smacking too hard on a vulnerable spot. One mother reported that 'sometimes the nearest bit of him to hit is near his head and I have boxed his ears, perhaps three times, which I regret'. One mother remarked that 'you don't realize what you've done until you see the bruises later'.

Over half (57%) admitted that on at least one occasion they had 'lost their temper completely and hit the child really hard' and 40% had entertained the fear that they might one day lose their temper and 'really hurt' the child. Comparing the group with those mothers who do not express such a fear we find that they have a greater tendency to report erratic discipline and frequent use of physical punishment. As a group they also report more irritation in response to the child's crying and are worried about the possibility of losing control over the child. Each of the relationships mentioned here is associated with a statistical probability of less than one in 1000. There is also a slight, though significant, association with social class, with working class mothers more frequently reporting a fear of harming the child.

The mother's mood.

A common theme in mothers' accounts of their reactions was that emotional reaction and punishment often reflected not the behaviour of the child but a predisposed ill-temper of the mother. Some mothers related this to their general temperament:

> I have a tendency to quick temper and am not a very patient person and I therefore fly off the handle without needing a good reason.

but most related it to particular feelings of tiredness or irritability at that time:

> I sometimes feel less patient because I am feeling extra tired.

In trying to understand how mood affects an aggressive reaction it is of interest to discover whether the effect is mainly on judgements about the situation or on the emotional or behavioural reaction produced. From the present study there is evidence of both types of involvement. Mood affects judgement and annoyance:

> If I am tired, what normally I would brush off annoys me.

> Depends on my personal mood. What's unacceptable one day could be quite amusing on another.

But in addition to this the intensity of the punishment given seems independently to reflect the mood:

Smacking is my first reaction to relieve tension when I'm feeling less patient than usual.

I smack, sometimes too hard, as a punishment, but I find that its a harder smack if I feel irritable.

Accounts of particular incidents.

Twenty-two respondents were able to give an account of a particular incident in which they had really lost their temper and hit the child and it was clear that in a few of these there had been a serious danger of injury.

It was with my eldest girl. When she was younger I was going out and she was getting in the way. Then I picked her up and I just threw her. She banged her head on the side of the wall. I was so frightened I had to pick her up and give her attention. I felt sorry for her. Never again.

With just one exception the child was reported as doing something to trigger the aggressive outburst, and in the exceptional case the mother had been suffering from severe pre-menstrual symptoms. Sometimes the trigger behaviour was almost incidental – one mother reported that it had been 'Just one small silly thing that triggered off built-in tensions within me' – but often it was an action which understandably brought about an intense emotional response.

Various elements recurred in the accounts of the children's actions leading to the incident. Irritating *nuisance* behaviour was predominant in one third of the cases and included persistent 'getting in the way' and loud continuous screaming in the early hours of the morning. *Defiance* was the apparent key feature in another one third of cases and this included 'throwing food all around the room' and 'deliberate' dirtying, especially after a recent change of nappy.

I had just completed changing her clothes after her messing everything, then she stood by the pot and wet the carpet and laughed.

As he often did, he looked me straight in the eye, pulling his pants down and dirtying on the floor.

In a few cases there was a real *cost* of effort or money involved. A glass wedding present had been smashed, scouring powder had been tipped over the floor, a room had been talcum-powdered, a television set chalked all over and nail varnish painted over a dressing table. Finally, certain actions of the children involved in these incidents

57

had exposed them to real *danger*, and it seems as though the fear which had been aroused had become translated into the extreme aggressive outburst – a phenomenon reported also in other sorts of aggression incidents.

> She frightened me because she was warned about using matches and she found some and lit them and put them in the bin still lit. She won't touch them now.

Another child had been playing with the dials of an electric cooker, and another had run across a busy road.

Most often, however, the child's action could hardly be seen as a sufficient condition for an outburst of the intensity indicated and in most cases the mother recognized that her reaction had also reflected her own current mood state. In response to a question about whether other things had happened to affect their mood on the day of the incident, half of the mothers did recall some such factor.

> I was tired. I had been up with the baby the night before, and then the child had been generally uncooperative the whole day long.

> I was looking for a coat for my daughter as well as my weekend shopping. We tramped miles, and I didn't get a coat. Everywhere they were too dear.

> It was just one of those days when everything seems to go wrong. Not enough time, too much to do, and a general feeling of edginess.

Other respondents mentioned children having been irritable or defiant, one mentioned severe premenstrual symptoms, and another remembered that there had been particularly heavy money problems at the time. Because of the interdependency between family members in their moods, experiences and behaviours, there may be widespread effects of any change for one individual and it may be impossible to disentangle the factors leading to a particular incident. The child's 'trigger' behaviour may itself be a response to the low attentiveness of a tired and irritable mother who then reacts to that trigger in an extreme fashion. Such a 'systems' effect is implicit in a number of accounts.

> Loss of sleep over a few weeks had made me irritable and quarrelsome with the family, and because of this we were all rather unhappy and tense.

Mothers were asked to indicate, using a mood check list, how they had been feeling immediately prior to the incident. Only five checked the adjective 'normal', and three of these were the mothers who had reacted to self-endangering behaviour of the child. The most commonly indicated moods were 'tired', 'depressed' and 'irritated' and all mothers who did not check 'normal' reported feeling at least one of these. 'Anxiety' and 'tension' were also indicated in a number of cases.

Those mothers who recalled a particular incident were more likely than others to see themselves in danger of one day losing control and hurting the child, they reported more frequent use of physical methods of discipline and were likely to admit to sometimes using punishment unjustifiably. As a group they also seemed to be more irritated by the child's crying and reported that they were frequently bored and lonely in the house. These statistically significant relationships indicate a complex multifactorial pattern of antecedents to the particular incidents and show that longer term factors such as punishment style and attitudes to discipline are involved in addition to the more immediate elements of mood and situation.

Data regarding these immediate factors suggests that in most of the incidents the aggressive act emerges from an interaction between the mother's current tired, irritated or depressed mood and the reaction to some perceived action of the child. The major exception to this pattern occurs in those cases in which the mother may be seen as reacting to the child's self-endangering behaviour. Those studies in the abuse literature which have analyzed incidents reveal a somewhat similar picture (Gil, 1970; Scott, 1973) though generally much of the research on abuse has focussed on longer term situations and more distant variables. The clinical case literature also reveals many instances in which the immediate aspects seem to be very similar to those found in incidents reported by the present non-injuring sample.

There is a notable similarity between those actions of the child which trigger serious incidents and those which are generally reported as 'getting on mothers' nerves', and indeed the elements found here among those things which annoy parents – irritants, costs and transgressions – are common to anger elicitation generally. Those things which make parents angry with their children, then, perhaps even to the point of physically attacking them, have a marked similarity to the things which more generally produce anger. This suggests that we might learn a good deal about the nature of abuse by considering it as one form of the more general phenomenon of 'assaultive behaviour', or the even wider phenomenon of 'anger reaction'.

This is not to suggest that abuse is an ordinary response to extreme external stimulation, since clearly it is not the situation itself which produces the reaction but the parent's particular appraisal of it and this may be quite idiosyncratic, reflecting individual attitudes, beliefs and sensitivities. Furthermore, the action consequences resulting from any perceived situation with the child are influenced by a large number of other factors such as behavioural style and the current social environment.

Response control strategies.

When I feel as if I'm really going to lose my temper I stop and remember her age. I then realize that my child's character and personality are mainly shaped by me and that I should take some of the blame for her behaviour.

I have sometimes felt obliged to get away from him. I either leave the room or send him into another room because he has made me feel very angry, but I return as soon as my temper has cooled in a few minutes.

Mothers know the likely dangers of letting their tempers flare, and many of them have developed effective strategies for avoiding such outcomes. Of the total sample, 84% said that there had been times when they stopped themselves losing their temper. Many of the classic anger control methods such as counting to ten, breathing deeply, leaving the room or stamping the foot are represented among the techniques reported, but some other methods are more elaborate and many of them are similar to the self-instructional and cognitive management techniques which have recently entered the therapeutic cognitive-behaviour modification repertoire (Meichenbaum, 1977; Novaco, 1975).

Some strategies were used to affect principally the mother's *appraisal* of the child's annoying behaviour, either by distraction or by setting a frame of mind to view the child sympathetically. Examples of setting a positive appraisal style include that of the mother who used the strategy of reminding herself that 'children know no better' and another who concentrated on thinking about how small and dependent the child was. A strategy which seems to combine such a technique with distraction is that of the mother who in times of such difficulty would call to mind 'scriptural references to how to bring up children and build a happy family life'. One mother reported distracting herself from current annoyance by systematically recalling moments from a very happy holiday, and two of the women said that when the older child provoked them they turned their attention to the baby, who evoked quite a different emotional reaction. One said 'I take a deep breath and look at my baby. He is so cute I cannot help laughing at him'.

Some other strategies let the appraisal take its course and seemed to be principally aimed at 'calming' the individual by directly affecting the level of *anger arousal*. Deep breathing and 'counting to ten' fit into this pattern and stamping the foot, screaming, 'screaming inside' or bursting into tears (all of which were reported by mothers in the study) may be regarded as classic examples of physical acts which may lead to aggression catharsis. Cigarettes were also used for their calming effect, and one mother reported that to control her anger she had sometimes taken a tranquillizer. Another reported putting on a favourite record, one had splashed her face with cold water and one reported using 'level B of the relaxation I learnt for the birth of my babies'.

Some strategies have their main effect at a stage subsequent to that of anger arousal. These techniques serve to substitute for or to directly inhibit aggressive *behaviour*. Inhibition-maximizing strategies reported included concentrating on the physical injury that could result from hitting the child and anticipating subsequent guilt. 'Anger may make me over-react', reported one mother, 'and I know that I'll feel guilt and remorse later. This realization of my responsibility for Peter's welfare acts as a powerful barrier'. Some mothers initiated specific actions which were incompatible with physical abuse – they started knitting, 'got on with the housework' or made a cup of tea – but the most common technique of all, and one which combines many of the features mentioned, involved simply getting out of arm's reach of the child, either by shutting the child in a room or by the mother getting away from the situation herself.

Considering the frequency with which mothers seem to become angry with the child and the fact that this emotional reaction is often intense, the reported number of incidents of extreme aggressive behaviour may be seen as low, and this might suggest that strategies for self-control are often effective. Where a parent does physically injure the child, then, it may be that 'safe' reactions are relatively low in the hierarchy of habitual responses to anger. On the other hand, perhaps we should not be too confident that the strategies reported would be effective for the mothers in the study under the most extreme conditions. Whereas nearly all of them reported that they used response control techniques, a sizeable proportion still felt that it was not impossible that control might at some point break down and that they could in some circumstances harm their child.

Implications.

There is nothing new or surprising in the finding that mothers of young children often have problems and that they often react with anger. The study did reveal some of the common antecedents of these reactions and some of the coping techniques which had been used. Many mothers are very good at dealing with and controlling such feelings, but angry hitting of the child is not rare and a substantial number of these parents seem to have rather complex and ambivalent attitudes towards discipline. They may feel that punishment is frequently necessary to avoid a certain danger of losing control over the child, but at the same time they often recognize that their own disciplining is sometimes erratic or unjust and that it could be a danger to the child.

Have we learned anything about abuse? Some obvious limitations in the scope of the study are that it deals only with maternal behaviour and only with mothers of children between 18 months and four years old. Much of the physical injury inflicted on children is the result of attacks by fathers or people other than the parents and the children involved are often outside the age range of those in the present study. Nevertheless, some of the accounts given here do show a marked similarity to case reports from the clinical abuse literature and it is suggested that the findings as a whole support the view that *some cases* of clinical abuse may best be regarded as extreme forms of the type of anger reaction which is relatively common in the general parent population.

The patterns of antecedents and reactions which have been elicited in this small-scale study may therefore bear some relevance to abuse. In several of the cases the actions reported by the parents could have resulted in physical injury and they were in fact lucky to escape such a consequence. Mothers reporting specific angry hitting incidents tended to use physical means of punishment as a routine and they admitted that their disciplining was somewhat erratic. On the day of the incident they had generally been feeling depressed, tired or irritable and there were often recent events or aspects of the current situation at that time which they recall as probably having made them particularly vulnerable to an angry outburst. Typically, the child was then seen to behave in some way which triggered the extreme reaction.

Optimistically, one might regard many of these incidents as events which required all of several elements – general behavioural style in disciplining (habitual physical punishment), mood disposition at the time, child's action as trigger, and absence of effective control motivation or technique. In terms of prevention one might therefore aim to reduce any of these, and the variety of interventions which might effectively decrease any one may be very considerable. Mood, for example, might be improved by direct social support, by helping difficult intrafamilial relationships or, in the case of pre-menstrual tension, by drugs. In many cases it is likely that the mother anticipated her outburst and if some early avoidance action could have been taken easily, and without embarrassment, then this might have been sufficient to prevent the incident.

Many mothers had learned strategies to avoid extreme reactions and used them to great effect. Perhaps it is in the recognition by the mother of danger and the use of such simple techniques that some powerful prevention strategies may lie. There can be no single or simple answer to abuse prevention, but it would hardly be paradoxical if it were found that an important key to abuse prevention were to be found in the study of parents who do not abuse their children.

REFERENCES

Gil, D.G. (1970) *Violence Against Children: Physical Child Abuse in the United States.* Harvard University Press, Cambridge, Mass.

Meichenbaum, D. (1977) *Cognitive-Behaviour Modification.* Plenum Press, New York.

Novaco, R. (1975) *Anger Control: The Development and Evaluation of an Experimental Treatment.* Heath and Co., Lexington, Mass.

Scott, P.D. (1973) 'Fatal battered baby cases'. *Medicine, Science and the Law, 13,* pp. 197–206.

5   Parental Punishment Strategies with Eleven-Year-Old Children

John and Elizabeth Newson

Whenever dramatic incidents of vandalism or juvenile crime are reported in the daily press, one can count on a spate of letters during the following days questioning whether parents nowadays are failing in their duty to discipline their children. This in turn revives the eternal debate about whether physical punishment should be condoned, or perhaps even encouraged, as a disciplinary strategy in the upbringing of children. How should professionals in teaching, social work or psychology address themselves to such questions?

In our view an informed social psychological appraisal has to start from the assumption that corporal punishment needs to be understood as a *communication* addressed to the offending child. It thus becomes impossible to predict what effect it will have unless we can also specify the social context – the complex network of explicit understandings and shared beliefs – within which this communicative act takes place. And the context must obviously include the feelings and intentions of the person who administers the punishment, the way the child regards that person, whether the fact of punishment is deliberately divulged to others, and how those who know the child – and that he has been punished – subsequently react in their future communications with him. At the human level, punishment is almost always consciously intended to humiliate the victim in the eyes of a particular audience, and it may be largely irrelevant whether it causes *physical* pain. For these reasons, we would argue that those psychological discussions which focus upon the effect of aversive stimulation on behaviour, and which have their base in experimental work with animal subjects, are of such tangential relevance to serious policy issues about the desirability of using corporal punishment on children that they merely make the psychologists seem naïve.

Perhaps at the outset in this kind of discussion it is important to state one's personal views and values, and to acknowledge them as judgements which cannot ultimately be strongly based upon evidence assessed in a totally value-free way. As enlightened, middle-class, liberal-minded, academic and professional parents, we ourselves are 'against' the use of physical punishment, though we also admit to having been driven to its use in moments of stress. Under stress or not, we subscribe to a value-system which holds that there are all sorts of 'better' and more effective ways to communicate with children which do not involve physical sanctions. We are also opposed to the use of corporal punishment by school teachers.

However, in the particular cultural context of British society, our work on child rearing practices in Nottingham, a not atypical city, forces us to acknowledge that, in practice, a substantial proportion of the parents we have interviewed do not share these sentiments with us. Not only do they threaten physical punishment in a fairly routine way as a natural part of socialization (something which our notion of 'being driven to it' would not allow us to do), but many also believe in its efficacy (or hope that it will eventually prove effective) and are quite happy to see such sanctions used in schools.

The data tables presented in the paper are all based upon a sample comprising more than 700 children whose parents we have repeatedly interviewed and they refer to interview data obtained at the ages of seven years and 11 years. The population is a class-stratified random sample of children living within the City of Nottingham and includes at least 100 respondents in each of the five social class categories shown.[1] Our questions on punishment formed only a small part of a long and comprehensive interview covering all aspects of child rearing. Table (1) is concerned with the actual incidence of smacking as reported by parents.

At seven years, 42% of all children (and more than half the boys) were being smacked as often as once a week. By 11 years the overall figure has dropped to 18%. In both sets of figures there are clear (and statistically significant) trends with social class and with the sex of the child. Relatively more smacking takes places as we move down the social scale, and boys are smacked more frequently than girls.

What lies behind this decrease in smacking between seven and 11? The verbatim comments of individual parents, tape-recorded during the interviews when their children were 11, can perhaps put some flesh on these statistical bones.

Housing Inspector's Wife (herself a Technician)
I feel when they're very young, a little slap – you can reason with them now – you can talk with them and I don't feel slapping's necessary; but if the occasion arose and we felt that it was a good thing to do. You see when they're very tiny children I sometimes think a quick slap and they know something's wrong from that – at this age one can reason and sort things out.

Sales Manager's Wife (herself a part-time shop manager)
Not as much now, I suppose, as he used to, we don't see one

Table 1

*Children who are smacked once per week or more at age 11 (age 7
bracketed), analyzed by sex and social class.*

	Social Class				
	I & II	III white collar	III manual	IV	V
Boys	9%(39%)	20%(47%)	22%(53%)	29%(52%)	42%(64%)
Girls	4%(19%)	10%(26%)	16%(33%)	16%(27%)	27%(49%)
Both	6%(29%)	15%(36%)	19%(43%)	23%(39%)	34%(56%)

Significance at age 11: class trend ↗ * * * *
(Chi-squared analyses used throughout).

	Summary		
	Middle Class	Working Class	All (Random)
Boys	14%(43%)	25%(54%)	22%(56%)
Girls	7%(23%)	17%(34%)	15%(31%)
Both	10%(33%)	21%(44%)	18%(42%)

M.class/W.class * * * *; between sexes * *

Note: Significance level convention: * * * * p less than .001;
* * * p less than .01; * * p less than .02; * p less than .05.

another quite so much! Oh, I shouldn't think a week goes by
without having one at least. (What about your husband?) Oh yes,
he will smack him, yes, if necessary. (About the same amount?)
Yes, I should think so, we're quite er . . . I think when they get old
enough, to try and reason with them – at least you try and do this
before – but whereas when they were naughty the *first* thing would
be to smack; they'd understand that more than a reasoning session,
wouldn't they? Insolent back-chat I think is the worst now.
Arguing with you when you know – well, they think they're right
and you *know* you're right. I think this is one of the worst.

Machine Operator's Wife (herself a part-time restaurant worker)
(Does she ever get smacked nowadays?) Well not now, but when
she was little and it was deliberate – not just an accident. I just used
to smack her legs. But no, I never smack her now. As I say, I'd
rather send her upstairs, you know. I think a child remembers you –
how you are – when they get older. And er . . . No, I wouldn't like
her to have really bad thoughts.

Display Manager's Wife (housewife)
Very rarely. I find that reasoning's better. But if it's something really wrong he'd probably get the slipper. Very rare nowadays. He's nearly as big as me now.

Given that parents are continuing to use smacking at this age, the indications are that it tends to be used less routinely and less formally, and much more often as a strategy of last resort. Thus it is either reserved for especially serious misdemeanours or it is something which happens when the child 'goes altogether too far' – as one mother put it, 'When I do smack her I give her a damn good hiding'. The reduced frequency of physical punishment with older children thus does not imply that when it is resorted to it will be of lesser severity. On the contrary, some mothers suggest that it needs to be rather more violent and painful to make much of an impression on an 11 year old as compared with a seven year old child (though that does not take account of the shock value of a smack given to a child who no longer expects it).

It is of interest that, although the majority of parents who have given up physical punishment gave as a reason that it now seemed socially inappropriate and perhaps demeaning for both punisher and punished, there were indeed instances where the main factor was that it was now ineffective because the mother was no longer able to hurt the child sufficiently with her bare hands.

Warehouseman's Wife (herself a part-time typist)
(Do you ever threaten to use something on her?) No, I wish I had thought of it because sometimes I hurt myself more than I do Janine. No – I would never.

GPO Driver's Wife (housewife)
No, I don't think smacking does them much good – it hurts me more than them. But if he's very naughty I tell *him* (father) and he'll deal with him.

Because smacking is now quite often the result of an escalating conflict in which parents finally lose control and lash out, they are now less likely than they were at an earlier age to justify its use in terms of training the child to discriminate right from wrong, and are more likely to stress the need for children of this age to appreciate certain rather basic rules of social conduct which also apply between adults – if you needle people too much, and drive them too far, you have to expect explosive and angry reactions, although it is very rare for parents to pursue the adult parallel to the extent of accepting that a child might be justified in smacking back!

Typically, smacking now seems to happen as the culminating act following a build-up of unresolved emotional tension. Parents who can no longer justify its rational use now see it as, at worst, a humiliating breakdown of normal self-control and, at best, a dramatic gesture which relieves an accumulation of exasperation and resentment and clears the air so that relationships can revert to a more 'normal' pattern.

The danger is, of course, that aggression released in this manner will be altogether too violent, and that loss of parental control may lead to the child being physically injured or 'marked' in some way. Some parents were clearly aware of this as a serious possibility.

Civil Servant's Wife (herself a nursing sister)
Sometimes I give him a slap. Sometimes I tend to get him upstairs and get him to come down when he's feeling better. And he says 'it wasn't me'. 'Out'. And he knows when I mean it, I mean it. And sometimes when he does something really bad, I know I really hit him and hurt him. I say 'Roger, go, because you know if I touch you once I shall really lay into you, so go for your own sake'. And he goes, 'cos he knows I will.

Bus Driver's Wife (housewife)
Well, with Evie he (father) only hits her gently. Now with Derek – when Derek used to pinch money and he used to give him real good hidings, he used to . . . he don't hit him with the flat of his hand, he punches out. And yet, you know, we get on all right. Yet if Derek pinches any more money or plays truant again, I think he'll kill him. He's threatened him with a carving knife once.

Director's Wife (housewife)
(Does she often get smacked nowadays?) Very rarely. If I'm cross. I've got a violent temper and I daren't – I've just got to get her out of the way – and take her upstairs you see.

At the age of 11 years the two situations which parents most commonly identified as leading to physical punishment were, first, cheek and answering back (i.e. not showing sufficient respect for the parents themselves or for other adults) and secondly, noisy arguments with siblings, for which parents judged the child in question mainly responsible. A third situation, less frequent but potentially more serious, was one in which the child had been reported by someone outside the family for rudeness, truancy, damage to property, etc. in such a way that the parents' failure to take rather dramatic action might place the reputation of the whole family in jeopardy.

Table 2 shows the use or threatened use of 'instruments' by these parents in punishing their children. These commonly include canes, straps and slippers, and less commonly rulers, the back of a hair brush, etc. It should be emphasized that these are responses freely admitted to by our sample parents in the context of a general interview about child rearing. We see no reason why they should wish to exaggerate on these issues, and it is plausible indeed to assume that the figures are reasonable *minimal* estimates of the extent to which parents actually resort to such threats.

Table 2

Instruments used or threatened in the punishment of the child at age 11 (age 7 bracketed) by sex and social class.

| | **Social Class** | | | | |
	I & II	III white collar	III manual	IV	V
Boys	26%(80%)	56%(97%)	52%(95%)	47%(80%)	66%(92%)
Girls	15%(51%)	19%(55%)	38%(57%)	33%(73%)	33%(69%)
Both	20%(65%)	37%(76%)	45%(76%)	40%(76%)	49%(80%)

Significance at age 11: class trend ↗ * * * *

| | **Summary** | | |
	Middle Class	Working Class	All (Random)
Boys	41%(87%)	55%(91%)	49%(91%)
Girls	17%(53%)	36%(62%)	31%(59%)
Both	29%(71%)	45%(76%)	40%(75%)

M. class/W. class * * * *; between sexes * * * *

At seven years, 75% of all children in a random sample are threatened in this way; for boys, the proportion rises to 91%! By 11 the figures have dropped substantially, to 40% overall, but still nearly half the boys are apparently subject to such threats. Threats of the cane and the strap seem to be a taken-for-granted part of child rearing for many British parents. Social class trends are again consistent and clearly significant, as are the sex differences, and both are in the same direction as in the previous table.

How often do parents actually carry out their threats? Before presenting information to answer this it is useful to draw some distinction between parents who slap in anger and the heat of the moment, and those who punish calmly and, as it were, 'on principle'. It seems reasonable to suppose that parents who threaten an implement do thereby in some sense commit themselves verbally to a belief in their *right* to exert physical force, as opposed to the mere loss of control expressed by lashing out with their hand. Parents who actually use an implement formalize the punishment still further by encapsulating it in premeditated ritual. Both implement-users and implement-threateners define themselves as willing to use the sanction deliberately rather than simply being driven to an unpremeditated act. Table 3 shows, for both 11 and seven-year-olds, how many parents had already used an implement to punish their children.

Table 3

Implements already used in punishing the child at 11 years (and 7 years) of age.

	Social Class				
	I & II	III white collar	III manual	IV	V
Boys	12%(29%)	21%(26%)	19%(27%)	13%(20%)	36%(25%)
Girls	6%(22%)	2%(18%)	5%(19%)	5%(17%)	14%(10%)
Both	9%(25%)	11%(22%)	12%(23%)	9%(18%)	25%(17%)

Significance: class trend n.s.

		Summary		
		Middle Class	Working Class	All (Random)
	Boys	16%(27%)	20%(25%)	19%(26%)
	Girls	4%(20%)	4%(18%)	5%(18%)
	Both	10%(24%)	12%(21%)	12%(22%)

M. class/W. class n.s.: between sexes * * * *

Here we find that the overall percentages are considerably smaller. More than twice as many parents only threaten, as opposed to actually carrying out, these threats (at seven years, 22% in a random sample actually carry out their threats compared with 53% who have threatened but have never put these threats into practice). From what parents say, it seems that for those who are committed to physical punishment, and believe in its ultimate effectiveness, the threat of a cane or strap (or of giving the child a 'good hiding') is used in the

70

sincere belief that it should only be necessary to carry out such threats infrequently, if at all. That parents comparatively rarely carry out their threats in practice should not, therefore, be seen as evidence of widespread inconsistency in parental discipline. More probably it indicates that such weapons are genuinely regarded as ultimate deterrents, whose usefulness might diminish if they were actually resorted to at all often. Sex differences are also quite striking and highly significant at both ages, but the relative incidence for boys as compared with girls *increases* as the children get older, so that by 11 years roughly four times as many boys as girls actually receive the strap, cane, belt, etc. A further intriguing finding is that the social class gradient is now quite non-significant both at seven and 11 years. This implies that there is a small proportion of parents in all social classes who believe in premeditated corporal punishment to the extent that they have actually practised it on their children. However it should be noted that this proportion is reduced substantially between seven and 11 years of age.

Some confirmation of the absence of class differences in resorting to 'formal' punishment can be obtained from the next table, which shows the percentages of parents who do use smacking, after excluding those who smack 'in anger only' i.e. informally. Our question was 'How often does he in fact get a smack from you or from his father?'

Table 4

Proportion of parents who use smacking as a deliberate correction, at least on occasion, as a function of sex and social class at age 11 years

	I & II	III white collar	III manual	IV	V
		Social Class			
Boys	20%	19%	24%	22%	28%
Girls	17%	21%	24%	28%	20%
Both	18%	20%	24%	25%	24%

Significance: class trend n.s.

	Middle Class	Working Class	All (Random)
		Summary	
Boys	19%	24%	23%
Girls	19%	24%	23%
Both	19%	24%	23%

M. Class/W. Class n.s.; between sexes n.s.

Here neither class differences nor sex differences are large enough to yield a significant result. This seems to lead us to the conclusion that class differences are more apparent in relation to unpremeditated forms of physical punishment – those to which parents feel driven. The social class gradient is much reduced in relation to more formal or deliberate acts of corporal punishment.

Punishment across cultures

In a broader cross-cultural perspective, the physical punishment of children seems to be taken for granted in Britain in a way which is not the norm in, for instance, the U.S.A. or many European countries. We have also been able to obtain some reasonably comparable data by using a uniform index of parental reliance on corporal punishment for our main sample and for two additional samples comprising 200 Punjabi immigrant and 200 West Indian immigrant families with children at around seven years of age[2]. It should be noted here that, in the interests of homogeneity, the main sample we have been discussing so far specifically excluded immigrant children. Plotting the frequency distributions of this index of corporal punishment shows in quite a dramatic way how the Punjabi parents resort hardly at all to physical acts of punishment with their seven-year-olds, whereas the West Indian parents punish their children still more frequently and severely than do indigenous white parents.

It is perhaps salutary to remind ourselves that historically West Indian parents derive their values from a hierarchical and rigid social system which institutionalized and condoned slave labour and the physical beating of slaves by our own forebears. Additionally, West Indian culture has since been influenced by a strong commitment to a revivalist religion (also imported from Britain) which stresses that pain to the body is of far less concern than damnation of the soul (Newson and Newson, 1974). By contrast, Punjabi parents come from a traditional and well established culture in rural India which emphasizes 'respect' towards parents (and to adults generally). These parents assume that a resort to physical violence between themselves and their children could only imply that the conventional and established norms of family life had broken down altogether. Paradoxically, Punjabi parents also believe that in later childhood their children may well need to be physically punished by their teachers if they fail to learn in school. They place a strong emphasis on the virtues of formal education and think that English teachers are too soft.

In fact, by the time their children reach the age of 11 years a surprisingly large proportion of indigenous Nottingham parents also believe that teachers should be permitted to use the cane on their pupils. Table 5 shows that in a random cross-section of ordinary parents more than half are of this opinion, and it is again interesting that consistent social class differences are not in evidence on this issue. From the qualitative answers given, however, it seems that the English parents were less often thinking about whether their own children should be punished in this way, and were mainly concerned that a minority of disruptive pupils should not be permitted to interfere with the progress of the majority.

Table 5

Do you think teachers should be allowed to use a cane or strap on children of N's age? (11 year old children).

Proportions of parents answering 'Yes', as a function of sex and class.

	Social Class				
	I & II	III white collar	III manual	IV	V
Boys	47%	74%	59%	57%	65%
Girls	40%	56%	48%	43%	50%
Both	44%	65%	54%	50%	58%

Significance: class trend, non-linear * * *

	Summary		
	Middle Class	Working Class	All (Random)
Boys	60%	58%	59%
Girls	48%	47%	47%
Both	54%	53%	53%

M. class/W. class n.s.; between sexes * * *

The actual proportion of children who, to their parents' knowledge, had received the cane or strap at school by the age of 11 years is shown in Table 6.

Drawing these various strands of information together, then, we have to recognize that the majority of British parents we have interviewed seem to believe that physical punishment is an inevitable and probably necessary aspect of ordinary child upbringing. This belief marks them out as being somewhat more committed to the use

73

Table 6

Proportions of children who have received the cane or strap at school by age 11

	Social Class				
	I & II	III white collar	III manual	IV	V
Boys	20%	30%	22%	22%	39%
Girls	5%	7%	5%	9%	7%
Both	12%	18%	13%	15%	23%

Significance: class trend ↗ *

	Summary		
	Middle Class	Working Class	All (Random)
Boys	24%	24%	24%
Girls	6%	6%	6%
Both	15%	15%	14%

M. class/W. class n.s.; between sexes * * * *

of physical punishment than is the case in Western societies taken as a whole. Contributory evidence on this point has recently been offered by the organisation STOPP (the Society of Teachers Opposed to Physical Punishment). They have drawn attention to the fact that Great Britain and Ireland are now alone among the countries of Continental Europe in permitting teachers to use corporal punishment in schools. They are also suggesting that individual parents who object to current British practices may be able to appeal successfully to the European Commission on Human Rights.

Prognoses for Socialization

Given that parents in Britain who habitually resort to physical punishment can be seen to be conforming to a cultural norm, it remains true that there are considerable variations between families, both in whether and how often punishment is actually used, and in whether it is thought to be desirable or effective as an instrument of socialization. A key question which may therefore be asked is whether such differences relate in any way to whether the children subsequently turn out to be 'good' or 'bad'. In practice this is a complex and difficult question to pose, and simplistic interpretations must be avoided. Gross quantitative associations are always difficult to interpret unambiguously. One must constantly bear in mind the crudity of the measures being employed, in contrast to the complexity and subtlety of the contextual factors informing individual instances of punishment, which we could not do more than barely mention in the introduction to this chapter.

Our method was to define an index of putative 'delinquency' to be referred to hereinafter as the *Delindex*. This is obviously only a rough and ready measure of potential deviance, based on the information we had available from the answers given to certain questions on the 11 year interview schedule. Table 7 presents a list of the questions which entered into the composition of the 'Delindex' and shows how the different categories of answer were scored to produce a composite measure for each child.

Table 7

Questions and answers from the 11-year-old interviews used to define the 'Delindex'

		Coding	Score
Q.10	Is he one of those children who is always in hot water, or does he manage to keep out of mischief mostly?	Hot water	2
		Varies	1
		Keeps out	0
Q.186	Sometimes children of this age go through a phase of taking things that don't belong to them, have you had this at all?	Yes	1
		No	0
Q.187	Has he ever been in real trouble with school so that you have really had to speak to him seriously?	Yes	1
		No	0
Q.188	Has he ever played truant from school, so far as you know?	Yes	1
		No	0
Q.190	Has he ever got himself in trouble with the neighbours?	Yes	1
		No	0
Q.191	Or the police?	Yes	1
		No	0

Possible score range: 0 to 7

An index was formed showing for each child whether he or she was 'constantly in hot water' or had already been in some kind of serious trouble with the neighbours, at school, over thieving, or with the police. The resulting 'Delindex' scores were distributed as follows.

In view of the shape of this frequency distribution and taking into account the content of the questions comprising the index it was decided to define as 'potentially delinquent' children who scored two

Table 8

Distribution of Delindex scores in a sample of 780 11-year-olds

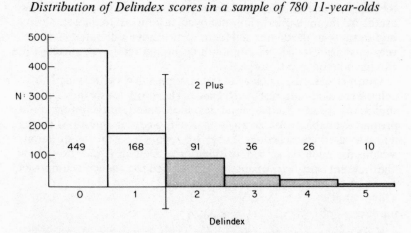

Delindex

or more points on this index. In a perfect random sample of such children, 22% would score two or more points.

There are various advantages and disadvantages in defining an index of pre-delinquency or proto-delinquency in this way. As the information is all based upon parental report, it is possible that some parents would not like to present their children in a bad light and would therefore dissemble in answering these specific questions, in which case this method of identifying such children would be missing some children who would be rated troublesome had their parents been more frank. Given that we may have missed a few children in this way, however, it seems reasonable to believe that those who do admit to troublesome activity to the extent that they score two or more points are giving us genuine information about a group of children who are somewhat deviant in the direction of delinquency. A further reason for credibility is that the questions being asked were posed in confidence and in the context of a long interview covering many different, and more pleasant, aspects of child behaviour and upbringing. The conversation was not seen by the respondents as addressed towards labelling their children by name as delinquent, and indeed was not intended for any such purpose. Other methods of defining a delinquent child, based upon whether he has been officially stigmatized as having committed some illegal act or broken the bounds of social convention enough to receive some formal reprimand from persons other than parents, are somewhat more likely to produce defensive parental attitudes, and perhaps class biased results. The situation may also have been less threatening because these children were on the whole still too young to be formally charged with having committed criminal offences. It was hoped, therefore, that the results based upon this index could give some useful clues about the factors which pre-date genuine delinquency as it is more conventionally defined. In the total actual sample of 11-year-olds' interviews (780 cases), the proportion of children scoring two or more on the 'Delindex' is 21%, which in a corrected 'random' sample would be 22%. Table 9 gives the proportions of these proto-delinquent children analyzed as a function of sex and social class and shows, firstly, that there is a general trend towards an increase in the proportion of two-plus scorers as we descend the social class scale and, secondly, that there is a notable increase in incidence as the middle class/working class borderline is crossed. There is also a highly significant sex-difference.

Table 10 shows the relationship between 'Delindex 2-plus' and a number of possible sociological factors.

It is noteworthy that, in contrast to the popular stereotype, the mothers who work full-time (or even those who work part-time) are, if anything, *less* likely than non-working mothers to have children who fall into the 'two-plus' category. Even though these two results

Table 9

Children who score 2 or more on the Delindex measure, as a function of sex and social class.

	I & II	III white collar	III manual	IV	V
		Social Class			
Boys	18%	16%	34%	31%	41%
Girls	11%	7%	16%	16%	15%
Both	15%	11%	25%	24%	28%

Significance: class trend ↗ * * * *

	Middle Class	Working Class	All (Random)
	Summary		
Boys	17%	35%	30%
Girls	9%	16%	14%
Both	13%	25%	22%

M. class/W. class * * * *; between sexes * * * *

Table 10

Association between Delindex 2-plus and other factors

Sample	Variable investigated	N = 173 DELINDEX 2 +	N = 607 The rest	
All (Random)	Mother works full-time	13%	12%	n.s.
All (Random)	Mother not working	42%	36%	n.s.
All (Random)	Family size *large* (4-plus children)	50%	40%	chi-squared = 5.50**
All (Random)	Family size *large* (social class controlled)	46%	40%	n.s.
Working-class boys	District of residence: central city	32%	19%	chi-squared = 4.98**

are not significant, their direction is of interest[3]. The findings also emphasize that the potential delinquency rate is higher in the city centre districts (districts within approximately one mile of the city centre) than in either the 'council estate' or 'suburban-other' residential categories. This effect is not simply an artefact of class composition, since it holds significantly even among the numerically reduced sample comprising working-class boys only. Taken together, then, these results provide a kind of rough validity check on the meaningfulness of the 'potential delinquency' measure we have used.

As a further check we were able, at a somewhat later stage in our longitudinal study, to identify a small number of children in our sample who had gone on to commit real offences and acquire a police record. Our method of identification has inevitably missed some such individuals – and of course the ball has not stopped rolling yet – but among a group of 54 children so far positively identified, 27 had Delindex scores of two-plus at the age of 11, which represents an incidence of 50%. Remembering that the incidence for the children as a whole was 21%, and calculating that it would be 19% for the total group of non-identified children, this presents a result which could not be attributed to chance (Chi-squared = 24.9, d.f. = 1, p less than 0.001). Such a clear-cut statistical association lends additional weight to the validity of 'Delindex 2 +' as a meaningful categorization. Of course, such evidence does not provide a clear prognosis in the sense of showing that a high proportion of children scoring two-plus at age 11 are inevitably on a pathway to adult criminal conviction, since the majority of them do not go on to get into serious trouble.

Delindex two-plus and parental punishment strategies

Table 11 attempts to examine the relationship between Delindex two-plus and various categories of disciplinary methods used by parents. All these findings derive from information obtained from interviews at the 11-year-old stage only.

Table 11

Association between Delindex 2+ and the use of physical punishment

Sample	Variable Investigated	N = 173 DELINDEX 2 +	N = 607 The rest	
All (Random)	Instrument used or threatened	60%	33%	Chi-squared = 35.10****
All (Random)	Instrument used	25%	9%	Chi-squared = 26.36****
All (Random)	Child smacked 1 plus per week at 11	34%	11%	Chi-squared = 48.15****
All (Random)	Mother smacks in anger only	70%	68%	n.s.
All (Random)	Mother uses smacking as a deliberate corrective (excluding 'None' and 'In anger only')	25%	22%	n.s.

It can be seen that, in every comparison made, mothers who punish more are if anything more likely, as opposed to less likely, to have children in the Delindex two-plus category. Such a finding, as yet unsupported by other evidence, must remain ambiguous in terms of any simple causal explanation. It could be that punishing parents produce naughty children or, equally, that naughty children drive their parents to adopt punitive methods of control. The only secure conclusion that can be drawn is the rather negative one, that the old-fashioned, simplistic adage 'spare the rod and spoil the child' is clearly not supported by this kind of statistical evidence in the context of contemporary child-rearing beliefs and practices. We are not justified in telling parents that if they punish their children more severely, in the physical sense, this will necessarily prevent them from getting into trouble.

Of more interest, perhaps, is a secondary implication arising from the pattern of differences shown. Parents who use physical punishment as a deliberate disciplinary strategy are not significantly more likely than the parents who feel 'driven' to smack, to have children who kick over the traces. It also appears, however, that they are not actually more successful in producing 'good' children than parents who manage to avoid habitual resort to physical punishment.

On the whole, these results do lend support to the well-known association between children's tendency to get into trouble with the community and the tendency of parents of such children to punish them with greater severity. There is also some suggestive evidence that this association is less strong when we take into consideration the deliberate and principled intentions underlying parental punishment strategies, rather than simply their severity.

NOTES
1. The sample is based upon the Registrar General's Classification of Social Class, but for our class categories we have chosen to combine his Classes I and II (upper and lower professional/managerial) and to divide his Class III into white collar (shop and clerical) and manual (skilled trades).
2. This work was carried out in the Child Development Research Unit at Nottingham by Dr J.S. Dosanjh and Miss Angeline Grace.
3. In practice, 'mother working' is ambiguously related to social class. Slightly more middle-class than working-class mothers are working full-time, slightly more working-class than middle-class mothers do part-time work outside the home, and slightly more Class V mothers do not work at all, which is probably related to their having, on average, larger families.

REFERENCES
Newson, J. and Newson, E. (1974) 'Cultural aspects of child-rearing in the English-speaking world'. In: M.P.M. Richards (Ed.) *The Integration of a Child into a Social World*. Cambridge University Press.

Approaches to the Study of Abuse

6   Contributions of an Ethological Approach to the Understanding of Abuse

Kevin Browne and Robert Parr

It is generally accepted that child abuse is a complex problem, not amenable to general explanation in terms of one or even a few causal factors. The purpose of this chapter is to review the ways in which an ethological approach to the study of behaviour may contribute to our understanding of abuse. Such contributions are seen as complementary to the sociological and psychological approaches rather than as representing an alternative.

In recent years ethology has become increasingly involved in the study of child behaviour (Blurton Jones, 1972), particularly in the examination of the interactive relationship between the mother and her infant (Lewis & Rosenblum, 1974; Schaffer, 1977b) and the theoretical interpretation of this relationship in terms of survival and evolution (Bowlby, 1969). This has encouraged a change of emphasis regarding the methods used by developmental psychologists, away from descriptive and psychometric techniques and towards those involving direct observation of behaviour. Such techniques have been usefully described by Hutt and Hutt (1970). Our work at the University of Surrey (described by Clare Hyman in Chapter 7) suggests that the application of an ethological approach, through the detailed observation and description of communication patterns between the infant and its caregiver, may lead to a better understanding of the problems in abusing families.

The Characteristics and Concepts of Ethology

Ethology developed through the naturalistic observation and description of animal behaviour pioneered by Charles Darwin (1872) and can be most simply defined as the 'Biology of Behaviour' (Eibl-Eibesfeldt, 1975). Following the classic works of Lorenz (1950) and Tinbergen (1951) the method can be seen as involving the prolonged observation of the animal under investigation, observation within the animal's natural environment, description involving anatomical terms rather than broad categories, and the study of a wide range of species.

83

As outlined by Tinbergen (1951), ethology focuses upon the reasons why an animal behaves the way it does, upon the functional aspects of the observed behaviour patterns and the development of these in order to determine which selection pressures have shaped their evolution. Just as zoologists have demonstrated the evolution of anatomical features through natural selection, ethologists endeavour to provide an evolutionary perspective to the study of behaviour. We have stressed, then, both the *methods* of ethology and the *theoretical stance* from which it originates. Methods and theory, however, may be separated. We are free to adopt either one without the other.

Ethological Aspects of Human Behaviour

It is generally accepted that pre-programmed, genetically determined, aspects of behaviour become less important as we ascend the phylogenetic scale. By 'less important' it is usually meant that the effects of learning tend to complicate the characteristics of behaviour, making it more varied in appearance. However, merely because this variety is due in large part to the effects of experience, this does not imply that biological bases of human behaviour are unimportant. A thorough understanding of human behaviour cannot develop without a recognition of the biological influences and constraints upon behaviour which affect learning and the impact of the environment.

Hinde (1974) considers that studies in animal behaviour, when used for the development of methods and the formation of general principles, can contribute significantly to an understanding of the biological bases of human behaviour. He adds a need for caution in any such extrapolation, however, and stresses the need for direct confirmatory evidence from human studies. With this proviso in mind we wish to consider examples of 'parental' aggression in non-human primates.

Most recently, Nash (1978) found that maternal aggression was rare in wild baboons even when quite minor behaviours such as 'threat' and 'push' were included in the analysis. On those occasions when aggression did occur there were identifiable situational contexts. The first of these involved resistance by the mother to her child's riding, the second was that of weaning and the third context was the situation in which the mother was in consort with an adult male. The aggressiveness of the mother in each of these kinds of situation may be considered as functional when seen in the light of contemporary evolutionary theory. Such theory holds that selection pressure operates so that an individual will tend to maximize the 'passing-on' of its own genes. Maternal aggression in each of the contexts cited may be seen as adaptive in that it increases the mother's own 'genetic fitness'. In the case of the resistance to riding the mother is forcing independence on her infant and thereby increasing her chances of mating and producing further offspring. The weaning of an infant not only increases the mother's independence from her infant but also increases her fertility, and the repulsion of the infant whilst the mother is in consort with a male clearly increases her chances of reproducing. DeVore (1963) has also reported that mother baboons forcefully reject their infants more frequently during oestrus.

These examples of aggressive behaviour towards offspring seem to have a functional basis and there is never any mention of serious injury being sustained by the infant. In view of these considerations it would be naïve to draw a direct parallel between child abuse in humans and the aggression reported here without first assessing the relevance of the application of evolutionary theory to parent-infant relationships.

The comparative data that are available from experimental studies in which social isolation or separation from mother have been used do suggest a closer link with child abuse in humans but even here we should be very careful in generalizing. Harlow et al. (1963) found that female rhesus monkeys subjected to social isolation in infancy were normally unable to successfully mate as adults. When matings were 'arranged', however, and offspring produced, the mothers showed little or no maternal behaviour – on the contrary they physically attacked their infants, treating them as they would an intruding member of another species. It should be remembered that Harlow's monkeys not only lacked a mother when young but were also socially isolated. Suomi (1976) on the other hand studied 50 rhesus monkeys which, although all motherless, had experienced varying lengths of social isolation in infancy. Again it was found that the 'motherless mothers' abused and neglected their offspring but Suomi reported that those mothers which had experienced shorter periods of isolation tended to be more competent mothers.

At first sight one might be tempted to refer to such studies as indicating the possible basis of the frequently reported fact that battering parents have often experienced unsatisfactory or abusive relationships as children. However, severe deprivation of the order of that imposed upon these rhesus monkeys occurs in only the most extreme cases in humans.

The importance of this work does not lie in its potential for supplying an experimental analogue of human child abuse, but in the effects that it has had upon our ideas about and approaches to the study of early social development in human infants. For example, Harlow has demonstrated that the rhesus monkey's attachment to its mother is not based upon the mother as a supplier of nourishment but is based upon contact comfort. Thus an infant rhesus monkey deprived of a real mother and given the choice of a terrycloth-covered artificial mother and a wire surrogate with a milk bottle and teat attached, will stay close to, or cling to, the terrycloth mother in preference to the milk-provider when confronted with a novel or alarming stimulus. The work of Harlow and his associates has been partly responsible for significant development in our understanding of social attachments in human infants.

The Theory of Attachment

It is now many years since Bowlby first published his views on the nature of the child's tie to the mother – 'attachment' – and a more comprehensive account of his ideas became available in 1969. A number of general considerations and lines of evidence led to Bowlby's particular views. Among these were the work of Harlow, described above, the study of imprinting and critical periods of development in certain precocial birds (Lorenz, 1942; Hess, 1959) and the wealth of literature linking the disruption of the child's early relationship with his mother to a whole range of later problems. More specifically, Bowlby set out to understand why infants become upset when separated from their mothers, why they show fear of strangers and how such behaviours are related to the exploration of the environment. He adopted an evolutionary perspective from which to view the attachment of the child to his mother, considering how the behaviours which are expressions of this tie may have served to contribute to the survival of the infant by increasing the protection which the mother gives.

Human infants are presumed to be predisposed to form specific emotional attachments during a relatively limited period of their infancy (it is now generally agreed that the period of attachment formation extends for the majority of children from about the fifth month to one year of age). As the principal caretaker, the mother is most frequently the primary object of the child's attachment, although some investigators have shown that this is by no means always the case (Schaffer & Emerson, 1964).

Attachment is presumed to develop as a result of specific 'attachment behaviours'. These behaviours (crying, smiling, tracking, and following) form a system which, when activated, is most likely to bring about proximity to, or contact with the mother. Exploratory behaviours are seen as forming a reciprocal system to attachment behaviours in that they involve loss of contact with and reduction of proximity to the mother. The evolutionary significance of attachment and the behaviours by which it is expressed lies in both the regulation of distance and separation from the mother and in the support of exploratory behaviour. Attachment behaviours are displayed either in response to strange objects or people or when separation from the mother occurs, thereby performing a protective function whereby nearness to the mother and therefore safety (in our evolutionary past, safety from predators) is maintained. On the other hand, the existence of the attachment to the mother also fosters exploratory behaviour and play by which experience of the environment is gained and upon which autonomous survival depends.

Bowlby's theoretical perspective has been adopted by Ainsworth and her associates and they have applied the observational approach to the study of attachment and exploratory behaviours. Ainsworth (1971) has developed a standard 'Strange Situation' procedure for directly observing individual differences in the balance between attachment and exploratory behaviours. Mary Main has described some studies involving this technique in Chapter 2. Ainsworth's procedure involves a one-year-old infant being placed in a strange environment and being confronted with a stranger in the presence and absence of the mother. Ainsworth has described three broad categories of response to the strange situation. The normative infants (Group B), although they showed some distress (particularly when left alone) showed positive responses to reunion with the mother and generally exhibited a desire for interaction with the mother in preference to the stranger. Group A infants on the other hand tended to show high levels of exploratory behaviour throughout the strange situation procedure and tended not to seek interaction with or proximity to the mother, frequently avoiding contact on reunion. The third category of response involved ambivalent behaviour, the infants in this group (Group C) showing elements of both approach and avoidance behaviour towards the mother on her return. These children also showed low levels of exploratory behaviour throughout and were more likely to cry.

Ainsworth warns against the use of a simple distinction between attached and non-attached infants and stresses that we should consider the *quality* of attachment. Thus she refers to the dimension of 'security of attachment'. In other work the relationship between the strange situation responses and the behaviour of both mother and child in the home has been examined and the results have suggested that the degree of maternal sensitivity is highly influential in affecting the child's reactions. In the homes of the securely attached infants (Group B) sensitive mothering was exhibited to the infant's behaviour. On the other hand anxiously attached, avoidant infants (Group A) were found to be rejected by the mothers in terms of interaction and it was suggested that the enhanced exploratory behaviours shown by these infants were an attempt to block attachment behaviours which had been rejected in the past. In the home environments of the insecurely attached ambivalent infants (Group C) a disharmonious mother-infant relationship was evident and the ambivalent behaviours shown were seen as a defensive reaction against insecurity.

The view of attachment behaviours as fulfilling a biological function and the belief in a period in infancy when the child is predisposed to form attachments have considerable importance in relation to child abuse. The literature on child abuse contains numerous reports regarding the high number of abusive parents who were themselves victims of abuse as children. It is our contention that in at least some cases the link between experience of abuse as a child and abusing as a parent is likely to lie in the experience of an unsatisfactory early relationship with the mother or other principal caretaker and a failure to form a secure attachment. In such cases intervention in the form of training for the mother in interaction with the child may be ineffective as we may not be dealing with a mother who has simply failed to learn certain types of maternal and caretaking behaviours but with a mother who may be emotionally unable to cope with the development of a stable relationship with her child. Kempe and Kempe (1978) estimate that of the abusive families in their experience, somewhere in the region of 10% are untreatable.

In postulating such a connection between early experience and later behaviour we are not claiming a 'one-to-one' relationship or advocating that certain groups of abusing parents be denied the opportunity to benefit from therapy and training. It is suggested, however, that those involved in the treatment of abusive families have a primary duty to the child and that they should recognize that in some cases treatment with the child remaining in the family may be ineffective and may in fact serve to perpetuate the 'abused becoming abuser' cycle.

The consideration of attachment theory, then, may change the focus of our attention when dealing with child abuse from the child's experience of abuse episodes to the wider context of the abusive relationship. If the quality of the relationship between the mother and child is the important factor determining the child's later development then perhaps treatment should be focused on this directly. 'Mothering the mother' may be successful in helping the mother to cope with other problems and yet leave the difficulties in her relationship with her child unaffected. It clearly follows from this that the assessment of treatment effectiveness must also be concerned with the development of the relationship of mother and child. It is not sufficient to evaluate treatment programmes on the basis of the occurrence or non-occurrence of subsequent abuse. Training parents to inhibit aggressive behaviour towards their children may still leave the harmful context in which the initial abuse occurred quite unchanged.

Mother-Infant Bonding.

In discussing the mother-infant relationship so far we have been concerned primarily with the child's attachment to his mother. We shall now consider the other side of the relationship and discuss the attachment of the mother to her child. In order to distinguish this mother-to-infant attachment from the infant-to-mother attachment already discussed, the term 'bond' will be used, as has become the convention.

An example of an experimental study of bonding in animals which illustrates the interaction of separation at the infant's birth and the prior experience of the mother is that of Meier's work with rhesus monkeys (1965). Meier used both feral and laboratory reared monkeys, delivering half of each group by Caesarean section and separating mother and infant for two hours, and allowing normal births for the remainder of the monkeys. Laboratory animals which had been delivered by Caesarean section and separated from their infants refused to accept their young when re-introduced, whereas feral animals subjected to the same procedures did accept their offspring. Both laboratory reared and feral animals which had given birth to their offspring in a natural manner and had not been separated accepted their newborn infants. Clearly, the effects of the period immediately following the birth are not absolutely determined, even though they are presumed to have a biological basis, but are modified by the mother's previous experience (laboratory animals are of course likely to have experienced some degree of social deprivation). This point should be borne in mind when considering the possible relationship between early separation of human mothers and infants and child abuse.

In their book *Maternal-Infant Bonding* (1976), Klaus and Kennel review clinical and experimental evidence relating to the importance of the immediate post-partum period for the development of the mother-infant relationship and hold that this supports their view that there is a sensitive period for the formation of the bond of mother to infant. During this period they consider it necessary for optimal development that close contact be made with the infant. In support of their case they refer to two studies which have examined the effects of the immediate post-partum period upon later maternal and infant behaviour. In the first of these studies Hales et al. (1977) compared maternal behaviour at 36 hours after birth in mothers who were given 45 minutes skin contact with their infants immediately after birth and mothers who received their infants at 12 hours. The early-contact mothers showed more looking at and talking to their infants and more fondling, caressing, kissing and smiling.

The effects of the post-partum period were demonstrated over a longer time period by De Chateau (1976). Observations of behaviour were made at three months for two groups of mothers and infants. The early-contact mothers were given 30 minutes of skin contact immediately after the birth whereas the control mothers had no such contact but had their babies placed in cribs close by their beds from 30 minutes to two hours after birth. At three months the early contact infants were observed to cry less and smile more than the controls. The early contact mothers more frequently adopted the *en face* position and kissed their infants more. Such differences, although relatively minor, do illustrate the effects of experience in the immediate post-partum period and point to its special importance.

It should be acknowledged that the belief in a sensitive period for the development of the mother-infant bond is not universal. Leiderman and Seashore (1975) concluded from a study of early mother-infant separation that their results did not support an ethological interpretation. However, these workers did not deal with a separation in the first 24 hours of the infant's life, which Klaus and Kennel (1976) believe to be the most important. They also adopt a rather naïve view of an ethological explanation in expecting the effects of other factors, such as social class, to be eclipsed if an ethological interpretation is to hold. In addition they suggest that later maternal behaviour is strongly related to social class, and yet they fail to control for social class in their sampling, thereby allowing the possibility that the effect of early separation may have been masked by the large degree of variability introduced.

It may be argued that the differences which have been reported are slight and that the significance of experience within the early sensitive period is unlikely to be great enough to have implications for child abuse. However, as we saw in Meier's study of rhesus monkeys, the effects of this early period are not simply or directly determined but may be modified by the mother's previous experience. It is suggested that the importance of this early period should be seen in terms of the effects that early disturbance of bond formation may have upon future interaction. That relatively minor modifications of experience in the post-partum period may affect both maternal and infant behaviour has been indicated.

A number of reports suggest a higher prematurity rate among

abused children. The estimate ranges from 13% (Skinner & Castle, 1969) to 30% (Elmer & Gregg, 1967). Lynch (1975) suggests that bonding failure may be a contributory factor in child abuse., finding that of the 25 abused infants she studied, ten of them had been separated from their mothers for at least 48 hours after delivery. Only two out of the 35 siblings of these children were found to have been separated. Rather than viewing the contributory factor as *failure* to bond, however, it is contended here that the initial disturbance in the bonding process may have operated through the establishment of a particular interactive style, involving less affectionate behaviour on the part of the mother and more irritable behaviour on the part of the infant. Two recommendations follow from this view – that separation after birth be avoided if possible and that if separation is unavoidable then support and therapy be provided in order to help the mother in the early development of her relationship with the child. Such intervention should be particularly considered if the family concerned displays high-risk characteristics (Kempe & Kempe, 1978; Lynch & Roberts, 1977).

Another area of work which relates to the establishment of mother-infant interaction and which may have implications for the higher incidence of prematurity and handicap amongst abused children concerns the ethological concept of the sign stimulus. Lorenz (1943) and Eibl-Eibesfeldt (1975) suggested that the characteristic head proportions and facial features of a newborn child, termed the 'Baby Schema', serve as a 'cute' sign stimulus in eliciting protective responses and inhibiting aggression from the parent.

More recently Hall Sternglanz et al. (1977) have conducted an experimental investigation of a range of infant facial characteristics to determine which evoke particular responses in adults. They conclude that their results support an ethological view and further-more suggest that the analysis of infantile characteristics may have implications for the treatment of disturbed parent-child interaction. It may be tempting to postulate, therefore, that abused children lack such stimulus characteristics and thereby fail to inhibit aggressive behaviours. Although this may be true in certain cases, any such connection between infant characteristics and child abuse will again be mediated by the *interaction* of the mother and her infant, rather than being simply directed from the child to the parent.

One analysis of the relationship between the lack of 'cute' characteristics and abuse therefore focuses on the point of potential attack – absence of 'cuteness' fails to bring about the inhibition of a mother's aggression. An analysis based on the longer-term effects can also be provided. It may be that certain infants lack from birth those facial characteristics which typically enhance positive affective responses in adults. These babies might be less likely to be fully accepted by the mother. Lack of initial positive attractive features would be more probable in the case of infants born prematurely or with some handicap and early interaction between the mother and such an infant might therefore be disrupted not only by their separation but also by the child's appearance.

However, prematurity, handicap and other conditions (Lynch, 1977) likely to make early interaction difficult, cannot be regarded as the only factors which enhance the risk of child abuse. Another communicative characteristic of a young infant that is reported to be a major irritant even in non-abusing families is that of crying. In the human infant, crying can be distinguished into at least three distinct patterns (Wolfe, 1969) – the 'basic' cry, the 'angry' cry and the 'pain' cry. The basic and angry cries occur when the infant wants to be fed or when there is an absence of adequate stimulation from the parent, for example in the form of comforting and cuddling. Such responses were probably in fact the normal maternal responses of our evolutionary ancestors. Indeed, Konner (1972) reports that in the bushman society the mother carries her infant close to her body and quickly responds to his needs, usually before the crying begins. Furthermore, Ainsworth (1977) has stressed the part played by the mothers' responsiveness to crying in the formation of a secure attachment and in reducing the frequency with which the infant cries. This will of course be affected by maternal attitudes, for example whether the mother believes in feeding and cuddling on demand, and in an abusive relationship these attitudes are probably related to the mothers' distorted expectations of the infant. Such distortion has now been reported in a number of studies (Martin, 1976; Kempe & Kempe, 1978).

It has also been reported that the infant's demands which are mediated through crying are often the most irritating aspect of his behaviour as far as abusing parents are concerned (Kempe & Kempe, 1978). This problem may be related to the confinement and isolation of the nuclear family, a feature which is of recent origin. Our ancestors probably lived in hunter-gatherer groups with an extended family environment of grandparents, aunts, uncles and related offspring, all of whom might contribute to caring for and responding to a mother and her infant.

The extended family environment is an important factor when one considers that part of modern evolutionary theory which suggests that an infant will tend to maximize the chances of the passing-on of its own genes by demanding more parental investment than the parents, in terms of their own genetic 'fitness', are able to give. Trivers (1974) has used the term 'parent-offspring conflict' to refer to this phenomenon.

In a situation in which the mother is left alone all day with her infant in a single family dwelling and in which the excessive demands of the child cannot be redirected to other caregivers such as grandparents, an anxious and stressed relationship may develop. Thus it is not surprising to find an over-representation in an abusing sample of single parent families (Hyman, 1978) and of families in which there is an unstable marital relationship (Baher et al., 1977).

Mother-Infant Interaction.

It is now widely accepted that the interactions between mother and infant are fundamental to child development in general and have a large genetic component. Viewing the child as an active rather than as a passive partner in mother–infant interaction forces us to consider those characteristics and behaviours that the infant brings to this interaction. The infant appears to have an innate predisposition to develop an 'attachment' to its primary caretaker and both Bowlby and Ainsworth propose that the behaviour through which this attachment develops may be compared with those which Piaget (1954) described as being crucial for cognitive development. Indeed it has been suggested by Schaffer and Emerson (1964) that the infant must attain a certain level of perceptual-cognitive development in order to form an attachment to its primary caretaker. This then facilitates further cognitive growth. Bell (1970) has also implied that the quality of mothering is related to the understanding of person permanence and that this in turn indirectly affects the appreciation of object constancy.

Schaffer (1971, 1977a) further elaborates on this interactionist viewpoint and suggests that there are infant-based structural and functional aspects to early interaction. He states that the infant is born with inherited structural features which help to bind it to the primary caretaker. Thus Fantz (1966) has shown that newborns preferentially gaze at some visual stimuli rather than others and Yarrow (1967) has found that infants can discriminate their mother from a stranger by one month of age and that most preferentially attend to their mother by three months. Schaffer goes on to consider the functional ways in which certain endogenous mechanisms are manipulated in the interactive relationships between the mother and her infant. He suggests that as a result of the mother's sensitivity to the on-off flow of the infant's behaviour the movement patterns of the infant change from being mainly internally regulated rhythms and become linked to external events – especially the activities of the mother.

93

It has been claimed that synchronized mother-infant interaction may be established within the first few months of the child's life (Trevarthen, 1974; Brazelton, 1975). With this reciprocal interaction the infant gradually becomes aware of the relationship between his actions and their effects in initiating interactive responses, leading to a differentiation between self and non-self. Indeed, Bruner and Sherwood (1976) have emphasized the role of 'person-to-person' games (e.g. 'peek-a-boo') between the mother and the infant in the development of interpersonal exchanges through which the infant learns to anticipate that others will respond in certain ways. Towards the end of the first year intentionality and anticipation are beginning to be exhibited fluently throughout the infant's interactive and attachment behaviours (Trevarthen, 1977).

Given certain preadaptations for interactive development, then, the infant requires the opportunity to participate in interactions and one important aspect of this is the turn-taking pattern of mother-infant exchanges (Schaffer, 1977b). Without a cyclic interpersonal process both the establishment of a secure mother-infant relationship and further cognitive growth of the child may be retarded.

The Application of Ethological Methods to the Study of Abuse.

We consider that ethology can make its most significant contribution to the study of child abuse by providing methods of research and analytical techniques for the investigation of early interactive development. The application of this ethological approach has been incorporated in our own research at the University of Surrey where we have used a procedure derived from Ainsworth's (1971) 'Strange Situation' procedure. By direct observation we have been able to show that abused infants, during separation and reunion episodes, show similar behaviours to those described by Ainsworth for insecure ambivalently attached infants (Group C), and that this may be partly due to the obtrusive interactive style of the mother (Hyman et al., 1979).

To establish differences between abusive and non-abusive mother-infant dyads by direct observation, video tape-recordings were made in a structured room setting. This had the initial advantage of standardization and control of the stimuli which the infant received. In addition, a structured environment is necessary in order to obtain a detailed and reliable behavioural description.

The catalogue of behaviour items which we used to describe the movement patterns of the mother and her infant was similar to that devised by Blurton Jones (1972) in his attempt to describe the full range of behaviours which might be encountered in a study of mother-child interaction. For example, the catalogue provides a number of items which may be observed whilst the mother and infant are at play. These include 'demonstrate', 'manipulate to person', 'proffer' and 'show'. In contrast, other workers (e.g. Lewis, 1972) use only a single category of 'plays with' when such behaviours are associated with the mother. The more detailed description of behaviour is necessary if we wish to detect differences in the interactive styles of abusing parents.

The method which has become most popular for observational studies of behaviour is that of time sampling. This technique involves the imposition of a time grid upon behavioural sequences, providing a systematic way of coding behaviour. It has also been referred to as 'one-zero sampling' (Altmann, 1974) because the behaviours are scored for display within each time interval, thereby yielding the frequency of intervals in which a given behaviour is exhibited. This technique has been criticized by Altmann (1974) because it does not provide for a very satisfactory analysis of contingencies, but the three-second time interval that we have applied was in fact short enough to allow us to analyze 'interaction bouts' between mother and infant. The length of 'interaction bout' was established by summing the time interval units containing on-going interactive behaviours that occur in sequence. The start and finish of such a sequence was determined with reference to the intervening periods of non-interactive behaviour.

The findings from the pilot study showed that non-abusing mothers have a significantly greater number of mutual interactions with their infants than abusing mothers, and that the abusing mothers show more failed interactive initiatives (Hyman et al., 1979). Therefore, it is hypothesised that non-abusing mothers will show significantly longer sequences of uninterrupted interaction with their infants than abusing mothers. Recent studies (Schaffer, 1977b) can be distinguished by their emphasis on temporal relationships and contingencies of behaviour in interactive situations. Dyadic interactions are based on the interweaving of the participants' behaviour and it has been suggested that sequential analysis might provide a possible method for measuring this behavioural flow objectively although there are some technical problems in its application (Slater, 1973).

In the mother–infant case sequential analysis can be applied in two ways – firstly to determine sequences displayed by each individual, highlighting any particular category of behaviour occurring most frequently before the behaviour in question, and secondly to determine interpersonal sequences of behaviour and to establish whether the infant's response was influenced by the preceding behaviour of the mother (and vice versa). However, it should be realized that an action on behalf of the mother or the infant may be dependent not only on the immediate preceding activity of the partner but also on the antecedent behaviour of both participants.

Within the interactive situation the mother must allow herself to be paced by the infant and build up routine sequences of a predictable nature, to maximize the opportunity for the infant to learn (Schaffer, 1977a). However, the developmental lag of abused infants and the fewer interactive responses shown by abusing mothers suggests that in their case this process has been distorted (Hyman et al., 1979) Such an effect would be reflected by short interaction bouts in abuse-related dyads. Thus, comparing flow diagrams of behavioural contingencies for abusing and non-abusing mother-infant pairs, it might be possible to detect cases in which the communication between an abusing mother and her infant is mismatched. It may be possible to show that while the non-abusing mothers exaggerate, repeat and slow down their actions to facilitate imitation by the child (Pawlby, 1977; Stern, 1977), the abusing mothers arbitrarily impose their behaviour upon the child in a non-synchronous manner.

This hypothesis has received support from the results of studies by Jeffery et al. (1978) and Burgess and Conger (1977) in which, using video-tapes and direct observation of interaction in the home, it has been demonstrated that there is a low rate of reciprocal interaction in the abusing families. (Incidentally, the evidence produced by this research also supports the claim that our findings from the laboratory 'Strange Situation' procedure reflect interaction patterns in the home environment.)

More recently, Burgess and Conger (1979) have provided evidence which suggests that there are higher levels of 'threatening' and 'complaining' interactive initiatives from the mother to the child in an abusing family, with 'affectionate' and 'supportive' interactive initiatives by the mother 40% lower than in a non-abusing family. Thus a lack of reciprocal interaction or exaggeration and repetition of positive interactive initiatives from the mother might indicate to a worker in the field that there is a mismatch in the relationship, and together with other high risk characteristics (Kempe & Kempe, 1978; Lynch & Roberts, 1977) this could give reason for concern.

Conclusion

It should be clear from the foregoing that a view of ethology which holds that its only contribution to the study of human behaviour lies in naive generalizations from animals to man, is inappropriate. Ethology is an objective approach concentrating upon the detailed study of individual species and is concerned only at a secondary level with the generation of 'behavioural laws' applicable to all species.

Animal studies do not supply simple models of human behaviour from which we may generalize with impunity, but they may assist in the understanding of basic processes. Theoretical contributions serve to focus particular attention upon particular processes and periods of development in the relationship of mother and infant and this should result in more effective prevention, identification and treatment of abuse. Finally, the methods derived from ethology provide ways in which a fuller understanding of mother-infant interaction may be developed, thereby allowing a more precise appreciation of the problems involved in an abusive relationship.

Much work remains to be done in the field of child abuse and the application of ethological theory and methods will give help by complementing, rather than displacing, the more established psychological and sociological approaches.

REFERENCES

Ainsworth, M.D.S., Bell, S.M.V. and Stayton, D.J. (1971) 'Individual differences in strange situation behaviour in one-year-olds'. In R. Schaffer (Ed.) *The Origin of Human Social Relations.* Academic Press, London.

Ainsworth, M.D.S. (1977) 'Infant development and mother-infant interaction among Ganda and American families'. In P. Leiderman., S. Tulkin and A. Rosenfield (Eds.) *Culture and Infancy,* Academic Press, New York.

Altmann, J. (1974) 'Observational study of behaviour: sample methods.' *Behaviour, 49,* pp. 227–65.

Baher, E., Hyman, C., Jones, C., Jones, R., Kerr, A. and Mitchell, R. (1976) *At Risk: An Account of the Work of the Battered Child Research Department, NSPCC.* Routledge and Kegan Paul, London.

Bell, S.M. (1970) 'The development of the concept of object as related to infant-mother attachment'. *Child Development, 41,* pp. 291–311.

Blurton Jones, N. (1972) (Ed.) *Ethological Studies of Child Behaviour.* Cambridge University Press.

Bowlby, J. (1958) 'The nature of the child's tie to his mother'. *International Journal of Psychoanalysis, 39,* pp. 350–73.

Bowlby, J. (1969) *Attachment and loss. Vol 1: 'Attachment'.* Hogarth, London.

Brazelton, T.B., Tronick, E., Adamson, L., Als, H., and Weise, S. (1975) 'Mother infant separation'. In *Parent Infant Interaction: Ciba Foundation Symposium 33,* Elsevier, Holland.

Bruner, J. and Sherwood, V. (1976) 'Peekaboo and the learning of role structures'. In: J.S. Bruner, A. Jolly and K. Sylva (Eds.) *Play: Its Role in Development and Evolution.* Penguin, London.

Burgess, R. L. and Conger, R.D. (1977) 'Family interaction patterns related to child abuse and neglect', *Child Abuse & Neglect. 1,* pp. 269–77.

Burgess, R.L. and Conger, R.D. (1979) 'Patterns of interaction in abuse, neglect and control families'. *Child Abuse & Neglect. 3* (Proceedings of the 2nd International Congress) In press.

Darwin, C. (1872) *The Expression of the Emotions in Man and Animals.* Murray, London.

(Papio anubis)'. *Animal Behaviour, 26*, pp. 746–59.

Pawlby, S. (1977) 'Imitative interaction'. In H.R. Schaffer (Ed.) *Studies in Mother-*
DeVore, I. (1963) 'Mother-infant relations in free-ranging baboons'. In H.L. Rheingold (Ed.) *Maternal Behaviour in Mammals*, Wiley, New York.

Eibl-Eibesfeldt, I. (1975) *Ethology, the Biology of Behaviour* (2nd edition), Holt, Rinehart and Winston.

Elmer, E. and Gregg, G. (1967) 'Developmental characteristics of abused children'. *Pediatrics, 40*, pp. 596–602.

Fantz, R.L. (1966) 'Pattern discrimination and selective attention as determinants of perceptual development from birth'. In A.H. Kidd and J.L. Rivoire (Eds.) *Perceptual Development in Children.* International Univ. Press Inc., New York.

Hales, D.J., Lozoff, B., Sosa, R. and Kennel, J.H. (1977) 'Defining the limits of the maternal sensitive period'. *Developmental Medicine and Child Neurology, 19*, pp. 454–461.

Hall Sternglanz, S., Grey, J.L. and Murakomi, M. (1977) 'Adult preferences for infantile facial features, an ethological approach'. *Animal Behaviour, 25*, pp. 108–15.

Harlow, H.F., Harlow, M.K. and Hanson, E.W. (1963) 'The maternal affectional system of Rhesus monkeys'. In H.L. Rheingold (Ed.) *Maternal Behaviour in Mammals.* Wiley, New York.

Hess, E.H. (1959) 'Imprinting: an effect of early experience'. *Science, 130*, pp. 133–41.

Hinde, R.A. (1974) *Biological Bases of Human Social Behaviour.* McGraw Hill, New York.

Hutt, J. and Hutt, C. (1970) *Direct Observation and the Measurement of Behaviour.* C. Thomas, Springfield, Illinois.

Hyman, C. (1978) 'Some characteristics of abusing families referred to the NSPCC', *British Journal of Social Work, 8*, pp. 171–79.

Hyman, C., Parr, R. and Browne, K. (1979) 'An observational study of mother-infant interaction in abusing families'. *Child Abuse and Neglect, 3*, pp. 241–46.

Jeffery, M., Wilbrey, L., Sanson-Fisher, B. & Raymond, J. (1979) 'Some observations of the communications and interaction patterns of abusing families'. Paper presented at the 2nd. International Congress on Child Abuse and Neglect, London.

Kempe, R.S. and Kempe, C.H. (1978) *Child Abuse.* Fontana/Open Books, London.

Klaus, M.H. and Kennel, J.H. (1976) *Mother-Infant Bonding.* C.V. Mosby, St. Louis.

Konner, M.J. (1972) 'Aspects of the developmental ethology of a foraging people'. In N. Blurton Jones, (Ed.) *Ethological Studies of Child Behaviour.* Cambridge University Press.

Leidermann, P.H. and Seashore, M.J. (1975) 'Mother-infant neonatal separation: some delayed consequences.' In: *Parent Infant Interaction: Ciba Foundation Symposium 33.* Elsevier, Holland.

Lewis, M. (1972) 'State as an infant environment interaction: An analysis of mother-infant interaction as a function of sex'. *Merrill Palmer Quaterly, 18*, pp. 95–212.

Lewis, M. and Rosenblum, L.A. (1974) (Eds.) *The Effect of the Infant on its Caregiver.* Wiley, New York.

Lorenz, K. (1943) 'Die argeborenon formen moglicher Enfahrung'. *Z. tierpsychol, 5*, pp. 235–409.

Lorenz, K. (1950) 'The comparative method in studying innate behaviour patterns'. *Symposium: Society of Experimental Biology. 4*, pp. 221–68.

Lynch, M. (1975) 'Ill-health and the battered child'. *Lancet, 1975, ii*, pp. 491–92.

Lynch, M. and Roberts, J. (1977) 'Predicting child abuse'. *Child Abuse and Neglect, 1*, pp. 491–92.

Martin, H. (1976) *The Abused Child.* Ballinger, New York.

Meier, G.W. (1965) 'Maternal behaviour in feral and laboratory reared monkeys following the surgical delivery of their infants'. *Nature, 206*, pp. 492–93.

Nash, L.T. (1978) 'The development of mother-infant relationship in wild baboons

DeChateau, P. (1976) *Neonatal Care Routines*. Ph.D. Thesis, Umear University Medical Dissertations, Sweden.

Infant Interaction. Academic Press, London.

Piaget, J. (1954) *The Construction of Reality in the Child*. Routledge and Kegan Paul, London.

Schaffer, H.R. (1971) '*The Growth of Sociability*'. Penguin London.

Schaffer, H.R. (1977a) '*Mothering*'. Fontana/Open Books, London.

Schaffer, H.R. (1977b) '*Studies in Mother-Infant Interaction*'. Academic Press, London.

Schaffer, H.R. and Emerson, P.E. (1964) 'The development of social attachment in infancy'. *Monographs for Research in Child Development*, *29*, No. 3.

Skinner, A. and Castle, R. (1969) *78 Battered Children*. NSPCC, London.

Slater, P.J.B. (1973) 'Describing sequences of behaviour'. In P.P.G. Bateson and P.H. Klopfer (Eds.) *Perspectives in Ethology*. Plenum, New York.

Suomi, S.J. (1976) 'Neglect and abuse of infants by Rhesus monkey mothers'. *Journal of American Academy of Psychotherapy*, *12*, pp. 5–8.

Stern, D.N. (1977) 'The infant's stimulus world during social interaction'. In H.R. Schaffer (Ed.) *Studies in Mother-Infant Interaction*. Academic Press, London.

Trevarthen, C. (1974) 'Conversations with a one-month old'. *New Scientist*, *62*, pp. 230–35.

Trevarthen, C. (1977) 'Descriptive analysis of infant communicative behaviour'. In H.R. Schaffer (Ed.) *Studies in Mother-Infant Interaction*. Academic Press, London.

Trivers, R.L. (1974) 'Parent-offspring conflict'. *American Zoologist*, *14*, pp. 249–64.

Tinbergen, N. (1951) *The Study of Instinct*, Oxford University Press.

Wolff, P.H. (1969) 'The natural history of crying and other vocalization in early infancy'. In B.M. Foss (Ed.) *Determinants of Infant Behaviour: Volume 4*. Methuen, London.

Yarrow, L.J. (1967) 'The development of focussed relationships during infancy'. In J. Hollmuth, *The Exceptional Infant: Vol. 1*. Special Child Publications.

7   Families Who Injure Their Children.

Clare Hyman

Introduction.

This chapter will report and inter-relate a number of different projects undertaken either at the NSPCC's National Advisory Centre in London*, where the author worked as consultant research clinical psychologist from 1970 until 1977 (Hyman, 1978a), or in Surrey, in cooperation with Surrey Area Health Authority, during the period from 1973 until 1977 (Hyman, 1978b).

The sections into which the chapter is divided represent the different types of research project undertaken in chronological order and this sequence reflects a gradual attempt to expand the range of approaches used. Starting with the necessity to introduce some quantification and objectification into the process of recording social work information, we went on to use independent psychometric and developmental assessment methods and finished by using direct observational description of mother-infant interaction. These approaches are described in sections 2, 3 and 4 respectively. In the final section I have attempted to inter-relate these sectional reports and evaluate their significance for the prediction and prevention of child abuse.

Demographic Factors Contributing to Child Abuse.

The data on which this section is based derive from 85 social work schedules completed by social workers at four NSPCC Special Units and from 72 similar questionnaires completed by Health Visitors

* Acknowledgement is made to the Social Workers and the families interviewed at the NSPCC's National Advisory Centre on the Battered Child, together with Ruth Mitchell and Geraldine Connor, colleagues who helped with testing and with data processing. Thanks are also due to the Health Visitors of Surrey and to Mrs Mair Owen, Area Nurse, Child Health and Dr John Radway, Area Specialist, Child Health who made the study of case conference data in Surrey possible. My gratitude is also offered to Robert Parr and Kevin Browne who have worked enthusiastically as research officers (funded by the DHSS) and to Richard Stibbs of Cambridge University and Trevor Bryant of Surrey University who have helped in the computer processing.

attending case conferences on abusing families in the Surrey Health Area. In reporting findings derived from sociological studies of small samples it is essential to specify the social class composition of those samples since many behavioural differences which fundamentally affect family dynamics are now well know to be associated with social class membership (Newson & Newson, 1977).

If cases come from the register of a city agency, as in the NSPCC study, then it is likely that the social class composition will be over-represented by working class families. Thus 70% of the NSPCC sample came from classes IV and V (according to the classification of occupations by the Registrar General), while only four families came from classes I and II. In contrast the Surrey sample was normally distributed and its social class composition was similar to that of the nation as a whole. Many of the differences in the data obtained from the two samples reflect this essential difference.

Thus mean maternal age of the NSPCC sample, in common with many other reports on families referred to social and health agencies because of known or suspected non-accidental injury (Smith, 1975), was relatively young – 23 years. In Surrey, however, the mean maternal age (28 years) was exactly that expected for a mother having a child under the age of five years (C.S.O., 1976). All that this seems to reflect is that working class mothers, as is well known, have their families earlier than middle class mothers. Thus much of the past emphasis in the literature (Gorell Barnes, 1978) upon the youthful-ness of abusive mothers may not be relevant to abuse *per se* but may simply reflect the social class membership of the sample. That most abusive parents who have been studied seem to come from the lower end of the social class spectrum is probably true (Gorell Barnes, op. cit.) but where that is not so, as in the second study discussed here, then several of these so-called predictors of child abuse will not operate.

In neither sample was there any suggestion that large family size was a particular precipitator of child abuse. In the working class NSPCC sample 85% of the abused children came from one- or two-child families, while in the middle-class Surrey sample the mean family size of 2.2 children per family was appropriate to the age of the parents concerned. With these broad age and family size factors accounted for, it is necessary to determine the particular stresses which are associated with child abuse. The answer to this seems to lie in the family's circumstances. In both of the studies discussed here there was an over-representation of single parent families and almost all of these were fatherless families. Single-parent families accounted for 20% of the working class sample and 30% of the middle class sample.

Where the families were technically intact there had often been a history of circumstances unconducive to family harmony. For example, in the NSPCC sample 40% had lived together for less than one year before the birth of the injured child, while nearly one third had had two or more house moves over the past three years. Similarly, employment patterns were typically unstable with 23% of fathers having had two or more changes of job in the preceding year.

Perhaps the most outstanding feature in this sample of 157 families was the large amount of reported ill-health among the mothers. In the highest social class this reached staggering proportions. For example, over half of the Surrey mothers were reported as having received treatment for psychological illness before the reported abuse. In the working class sample this figure was halved but still high at 25%.

Physical health was also poor in both groups of mothers and there was a high rate of known drug prescription. There was also a low incidence of maternal employment – 9% for the NSPCC sample and 37% for the Surrey sample. In some ways the circumstances for these mothers are strikingly similar to those which Brown and Harris (1978) found to be associated with high levels of depression in a sample of young urban women – non-working, poorly supported or unsupported by a spouse, and having to care for a child in difficult circumstances.

If house ownership is regarded as ideal for raising young children, then a particular reflection of likely home stress may be lack of ownership and it is therefore of some interest that ownership was in fact relatively low in both groups.

Table 1: Housing of NSPCC and Surrey Samples

| | NSPCC 84 cases (Hyman, 1978a) | | | Surrey 72 cases (Hyman, 1978b) | | |
	NSPCC	C.S.O. 1976*		Surrey	C.S.O. 1976*	
Owner occupied	13	44.5%	p < .001	23	38%	p < .02
Rented	71	39.5%		49	34%	

Figures based to 84   Figures based to 72

*C.S.O. Central Statistical Office figures, 1976.
Both sets of figures show significant differences.

To what extent abused children themselves contribute to the pattern of stress so far described has always been a matter for debate. Lynch (1977) has always stressed the relatively poor health of abused children compared for example to their non-abused siblings, but this is not the only relevant comparison to be made. Given an 'abuse-prone' mother there may well be differential factors affecting the probability that any one child will in fact be abused. Age is clearly one such factor, since children under four years of age are predominantly at risk and in our samples between 80 and 90 percent were in this age group. There is no doubt that it is the youngest children who are most vulnerable to abuse (and most likely of course, to sustain serious injury if they are hurt).

A further relevant factor appears to be prematurity, since the infant of low birth weight is often more difficult to care for, being small, often difficult to feed and subject to crying and colic. In fact we have found a significantly raised incidence of prematurity in the children we have studied but at its highest (as would be expected in the working class sample), it has not exceeded 13%, which is approximately twice the national figure. Putting this another way, we can say that the great majority of abused children are not premature. A similar point can be made with regard to the incidence of handicap. Although the figure (14%) was higher than would be expected in such a sample, few of the abused children were handicapped.

These findings hardly support the idea that abuse is due to 'impaired bonding' and they are not unique in this respect (Martin, 1976, provides one other example) and it is therefore worrying that this issue has received so much attention and was, for example, discussed at considerable length in the Report of the Select Committee on Violence in the Family (House of Commons, 1977). There may be enhanced risk, perhaps, when a mother whose capacity for coping with her young infant is already impaired by immaturity, by anxiety, or by lack of support, then experiences post-natal separation from her premature infant as undermining and worrying. It would, however, be quite wrong to suppose that giving enhanced contact for a few hours in the post-natal period will safeguard her against the stresses of caring for her infant in the long term.

Kennel and Klaus are often quoted in support of this thesis (Kennel, Voos and Klaus, 1978), but the evidence for the long-term effects on mothers of either separation or of enriched contact with their premature infants is convincingly challenged by Leiderman and Seashore (1975). As these authors point out, the sex and parity of the infant, and especially the social class membership of the mothers, with all that this implies about attitudes toward child rearing, far outweigh the effects of prematurity or of the degree of contact in the immediate post-partum period. In any case, as Dunn (1975) has shown, the notion of consistency in relation to mothering is neither simple nor absolute. What mothers do in the first ten days after an infant's birth does *not* correlate highly with their later behaviour toward the infant. As Dunn herself says, 'The lack of correlation between co-ordination measures from the early feeds and the later consistent maternal measures suggests that the post partum period, rather than being a sensitive period, may be a time when the relationship between mother and baby is buffered against difficulties of adjustment' (Dunn, op. cit., p. 169).

The idea, therefore, that the infant himself contributes materially toward his own attack and that he in some way fails to inhibit his mother's aggression toward him seems to be over-emphasizing the biological evidence. There is little evidence that mothers rely substantially on predetermined behaviours to mother their infants successfully. Learning, both in childhood when they themselves were being parented, and much later through direct observation, instruction and modelling seems to be of much more consequence.

Equally, while there is no doubt that infants possess pre-adapted innate responses such as visual tracking, sucking, etc. which predispose them to pay attention to their caretakers, they require five or six months to 'learn' the mother as a 'continuous object'. Without the build-up of person permanence there can be no 'bonding' and such permanence probably takes months rather than days to establish.

Even the fact, as we found in about a third of our cases, that many abused infants are perceived by their mothers as 'difficult', crying excessively, and proving hard to feed and comfort, is no proof that they are in fact unusually difficult to rear. Battering mothers are known to have a distorted expectation of their children which may often lead them to regard as 'difficult' what another mother accepts as merely childish and to be expected (Martin 1976).

The early literature on child abuse was particularly biased towards the need to 'mother' the abusive mother and thus to infuse her with the emotional capacity to respond nurturantly toward her infant. Such a view tended to seek some reason related to the child's behaviour or appearance for her violence towards him. It is this approach which has led to the emphasis, which I believe is mistaken, upon characteristics of the child which are said to facilitate a mother's attack, especially if her 'natural bonding' with him has been disrupted by a difficult or abnormal birth process or his abnormal perinatal condition. The facts, however, seem to point to a major psychological disruption in the mothers of these children, in part derived from their difficult home circumstances and in part from their own poor health.

The stresses that precipitate child abuse may be considered to lie along a continuum. The younger working class abusing mothers seem to be responding more to external pressures arising from their poor social circumstances, made less tolerable still because of their youth and inexperience and the inadequate modelling opportunities in their own childhood homes. In addition, the risk of bearing a premature child is higher for them by reason of their social class and the deprivations which this entails.

The middle-class abusing mother, in contrast, resorts to violence less as a response to external frustration and more as the outcome of inner disharmony. This is shown by the much higher incidence of psychiatric disorder in the middle-class sample than in a largely-working class sample, together with better living conditions and a lower incidence of prematurity. In addition there are specific psychological traits which contribute to child abuse over and above those aspects of behaviour associated primarily with broader social circumstances and familial stresses.

Psychological Traits of Abusive Parents.

The data upon which this section is based are derived from the short form of the Wechsler Adult Intelligence Scale given to 44 parents attending the NSPCC's National Advisory Centre on the Battered Child in London. In addition 37 of these parents completed form C of Cattell's 16PF questionnaire. Referrals were from a variety of sources – Health Visitors, General Practitioners, Hospitals, etc. An equal number of normal control parents of matched age and social background, whose names were obtained from Health Visitors' files in the same health district, also completed the 16PF questionnaires. All cases were tested within two months of referral.

Intelligence. The battering parents in this sample conformed closely to normal expectation in intelligence with a mean verbal IQ of 95 and a mean performance IQ of 97. There were no significant differences between the IQs of the mothers and fathers in the sample, nor between the great majority (35) who had actually injured their children and a small minority (9) of parents referred either on account of others' fears or their own fears that they might injure their children. While there is a trend for battering parents to lag slightly behind the population mean of 100 this is an insignificant difference with a chi-squared value of 6.11 for the verbal IQ and a chi-squared value of 0.838 for the performance IQ. As with other delinquent populations there is a tendency in our battering parents' sample for verbal IQs to fall marginally below performance IQs. This may reflect once again the social class skew or may, as Glueck and Glueck (1950) suggested, represent a real difference in abstraction.

What is most noteworthy is the essential normality of the intellectual capacity of the abusive parents participating in this study. There is no confirmation at all in these results for Selwyn Smith's finding that over 50% of his battering mothers were of borderline subnormal intelligence (Smith 1975). In the present study, six out of 31 mothers (19%) fell below an IQ of 84 on verbal tests and four (13%) on performance tests. It is likely, of course, that between relatively small samples such as Smith's and the current one there will be major differences due to sampling. Smith's sample consisted wholly of hospital referrals whereas the NSPCC referrals were mixed, some coming from hospital casualty departments but others from social service departments. It might be that less severely injured cases have more intelligent parents. On the face of it this seems unlikely since the degree of injury is frequently a matter of chance and of the age of the child. A further possible reason for the differences could be the fact that Smith averaged short-form verbal and performance IQs; this could mask the relative differences between performance scale results and verbal scale results.

Workers in the field should not therefore assume too readily that intelligence as such is necessarily impaired in parents who commit an assault against their children or are at risk of so doing. Rather, the battered child syndrome appears to be part of a multifactorial complex, of which low intelligence, especially verbal (symbolic) thinking, may form a minor contributory part.

Personality. The results of the 16PF questionnaire administered to 37 pairs of abusive and matched control adults are shown in Table 2. The results have been reported in raw score form since British norms for this form of the test were not available.

The results generally confirm those reported in *At Risk* by the NSPCC Battered Child Research Team (Baher et al., 1976) which were based on a subsample of the present cases. The main finding for the fathers is a confirmation of their relatively introverted temperament. Although none of the individual factors at trait level (with the exception of factor F) differentiated between the battering and control fathers, the second-order factor of extraversion/introversion did do this.

Thus this group of battering fathers seen at the National Advisory Centre for the Battered Child tended to be generally shy, self-sufficient and socially inhibited and (Factor F) were particularly lacking in enthusiasm, cheerfulness, and the ability to express themselves without undue restraint. Not surprisingly, such clients are unusually uncooperative with social workers and other helpers, as

Table 2

Significant differences between 37 battering and 37 control parents' mean 16PF
scores

Factor	Battering	Control	p (Mann-Whitney test)
Fathers	(n = 14)	(n = 16)	
Extraversion/introversion	3.8	5.8	< 0.01
F	5.1	7.2	< 0.01
Mothers	(n = 23)	(n = 21)	
Anxiety/adjustment	7.0	5.6	< 0.05
C	5.5	7.8	< 0.01
Q3	5.9	7.3	< 0.05
L	6.3	4.4	< 0.01

reported in *At Risk*. (Baher et al., 1976).

The outstanding feature of the battering mothers' scores was the confirmation of their immaturity in comparison with the control mothers. Thus their C-scale scores were again significantly lower, reflecting their relatively poor ego control. This would imply difficulty in tolerating frustration, changeability, and susceptibility to emotional upset. In addition, factor Q3, representing the capacity for personality integration, was also lower for battering mothers. Factor L, representing the capacity for basic trust, was also skewed towards greater suspicion in the clients group.

All these factors contribute towards a weighted second-order factor of 'anxiety versus adjustment'. Overall, battering mothers scored as less well adjusted than the control mothers. However, it is of great interest that the actual scales contributing to this lower adjustment were demonstrably those of control and confidence in others rather than scales O and Q4 which reflect anxiety, apprehension and tension. These findings offer significant qualification to those of Smith (1975) who, using the global measure of neuroticism from the EPI, reports higher scores for battering mothers. It is of some importance for clinicians to appreciate that mothers who abuse their children physically, though less well adjusted than non-battering mothers, tend to show not raised levels of guilt and apprehension but rather lowered levels of integration and control.

It is not difficult to see why, in psychological terms, the children of these parents are at risk. On the one hand we have the disruption in the home already described, together with the actual absence of support from a father figure (in a substantial minority of cases) or a non-participant withdrawal on the part of those fathers who were present. On the other hand there is impulsivity and immaturity in the mothers whose own childhood has often been, if not actually abusive, frequently upset and discontinuous (Hyman 1978a).

The features which psychometric testing have revealed are clearly not peculiar to battering parents alone. What will become clear, however, is the way in which a variety of studies can highlight circumstances or traits which in isolation may not render a mother highly prone to violence but which in combination can create a set of pressures, external and internal, which potentiate the risk that she will become unable to control her aggression when faced with the considerable demands of a young and dependent infant.

Interactional Style of Abusive Mother Child Dyads.

The investigations of demographic and psychometric factors so far described have led inexorably to our focussing upon the essentially psychological nature of child abuse. It seems that even when social factors have been accounted for there remains a central area of personality dysfunction contributing to the violent acts committed by some parents against their children. We had already had some evidence of such disorder and its effects upon the children from a small study using the Bene Anthony Test of Family Relations carried out by Ruth Mitchell (Hyman & Mitchell, 1975). In this projective test, given to sixteen matched pairs of abused and non-abused pre-school children, significant differences were obtained in the way the two groups of children responded to the mother figure of the test. There was a general avoidance of this figure by abused children, responses being re-allocated to other family members.

In this test each child selects the cut-out figures which appropriately represent his own family and is then asked to 'post' a number of statements such as, 'whom do you like to cuddle?' 'who smacks you when you are naughty?', etc. Rather than showing either positive or negative involvement with the figure representing the mother the abused children allocated their responses either to the father or to siblings, or to the 'Mr Nobody' character supplied and whose use is viewed by Bene and Anthony (1957) as largely an avoidance or denial response.

Of particular interest here is the fact that both feelings toward and feelings perceived as emanating from the mother were denied and the results are the more striking for the fact that the controls used were other deprived (but not abused) children attending NSPCC day nurseries. Thus the denial and the distortion of mother–child interaction implied is the more remarkable for being contrasted not with the responses of normal home-reared young children, but with those of other underpriviledged children who also spent a substantial period of each day in a day nursery.

With this indirect evidence of maternal psychological impairment impinging upon mother-child interaction, we decided to directly confront the question of distorted interaction and we set about making video recordings of mothers and infants attending the NSPCC's National Advisory Centre. At the time of writing some 25 abusing dyads and an approximately equal number of matched control dyads have been filmed. To date 12 experimental and 12 control video tapes have been analysed and this sample forms the basis of this report.

The experimental and control families have been matched for sex, infant's age, ordinal position, parental age, ethnic group and home accommodation. All the infants ranged in age from 6 to 24 months with a mean age of 13.8 months for the abused infants and 13.6 months for the control infants – a non-significant difference. There were equal numbers of boys and girls in each group. Bayley developmental quotients showed developmental lag in the abused infants, with a mean motor scale quotient of 95 and a mean mental scale quotient of 89 for the abused infants. Such differences have been shown both by us (Hyman & Mitchell, op. cit.) and by Martin (1976) to arise through inhibiting influences in the abusive environment and they are reduced when there is effective therapeutic intervention, as for example at the special therapeutic nursery attended by many of the children at the NSPCC's National Advisory Centre.

It was decided that a short standard sequence should be used which would include the separation and reunion of mother and infant. Because of the use of a fixed angle video camera the child was placed in a high-chair for the duration of the observation session. The video recordings of the referred cases were made at roughly one month after referral and were carried out at the National Advisory Centre on the Battered Child. The occasion of the recording was the first visit that each mother and infant made to the centre. Clients were asked to participate in the research by their social workers. It was explained to each mother that this would involve a visit to the NAC during which testing would be carried out and a short film made of her child. Thus, the actual recording formed only a small part of the whole visit and no particular emphasis was placed upon the filming. In later discussion few mothers indicated any awareness of being filmed. Control cases were obtained from Health Visitor files of the same London Borough from which the majority of the referred cases came.

After being escorted to the centre all mothers were shown into the observation room by a social worker. The observation room was furnished as an office but with two arm-chairs and the child's high-chair placed in a shallow arc perpendicular to the line of the camera, which was mounted on the wall in one corner. The infant was placed in the high-chair and the mother shown to a chair beside the infant. The mother was told that someone would be in to see her shortly and recording began as the social worker left the room.

This first episode (A), with the mother and infant alone in the strange room, lasted three minutes and ended with the entry of a stranger. The stranger introduced herself and took a seat next to the child. After 30 seconds another stranger entered and asked the mother to accompany her in order to answer a number of questions (B). Episode C began as the mother left the room and this lasted three minutes. After the return of the mother to the observation room a further two minutes of recording was completed (Episode D). The mother was then told that she had been filmed, was shown the recording and told that the tape would be wiped clean if she wished.

The first stage in the analysis of the recorded behaviour of mother and infant was the compilation of a behaviour catalogue which in its final form consisted of over one hundred items, defined where possible in anatomical terms. The transcripts of behaviour produced by applying the behaviour catalogue in accordance with a set of scoring rules were then analyzed in two ways by the 'Primate' computer package (Humphreys, 1974). Amounts of individual categories of behaviour were obtained by a behaviour frequency analysis which merely counted the number of times specified behaviour items appeared in a transcript. In order that these analyses should accurately reflect amounts of behaviours a three-second time grid was imposed upon the behavioural sequences. (Further details of the procedure are given by Browne and Parr in Chapter 6). Behaviour frequencies were also analyzed using groups of items. The main items contributing to the grouping of manipulative behaviours, for example, were – general handling of a toy; inspection of a toy; banging of toys; dropping a toy and picking up a toy.

The analysis of interactions was accomplished by coding interactive initiatives, for which Primate supplies a special symbol, in the behaviour transcripts.

Instances in which an interactive initiative on the part of one individual is responded to by reciprocal directed behaviour are labelled as 'mutual interactions' in the results which follow, and those which meet with no response, as 'failed interactive initiatives'. Reliability coefficients of between .82 and .99 were obtained for distributions of behaviour items and there was 67% agreement for the coding of the interactive initiatives.

Results 1. Frequencies of Infants' Behaviours.
Significant differences were found in the separation (C) and reunion

(D) episodes. These differences are illustrated in Figure 1 and Figure 2 respectively. In episode C there was less looking at the stranger by the abused infants as a group. Consistent with this significant deficit was a non-significant tendency for the abused children to look for the mother more than the controls. Furthermore, the male abused children showed significantly greater signs of physical discomfort (e.g. struggling) than the controls. The abused boys also showed less looking at toys and less overall manipulation than their control counterparts (Figure 1) and while these differences were not significant for these broad categories the individual behaviours of 'gazing at toy' and 'handle toy' did significantly discriminate between the male infant groups.

These signs of emotional distress in the abused children as a group continued into the reunion episode. The abused children showed significantly more distress behaviour and lower levels of vocalization than the controls. For the abused boys this distress was again underlined by significantly lower levels of visual regard of toys and of manipulation (Figure 2). The distress aroused in the abused children by the mother's departure was therefore not allayed by her return, especially in the case of the male infants. Thus although in the low stress situation in which mother and child are alone together the abused and control infants showed similar patterns of behaviour, the introduction of the stranger and the departure of the mother potentiated different types of response in the two groups of children, with more negative reactions characterizing the abused children's behaviour.

Results 2. Frequencies of Mother's Behaviours.
Turning to an examination of the mothers' behaviours, few differences were found in episodes C and D. However, in episode A an interesting contrast was found between control and abusive mothers. While the abusive mothers looked at their infants more, the control mothers visually explored the room and manipulated the toys more, and this was especially pronounced for the mothers with girls (Figure 3). We conclude from these results that the control mothers were less anxiously preoccupied with their infants than were the experimental mothers.

Results 3. Interaction Analyses.
While none of the infants' response patterns to the mothers' initiatives showed any differences between the abused and normal children, differences in the mothers' interactive behaviours were of two types:
1. Mothers' responses to infants' initiatives (mutual interactions)

111

2. Mothers' failed interactive initiatives, in which behaviours are directed at the infant but a response is not forthcoming.

Figure 4 shows that the abusive mothers responded less to infant initiatives both in the initial episode A, in which mother and infant are alone, and in the final reunion episode D. They also showed more failed interactive initiatives in the reunion episode than the control mothers. This is primarily due to the mothers of boys, for whom this difference is significant.

Thus these interaction analyses suggest that the disturbances in infant behaviour shown in the separation and reunion episodes form part of a broader pattern of disturbance which involves the style of interaction between battering mother and infant, observable from the outset of the Strange Situation experiment. Abusive mothers of male infants, in particular, seem to have a more intrusive manner of relating to their children and appear to generate more behavioural initiative than their infants can effectively respond to. In addition, the style of the abusing mothers involves a generally less reciprocal manner of interaction throughout the experimental period. These important differences were not the result of the infants' being more disturbed, for the correlation between distress behaviours in the infants and failed initiatives in the mothers in episode D was not significant for abused dyads ($r = 0.35$, $p > .05$).

The results so far obtained in this ongoing observational study suggest that in the period of infancy and early childhood it is possible to detect differences in child, in maternal and in dyadic interaction which differentiate abused from normal pairs. Comparing our results with those of Ainsworth, who originated the 'Strange Situation' procedure, we were struck by the similarity between our abused infants and a small group of insecurely attached children who she described as having been mothered in an inconsistent and insensitive fashion (Ainsworth, 1971). The intrusiveness of our mothers' interactions is also very similar to the coerciveness reported by Burgess and Conger (1977) with an observational study of older abused children and their families. They too reported a lack of reciprocity in adult–child interactions.

While the results derived from our observational study must be interpreted with due caution given the small size of sample tapes so far analyzed, they derive greater significance from their consistency with these very different studies and such diagnostic importance as they show is further enhanced when taken together with the other investigations already reported here. The implications of all our studies for prediction and prevention will now be discussed.

The Psychology of the Child Abusing Parent

The research into child abuse which has been carried out so far tends on the one hand to be too circumscribed while on the other it seems too diffuse. Diffusion arises from a tendency to blunt the fine edges by inclusion of cases of neglect, of psychological abuse and recently of sexual abuse. This cannot help the understanding of violent injury since there is no prima facie reason why a man, for example, who sexually 'exploits' his child for pleasure is in any way motivated by the same uncontrolled rage which a lonely, anxious and overwrought mother experiences when she cannot comfort her persistently crying six-month-old infant. Much can be said along similar lines when criticizing the lumping together of abuse and neglect cases. Circumscription arises from the inevitably small sample sizes available to researchers in the area. Limitation to such numbers means that we are sampling samples, as it were, and unless we can really specify the broader groups of whom our studied cases form a part, we do not know how representative are the results which we obtain. Such criticisms are particularly relevant where researchers have not made clear the predominant socio-economic background of their samples.

It is necessary, for example, to consider social class effects before drawing any general conclusion regarding the youthfulness of abusive mothers. Similarly the lower the social class the more likely there are there to be housing and other economic pressures. The higher the social class the less such external pressures impinge and the greater is the contribution of inner psychological stresses. This is a matter of degree, however, for the great majority of the abusive parents we have tested reveal some disturbance of personality so that emotional immaturity (whatever the real life age) and behavioural impetuosity appear to be real problems for abusive mothers regardless of their external social circumstances. Equally, abusive fathers appear to be introverted and emotionally unsupportive to their partners, and this again is not directly related to social background as such.

The violent outbursts which characterize child abuse seem to be particularly provoked by young children mainly under four years and often under two years of age. This suggests that it is the dependency and the irrationality of the young child that particularly provoke his caretaker. This is not surprising since the quality essentially lacking in abusive mothers is maturity and self control. This must raise questions regarding the extent to which we are dealing with temperamental traits which predispose such parents to experience difficulty in meeting the demands of young children – traits which are likely to be linked to their biological endowment as much as their

113

early experience. Such a possibility has been discussed by the author at some length elsewhere (Hyman, 1973).

What needs emphasizing here is the often unacceptable idea that a diathesis toward a withdrawing unenthusiastic temperament may derive from inherited factors and that emotional immaturity may be similarly influenced by genetic factors (Eysenck & Eysenck, 1969). Heritibilaty is reported by Eysenck to be moderate for both the second order factors of extraversion-introversion and neuroticism and, although controversy regarding heritibality of such 'dimensions of personality' is lively, there seems little reason to ignore this possible influence upon abusive parents, particularly as the social factors involved, both in terms of childhood and current experience, are shared by a large number of non-abusive parents. This is not at all to deny the role of experiential factors both in the past history of the parent and in the present. The disruption so typical of the abusive parent's childhood can only make her 'natural' impulsivity less controlled by lowering the threshold of frustration and reducing her inner sense of security. Additionally it will deprive her of adequate modelling opportunities for good parenting. These two sets of factors must be thought of as acting in unfortunate unison. When to this is added the current isolation all too typical of the abusive family, then one can see how a multiplicity of influences interact to make the problems of being a 'good enough parent' insoluble.

But, as we have seen, the situation does not merely escalate to the point of catastrophe on one or two unpredictable occasions. It is a continuous problem, probably detectable from the point of the abused child's birth, if not from conception. This is not meant to suggest that difficulties in the 'sensitive period' of pregnancy and birth have some kind of mystical impact, but rather that an inadequate capacity for self control may combine with inadequate learning of parental skills and attitudes. This combination is catalyzed by current tensions and past recollections of abuse and neglect so that a mother's transactions with her infant are distorted and distorting from the outset.

Such mis-matching tends to be self-sustaining and cumulative in its effects. A mother who insensitively responds to her infant's needs may actually provoke such an infant to cry more, or feed less successfully (Ainsworth, 1971; Dunn, 1975). Hence the perception of the abused child as being inordinately difficult may be in part due to the abusive mother's unreal expectation of the infant, this then becoming a self-fulfilling prophecy because of her inability to comfort him and contain his distress. This would mean that, as he grows, the child's attachment to his mother will become more ambivalent and uncertain in the way we have been able to show directly. This, in turn, will lead to excessively demanding behaviour and an unusual need for reassurance on the child's part. But it is just this which undermines the inadequate and insecure mother and makes her feel both frustrated and angry.

To hope that we can avert all cases of abuse by team collaboration and proper exchange of information is futile. While these do help to reduce the incidence of the most serious abuse and re-abuse, bureaucratic measures alone cannot hope to provide full prophylaxis. Greater awareness of early malfunctioning in the new mother's interaction with her infant is required. Not only can help then be offered to reduce social and economic pressures but also, and of even more importance, sensitive intervention can be made regarding the transactions which are occurring between mother and child. Failures by a mother to react appropriately to her infant need to be accurately detailed and the inappropriate responses modified. We are currently extending our observational study into the homes of child abusing families to validate and refine our video findings. This may help with the question of early prevention, by providing behavioural clues to malfunctioning.

A large increase is needed in the availability of Health Visitors specially trained to help mothers cope with their infants' crying, sleeping, and feeding and other handling problems on an intensive daily basis. Additional residential centres are urgently needed so that such facilities can be made available on a 24 hour basis and where mothers, and hopefully fathers too, can gain confidence and experience in caring for their infants. Mothering aids and 'drop-in' foster-mothers are also required in greater numbers than presently available. All these measures are described by White Franklin (1978) and the recommendations are not new. What is required now is action based on such suggestions.

Without early and intensive intervention – not merely surveillance – there is little likelihood that this complex and enduring problem is likely to disappear. Child abuse has no simple explanation. It represents a complicated aberration in a basic social function, that of caring for and socializing a child until he reaches independence. This is the most basic function left to the modern nuclear family. Unless those who are unable to discharge this function receive appropriate help in sufficient degree to make it genuinely effective in the long term, or are relieved of this responsibility by due process of law, not only will children continue to suffer death and injury but they will in their turn fail to develop their own potentiality for good parenthood. The emphasis throughout the present decade has been upon case finding and case prediction. This now needs to change and the stress should be placed upon prevention and treatment. Both of these aims require

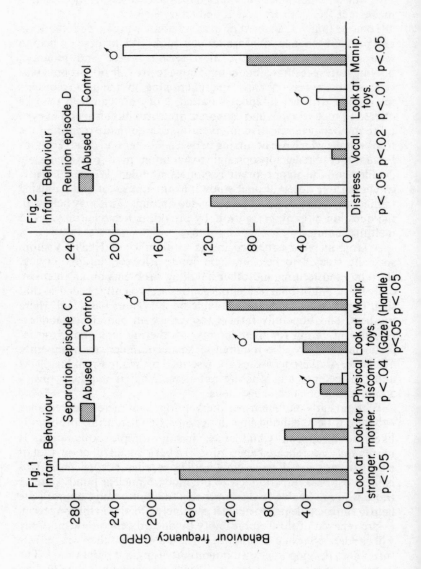

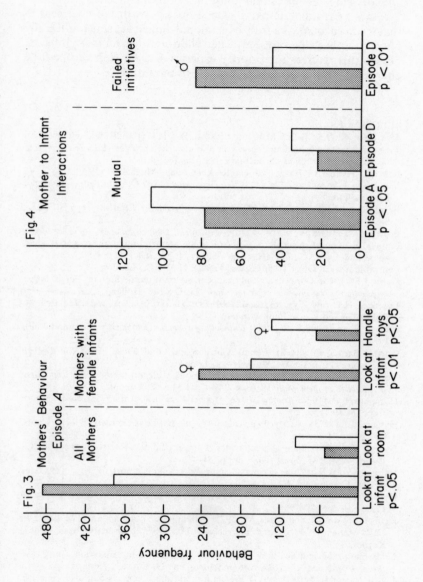

Fig. 3 Mothers' Behaviour Episode A

Fig. 4 Mother to Infant Interactions

that the 'latent abuser', that is the adyadic mother, be recognized at an early stage before actual abuse has been manifested.

Far more is still required to extend our knowledge of treatment so that it can encompass a truly educational dimension which will really alter a mother's perception of her child and her handling of him. Unless this receives the priority it deserves there seems to be little chance of a reduction in child abuse in the future.

REFERENCES

Ainsworth, M.D.S., Bell, S.M.V. and Stayton, D.J. (1971) 'Individual differences in strange situation behaviour of one-year olds'. In: H.R. Schaffer (Ed.) *The Origins of Human Social Relations*. Academic Press, London.

Baher, E., Hyman, C., Jones, C., Jones, R., Kerr, A. and Mitchell, R. (1976) *At Risk: An Account of the Battered Child Research Department, NSPCC*, Routledge and Kegan Paul, London.

Bene, E. and Anthony, E.J. (1957) *Manual for the Family Relations Test*. N.F.E.R., Slough.

Brown, G. and Harris, T. (1978) *Origins of Social Depression*. Tavistock, London.

Burgess, R.L. and Conger, R.D. (1977) 'Family interaction patterns related to child abuse and neglect'. *Child Abuse and Neglect, 1*, pp. 269–77.

Central Statistical Office (1976) *Social Trends*, H.M.S.O., London.

Dunn, J.F. (1975) 'Consistency and change in styles of mothering'. In: *Parent Infant Interaction: Ciba Foundation Symposium, 33*. Elsevier, Holland.

Eysenck, H.J. and Eysenck, S. (1969) *Personality Structure and Measurement*, Routledge and Kegan Paul, London.

Glueck, E. and Glueck, S. (1950) *Unravelling Juvenile Delinquency*. Commonwealth Press.

Gorrell Barnes, G. (1978) 'Family violence and child abuse'. In: *Good Enough Parenting*, C.C.E.T.S.W.; Study No. 1. London.

House of Commons (1977) *Violence to Children: First Report for the Select Committee on Violence in the Family, Session 1976–7*. H.M.S.O., London.

Humphreys, P. (1974) *Primate: Users Manual Version 4*. Brunel University, Monograph 74/1.

Hyman, C. (1973) *A Psychological Study of Battering Parents*. Ph.D. Thesis, University of Surrey.

Hyman, C. (1978a) 'Some characteristics of abusing families referred to the NSPCC'. *British Journal of Social Work, 8*, pp. 31–36.

Hyman, C. (1978b) 'Non-accidental injury: a research report to the Surrey Area Review Committee', *Health Visitor, 51*, p. 168.

Hyman, C. and Mitchell, R. (1975) 'A psychological study of child battering', *Health Visitor, 48*, pp. 294–96.

Kennel, J., Voos, D. and Klaus, M. (1975) 'Parent infant bonding'. In: C.M. Lee (Ed.) *Child Abuse: a reader and sourcebook*. The Open University Press, Milton Keynes.

Leiderman, P.H. and Seashore, M.J. (1975) 'Mother-infant separation'. In: *Parent Infant Interaction: Ciba Foundation Symposium, 33*. Elsevier, Holland.

Lynch, M. and Roberts, J. (1977) 'Predicting child abuse'. *Child Abuse and Neglect, 1*, pp. 491–92.

Martin, H. (1976) *The Abused Child: A Multidisciplinary Approach to Developmental Issues and Treatment*, Ballinger, Cambridge, Mass.

Newson, J. and Newson, E. (1977) *Seven Years Old in the Home Environment*. Allen and Unwin, London.

Smith, S. (1975) *The Battered Child Syndrome*. Butterworths, London.

White Franklin, A. (1978) *Child Abuse: Prediction, Prevention and Follow-up*. Churchill Livingstone, Edinburgh.

8   Emotional Expression in Abused and/or Neglected Infants*

Theodore J. Gaensbauer, David Mrazek and Robert J. Harmon

Since the pioneering observations of Kempe et al. (1962) there has been a dramatic increase in public concern about child abuse and neglect. The widespread incidence of abuse and neglect has been well documented (Gil, 1969), the variety of social and psychological factors which can contribute to such abuse have been described (Elmer, 1967; Parke & Collmer, 1975; Steele & Pollock, 1974), and a variety of strategies for prediction and therapeutic intervention in these families has been proposed (Kempe & Helfer, 1974).

Unfortunately, disproportionately little attention has been given to the specific impact of neglect and abuse on the children. Such research is crucial for at least two major reasons. First, a growing body of research in infancy has demonstrated that infant temperament has a profound effect on caretaker-infant interaction (Lewis & Rosenblum, 1974; Sander, 1964; Thomas et al., 1963). Study of these infants will help determine the extent to which characteristics in the infant contribute to difficulties with parents that lead to abuse and neglect. Such a hypothesis has been previously articulated (Martin, 1976; Milowe & Lourie, 1964) and is supported by the finding that a large percentage of these infants are premature (Elmer & Gregg, 1967; Klein & Stern, 1971; Weston, 1968) and by clinical reports that some children are abused in more than one home (Milowe and Lourie, 1964). A second reason would be to delineate more precisely the distorting effects of abuse and/or neglect on the infant's development, and the extent to which such distortions may be alleviated by specific remedial measures.

Studies of these children have documented the severe, though

* This research was supported by grants from the Grant Foundation Endowment Fund of the Development Psychobiological Research Group of the University of Colorado Medical Center and by BRSG RR-05357 awarded by the Division of Research Resources, National Institute of Health. Author Gaensbauer is supported by Research Career Development Award 1–K04–HD–214–01.

variable, effects which abuse and neglect can have on physical and mental development (Elmer, 1967; Martin, 1972; Martin et al., 1974; Martin, 1976a). Much less has been written about their emotional development, particularly in infancy, Descriptions have highlighted general characteristics, such as inhibition of pleasure, distractibility, provocatively aggressive behaviour, extreme fearfulness or, conversely, emotional apathy in situations typically upsetting to children (Elmer, 1967; Galdston, 1965; Martin & Rodeheffer, 1976; Morse, Sahler & Friedman, 1970; Silver 1968; Terr, 1970) without focussing on individual adaptive styles. Yet as Martin (1976a) has emphasized, these infants do not present a unitary picture. Defining specific patterns of infant response and the experiences leading to a particular outcome in a particular infant is critical for understanding the impact of the abusive environment.

A major reason that little has been written about the emotional development of these children during early infancy has been the lack of adequate methodology for systematically evaluating such infants. The need for a standardized psychiatric appraisal of infants has been emphasized by Cytryn (1968) who outlined the major components of such an evaluation.

As part of a larger project devoted to the study of emotional development in infancy, the authors observed a group of children referred for evaluation because of suspected or documented abuse and/or neglect. Using an experimental paradigm originally designed to study infant emotional expression, we have been able to make observations on many of the variables suggested by Cytryn, including affective responses, mother-infant interaction, free play, differential social responsivity to the mother and to a stranger in several contexts, developmental testing, frustration tolerance, and a brief maternal separation and reunion. Widespread use of experimental situations similar to those incorporated into our paradigm has provided normative data regarding infants' typical behaviour in such situations (Ainsworth and Wittig, 1969; Ainsworth, Bell and Stayton, 1971; Bretherton and Ainsworth, 1974; Emde, Gaensbauer and Harmon, 1976; Gaensbauer, Emde and Campos, 1976; Harmon, Durfee and Klein, 1976; Klein and Durfee, 1976; Lieshout, 1975; Rheingold and Eckerman, 1970). In addition, over 70 normal, primarily middle-class children between the ages of 9 and 20 months have been studied in our laboratory using the same experimental sequence. This extensive experience with normals provides baseline data for comparison with the responses of these high risk infants.

121

Subjects and Methods

The sample consists of 30 infants. Twenty-eight infants were seen in our playroom laboratory; 19 of these were seen with their natural mothers, and 9 infants were seen with foster mothers. An additional two infants were observed in a crisis nursery in the presence of a housemother.

Ages ranged from 12–26 months with a mean of 20 months. The infants were referred from social service agencies in Denver and outlying counties, including the Adams County Family Learning Center, (research and demonstration project in the area of child abuse funded by HEW-OCD Grant 90–C–73) and were primarily from lower socio-economic groups. The amount of background information available to us about the caretaking environment and the extent of abuse and/or neglect was often quite sketchy, resulting from the parent's reticence to volunteer such material as well as caseworkers' lack of opportunity to gather detailed information. For this reason, the children's behaviour will be emphasized in these descriptions, and speculations about the caretaking environments must be considered tentative.

The parents were aware that after the playroom visit a report would be written that might affect administrative decisions regarding them and the children. Though this knowledge influenced parental behaviour, usually in the direction of increased attentiveness to the child, the child's behaviour seemed less affected. For example, infants who were unused to reciprocal interaction with mother in the home would tend to ignore even strenuous efforts to engage them in play in the laboratory. Reports from mothers and caseworkers tended to confirm that the infant's behaviour was consistent with behaviour observed at home.

The experimental paradigm consisted of five phases: 1) a 7-minute play period with mother and infant alone in the playroom; 2) a 4-minute stranger (in all cases the senior author) approach sequence, proceeding from talking to the infant to a near approach, and finally to a pick-up of the infant, followed by a maternal approach and pick-up similar to the stranger's; 3) a 15-25 minute period which a Bayley developmental test was administered and several mild frustrations took place; 4) a 3-minute mother separation and 2-minute reunion sequence with the stranger remaining in the room throughout; 5) a 3-minute period of mother-infant play following the stranger's departure; the sequence concluded with the stranger's return. The testing occurred in a brightly decorated playroom containing two chairs for the examiner and mother and a large number of attractive toys placed equidistant between the two chairs. The entire sequence was videotaped through a one-way mirror for subsequent analysis.

Material reported in this chapter is based on consensus judgments of the authors as clinician researchers who reviewed the tapes and compared the infant's responses with the responses of normal infants observed in our laboratory. Although detailed microanalyses of affective responses, free play behaviour, differential social responsivity and attachment behaviour to mother and stranger are underway, this initial report will provide careful clinical description of the infants' behaviour in a structured playroom setting.

Given the lack of similar data in the literature such clinical description might well provide clinicians with a sense of how such infants might present themselves and stimulate thinking about the various factors contributing to the clinical picture.

Results

Some behaviours appeared to be characteristic of most of the infants tested and will be described in the context of general observations. In addition to these general features, four affective behavioural patterns were delineated. These affective patterns, a clinical description of an infant demonstrating each pattern, and some preliminary speculations about experiences which may lead to such patterns will be presented.

General Observations

Affective Responses.
There were differences from normative samples both in the quality of the responses and the manner in which such responses were modulated. Pleasurable responses during the free play and testing situations were less frequent. At the same time, overt expressions of fearfulness during the stranger approach were less often seen, as were distress responses to mother's leaving the room. Unusual affective responses were present which were not often seen in a normative sample. For example, fearfulness or sadness might be observed during the free play situation with mother, and expressions of anger were much more frequent throughout. In terms of modulation of affect, some infants showed a quite narrow range of affect, with little affective response regardless of the situation. Other infants showed a tendency to erupt with very strong and quite destructive displays of affect, particularly anger and distress.

Mother-Infant Interaction.
Characteristically, there was lack of sensitive and contingent reciprocity in the interaction between mother and infant. The behaviour of

mothers varied widely. Some mothers were quite uninvolved with their infants, while others made considerable efforts to interact. Regardless of mother's behaviour, if the child was unaccustomed to this type of interaction, he would not respond. The frequent result was a form of parallel play in which sustained reciprocal interactions were rare. Interestingly, this was the case with foster mothers as well; despite sensitive efforts to engage them, these children were often unresponsive. When social contact was left to the infant's initiative, proximity-seeking to mother and verbal and social bids for attention were less frequent than in the normal population. Mother was not used as a 'secure base' from which to explore (Ainsworth, 1967).

Free Play.
Most infants actively explored the room and the toys, though their play lacked the persistent and creative qualities of our normative sample. Instead, it appeared disorganized compared to normative sample infants of the same age. An aimless quality with a lack of ability to sustain interest in specific items was typical. A number of infants showed marked inhibition in activity. In some, this was associated with 'frozen watchfulness' accompanied by frequent uneasy glances toward mother, while in others it seemed related to depressive qualities of listless motoric retardation and lack of energy. This was in marked contrast to the play of normal infants who actively combine objects, make them work appropriately, and use them to produce interesting effects. Only those infants who were rated as 'ambivalently attached' (Harmon, Durfee and Klein, 1976) in a normative sample showed the aimless movement from toy to toy seen in these infants.

Mother-Stranger Comparison.
Since both stranger and mother approached the infant in a similar manner, the infant's responses could be directly compared. Though many infants will show positive reactions to strangers, it is unusual for a normal infant to respond more positively to a stranger than to mother (Harmon, Durfee and Klein, 1976). Such reactions were not uncommon in the abused sample. Indeed, in approximately 20% the response to the stranger was more positive than to mother, while an additional 40% responded similarly to both mother and stranger; only 40% were clearly more positive to mother.

Bayley Developmental Testing and Responses to Mild Frustration.
Bayley Developmental Test scores (mental scale) varied widely, ranging from 50–122, with overall scores somewhat below normal. The mean score for all infants tested was 95.5. The low scores were no

doubt related to the infants' lack of abilities, to temperamental characteristics which interfered with their performance (Rodeheffer and Martin, 1976) and to the fact that test conditions were not conducive to best performance. The infants had difficulty maintaining the sustained attention necessary for completion of the tasks. The frequent substitution of test items led to frustration, overt angry reactions, or regressed fussing. Withdrawal would frequently follow the removal of a toy if another test item were not immediately available. Difficulties in cooperating involved not only intentional resistance, but passive inattention as well. Being unaccustomed to interactions with adults, these infants would often pay little attention to the examiner's requests. Successful performance on a particular item would depend on catching the infant's attention during the brief span of time in which he would be willing to pursue the task. As a result, considerable test scatter was seen.

The response to a mild verbal prohibition occurring during the testing could be quite striking. Some infants responded with a temper outburst. However, several infants responded with an instant freezing reaction associated with a fearful or sad expression that persisted until the examiner reassured them.

Separation and Reunion.
The infants' reactions to mother's departure and reunion supported the hypotheses of Ainsworth and her colleagues (Ainsworth, Bell and Stayton, 1971). According to these investigators, a lack of search or distress behaviour following mother's departure, and the lack of positive greeting and avoidance of, or angry resistance to, mother following reunion, can reflect insecure and/or ambivalent infant attachment. These infants showed relatively little distress when mother left the room. When distress *was* evident, it often included an angry component which persisted for prolonged periods following mother's return in the form of avoidance or provocative attention-seeking behaviour. The comparison of the infants' responses to a separation from and reunion with the stranger, as contrasted with mother, was at times notable. In our normal sample, despite frequent positive interactions with the stranger up to this point, no infants showed more 'attachment' behaviour during separation or reunion to the stranger as compared to mother. In the abused group, six infants showed more 'attachment' behaviour to the experimenter, including search behaviours following departure, and positive approach behaviours following reunion.

Description of Affective Behaviour Patterns

Though there was heterogeneity in the kinds of responses observed in these infants, four relatively consistent affective patterns emerged. These patterns were associated with characteristic patterns of mother-infant interaction in the laboratory. While there was considerable overlap, it was posssible to place each infant within one of the four groups after careful consideration of the predominant picture. The groupings represent crystallizations of what we believe to be the essential elements of the developmental disturbances present in these infants. The major differences between the groups related to the quality of the affect expressed over the course of the experimental sequence. Each pattern will be presented separately, accompanied by one or two case vignettes.

Developmentally and Affectively Retarded

These infants had not only been deprived physically and emotionally, but had experienced a marked deficit in caretaker-infant interaction involving significant stimulus deprivation. Approximately two-fifths of our sample fell into this group. Such infants were reminiscent of the 'hospitalism' cases of Spitz (1945), institutionalized infants described by Bakwin (1942) and Provence and Lipton (1962), developmentally retarded infants living in families (Coleman and Provence, 1957; Prugh and Harlow, 1962), and infants experiencing 'sensory privation' (Rutter, 1972). We agree with Martin (1976a) that this is the most devastating form of neglect, since these infants lack the requisite experiences for development. They tended to be emotionally blunted, socially unresponsive, inattentive to their environment, and retarded in all spheres – cognitive, emotional, and motoric. Not only was their play repertoire limited, but they lacked the skills which would make adequate progress possible. Responses to strangers and to mothers revealed little discrimination and their emotional reactions in general were of limited range. One might see a kind of stimulus hunger in these infants, and increased activity and responsiveness to social stimulation could be seen over the course of the examination. Some demonstrated self-stimulating behaviours such as rocking and head nodding, as described by previous investigators (Spitz, 1945; Bakwin, 1942; Provence and Lipton, 1962).

Case of Matthew – a Developmentally Retarded Child

Matthew was 14 months and 7 days old when tested in our playroom with his mother. During the free play situation he neither walked nor crawled but sat in one place the entire time playing aimlessly with the toys. His movements were slow, awkward, and characterized by listlessness and lack of energy. The quality of his play was more typical of an 8 to 10-month-old infant with much banging and noise-making but little organized use of the toys. His affective responses were quite blunted and displayed little range; a blank, sober facial expression predominated with neither distress nor pleasure observed.

He was unresponsive to both mother and to the experimenter, and never initiated contact. Efforts to interact resulted in his flailing his arms in a rhythmic, uncoordinated, almost stereotypic fashion as he became more activated, but without any change in expression. Though he did not resist being picked up, holding him was like holding a dead weight or 'sawdust' doll as described by Provence and Lipton (1962) in their institutionalized infants. There was no effort to mould or adjust to the person holding him.

He scored 82 on the Bayley Mental Development Scale (MDI). Continuous encouragement was required to keep Matthew engaged. He was inattentive to the examiner, tending to play in his own way. When toys were removed, he would fuss briefly without any explicit communicative gestures, and would then quickly give up and withdraw.

His social unresponsiveness was also evident in the separation and reunion sequences. Except for a brief glance when mother left and after she returned, he showed no emotional reaction. When the experimenter left and returned, there was again little reaction. Instead, he continued to sit, playing listlessly with a few toys.

Depressed Infants

Approximately one-fifth of our sample showed predominant elements of sadness and depression of varying degrees of severity. The pathognomonic signs of depression in infants were present, as described by Spitz and Wolf (1946). These included motor retardation, inhibition, withdrawal, aimless play, proneness to fussing under minimal stress, and typical facial patterns associated with sadness and depression.

These infants were distinguished from the deprived infants in that, although their play was markedly inhibited, with considerable encouragement they could brighten up, engage the environment, and perform at their age levels. However, they seemed quite vulnerable to rebuffs of whatever nature, and during lulls in activity, depressive qualities might quickly surface. For example, during the separation sequence, an infant might show a marked depressive reaction with a sad facial expression and cessation of all activity or else marked distress, particularly if the ongoing depression itself was related to abandonment or recent separations.

These infants appeared to have experienced a period of at least adequate caretaking followed by a relative decrease in quantity or quality of caretaking. This decrease might be the result of abandonment, separation, maternal depression, or abuse which interfered with the infants' expectations regarding the availability of his caretakers. The crucial variable seemed to be the discrepancy between level of expectation derived from previous experience and current deprivation (i.e., the quality of 'having loved and lost').

Case of Michael – A Depressed Infant

Nineteen-month-old Michael had been placed in a foster home three weeks earlier, while his quite depressed mother tried to straighten out her own life. Mother was a very dependent person who had experienced a series of losses, leaving her unable to adequately care for her son. Michael was tested with foster mother, but his natural mother was requested to come at the end of the session so a comparison of responses could be made.

During the free play sequence, Michael had a dazed, waif-like look about him as he sat by his foster mother and warily surveyed the room. His foster mother attempted to interest him in the toys, but he was inattentive and scarcely acknowledged her interventions. After several minutes, he slowly crawled to the toys and began playing with them in an absent-minded manner. His facial expression was a predominantly wary one, interspersed with downcast, sad expressions lasting as long as five to ten seconds.

When the experimenter entered, his play became even more listless, and he avoided eye contact. He passively accepted being picked up, leaning his head on the examiner's shoulder and looking into the distance with a pathetically sad facial expression. He was somewhat more active in response to foster mother's approach; however, when she offered to pick him up, he impassively turned and began moving away from her. While being held, he avoided eye contact with her as well, but briefly smiled for the first time in the session.

Rearranging the room for developmental testing was unsettling; he began whimpering as foster mother adjusted his position in her lap. He was very hesitant in reaching for any of the toys offered, though, once engaged, he did complete several age-appropriate items. There were frequent gazes into space with a vacant or forlorn look. Over time, he became increasingly inhibited and fussy, and eventually testing had to be suspended.

The separation experience was quite stressful. When foster mother left, he went to the door and began screaming desperately. He continued to cry until her return. Upon seeing her, he walked toward her but stopped four feet away, giving no indication of a wish to be picked up. She proceeded to pick him up, whereupon he stopped crying within 15–30 seconds. However, when the foster mother attempted to engage him in play, he turned away and played by himself within several feet of her.

After the experimenter left, Michael's natural mother entered the room. As soon as he saw her, he immediately got up and walked toward her, holding his arms up and vocalizing a wish to be held. There was a prolonged and touching hug between mother and child. Over the next ten minutes he began playing with her in quite a different fashion than with the examiner or foster mother. He moved about the room more actively and confidently, vocalized happily to her, intermittently smiled, and engaged in reciprocal play. At the same time, a readiness to withdraw persisted; when mother offered to pick him up, he passively ignored her outstretched arms.

Ambivalent, Affectively Labile

Though almost all the infants tested showed some evidence of conflicting positive and negative responses in social interaction, approximately a quarter of the infants showed such mixed or ambivalent reactions in a consistent and marked fashion. These infants differed from the first two groups in that they did not appear to be overtly depressed. They were quite capable of functioning at their age levels and did not appear to have been significantly deprived. They showed pleasure and positive responses at times and could be socially engaging. However, such pleasurable responses and social approaches lacked stability, and distress responses, such as withdrawal or anger, could quickly emerge under stress.

These infants seemed to have experienced inconsistent mothering, with sensitive nurturing and reciprocally rewarding interaction alternating with periods of abuse and/or neglect. During periods when interaction was disturbed, two outcomes were frequently seen. First, the mother might attempt to reduce tension by withdrawing from the situation, leaving the child somewhat at a loss. Alternatively, the mother might respond punitively, resulting in an angry interaction. The inconsistency in affective responses of these infants could relate not only to inconsistencies in mother, but also to experiences with different caretakers of varying sensitivity and skill. This was particularly true of infants who had spent time in foster homes or day-care settings.

During the initial play period, the infants often demonstrated interest and pleasure with positive interchanges with mother. With the stranger approach, several responses were possible. Shyness might be seen and a clear mother preference indicated. For infants whose positive experiences were outside the home, an 'indiscriminate' prompt positive response might occur, such as immediately approaching and offering the stranger a toy. These infants might show preference for the examiner during both the approach and pick-up sequence and the later separation and reunion. Throughout the session there were conflicting tendencies of approach and avoidance, and of positive and negative reactions.

Case of Peter – An Infant Whose Positive Experiences Were Outside the Home

Peter was 12 months and 9 days old at the time of referral. Between the ages of five and eight months he had been in a foster home with quite adequate caretaking. For the three previous months, he had been in the natural home with mother with intermittent baby sitting at a day care centre.

During the entire sequence, mother remained almost totally uninvolved. As a result, Peter seemed uncertain. Though he went immediately to the toys, he played with them hesitantly. His uncertainty about mother's support, and conflicting tendencies to approach and avoid, were manifest throughout the sequence. At times he would play near her while making no direct bids. On other occasions he would take several steps toward her and then turn away. This conflict was perhaps most poignantly demonstrated at a moment when he turned toward her with a smile and expectant look. Receiving no response, he turned away with a sad, disappointed look, stopped playing, and stared into space.

Though initially wary with the experimenter, once Peter discovered that interaction was possible, he quickly warmed up. In fact, when he was put down by the experimenter following the pick-up episode, he immediately crawled over to the experimenter's chair, smiled broadly, and pulled himself up against the experimenter's legs.

He approached the testing in an interested and competent manner (MDI = 102), though his frustration tolerance was low. He would fuss when items were removed or placed out of sight. However, once the item was replaced, he would readily accept it. As the testing proceeded, he became more fussy and finally, when a favourite toy was put away after the testing was completed, he had a temper protest. This quickly subsided when the item was returned to him.

Ambivalence was quite marked during the separation and reunion sequences. There was little response to mother's departure, and he initiated and sustained social interaction with the experimenter during mother's absence. When she returned, he fussed briefly, crawled over to her, and reached toward her leg. Mother made no attempt to pick him up and he quickly moved away from her, making no further effort to engage her. When the experimenter left, he showed 'attachment' behaviour. He immediately crawled to the door, tried to open it, and remained there while vocalizing with appeal calls for approximately one minute. When the experimenter returned, he smiled broadly, immediately crawled over, and pulled himself into the experimenter's lap.

Case of Becky – Inconsistent Mothering

In contrast to Peter, the inconsistencies in 16-month-old Becky's life occurred in the context of the single relationship with mother. Matters had apparently gone well between Becky and her unwed mother during the first year of life, but had become more problematical when Becky turned one year and became 'willful'. Though often extremely frustrated with Becky, mother had left her with babysitters only on rare occasions.

The capacity for reciprocally pleasurable interchange was seen during the free play sequence. Becky frequently looked and smiled at mother and after a time moved over to play in mother's area. She was quite shy with the experimenter, looked to mother as a source of security and responded positively to mother's approach and pick-up.

Though she scored 109 on the Bayley test, she was very aggressive and easily frustrated in an unpredictable fashion. The fragility of her good mood was most clearly revealed following the maternal separation and reunion. There was angry fussing for approximately one minute following the separation which quickly subsided. Following her return, mother did not respond to Becky's gesture to be picked up, whereupon Becky became more aggressive in her play.

Mother eventually picked her up and attempted to comfort her by getting her to put her head on mother's shoulder, but Becky resisted. Mother then became angry and began poking at Becky in a teasing, provocative fashion. The interchange ended with Becky crying angrily on the floor at mother's feet, while mother sullenly tried to ignore her. From the child's standpoint, both the wish for comfort and the anger which interfered with receiving such comfort, were readily observed.

Angry Infants

Somewhat less than one-fifth of the infants showed very high arousal and extreme amounts of anger throughout the sequence. These infants had been exposed to chaotic, highly charged environments with frequent, harsh punishments administered by caretakers who often had difficulty with consistent limit setting. Provocative be-

131

haviour often seemed the most reliable means of gaining mother's attention. These infants were extremely active, showed disorganization in their play, lack of perseverence, and frequent angry outbursts and destructive behaviour. Frustration tolerance was very low. The response to separation was an angry one, often developing into a fully-fledged temper tantrum which could be abruptly turned off or could persist for long periods.

Case of Tommy – An Angry Infant

Although, at 26 months, Tommy was somewhat older than many of our infants, similar behaviours were seen in younger infants. His mother was a very immature, inadequate woman with an explosive temper. Except for two two-week stays during his second year in the crisis nursery during family upheavals, Tommy had been raised at home.

Hyperactivity and disorganized play were clearly evident during the initial sequence. He moved about the room without playing with any toy for more than 15–30 seconds. Within the first minute, he had protested against playing with a toy that mother had wanted him to have. At another point, an unexpected noise caused him to wince in fright. His play was aggressive with much hitting and throwing.

Social interaction was as transient and inconsistent as his play. For example, he allowed himself to be picked up by both mother and experimenter, but within five to ten seconds squirmed to be put down. Developmental testing was extremely difficult. He was constantly on the move, easily frustrated, and given to marked displays of anger. Though his overall score was above average (MDI = 122) he would comply with requests only for brief periods of time. If he were displeased with or tired of a task, he would push it away and refuse all further efforts to interest him, usually by throwing the toy on the floor. During the testing, mother initiated frequent contests of will by telling him what he should or shouldn't be doing.

When mother left, he wanted to leave with her and after being pushed back into the room (somewhat roughly), he began screaming and threw himself on the floor. This lasted about 30 seconds, after which, refusing an offer to play, he hit the experimenter on the arm. He then hit a doll and began provocatively to throw a variety of toys on the floor. This angry, provocative behaviour persisted throughout mother's absence and following her return. After the experimenter left, mother began to lose control of her own temper, especially after Tommy had grabbed a toy she had been playing with. Mother grabbed the toy back, and a power struggle between the two of them ensued. Mother's lack of impulse control was demonstrated by her threat that 'if you don't stop it, I'm going to punch you right in the kisser'.

Comment

Clinical descriptions of this sort represent only an initial step toward understanding the variable impact of abuse and neglect on very young children. Further understanding will depend on more precise analysis of these infants' affective and social behaviours and comparison to matched normal infants. Some techniques for dealing with such microanalyses have been developed and issues of reliability, the use of naïve raters, and multivariate statistical approaches to data analysis (including time series techniques) are important for more systematic description and rigorous hypothesis testing.

We nevertheless believe that the attempt to distill out the prominent affective elements in these infants can further our understanding of the specific impacts of abuse and neglect on emotional development. The hypotheses regarding the association of specific caretaking variables with specific patterns of affect behaviour are tentative, but provide leads for more detailed investigation. In addition to the caretaking environment, factors within the infant are likely to play an important part in the clinical picture. More detailed developmental studies, including longitudinal approaches, focused on the interplay between constitutional and environmental factors which may influence the infant's basic response tendencies, such as toward depression and withdrawal versus hyperactivity and aggressiveness, are needed. The question of whether particular patterns may be age-related is also an area requiring further research. In our sample, examples of each pattern were found throughout the age range studied, with the exception that the 'angry' infants tended to be somewhat older. Beyond this, we have no firm impressions.

The degree of 'fit' between the affective behaviour of the child and the mothers pointed to the potential value of research strategies which, rather than considering mother and infant separately, focus within the sphere of their affective interaction (Emde and Robinson, 1976; Sameroff and Chandler, 1975). It is likely that characteristic interactive modes established, not just at moments of crisis when an abusive incident might occur, but in the day-to-day interchanges between caretaker and child, are most likely to have the greatest impact on the affective response patterns established in the child. We also believe that such affect patterns assume considerable consistency over time, even at these very young ages, and can thereby significantly influence how the child is responded to by caretakers and others (Gaensbauer and Sands, 1979).

REFERENCES

Ainsworth, M. (1967) *Infancy in Uganda: Infant care and growth of love.* Johns Hopkins University Press, Baltimore.

Ainsworth, M., and Wittig, B. (1969) 'Attachment and exploratory behaviour of one-year-old infants in a strange situation'. In: B.M. Foss *Determinants of Infant Behaviour, Volume 4* Methuen.

Ainsworth, M., Bell, S., and Stayton, D. (1971) 'Individual differences in stranger situation behaviour of one-year-olds'. In *The Origins of Human Social Relations,* H.R. Schaffer, (Ed.) Academic Press, New York.

Bakwin, H. (1942) 'Loneliness in infants'. *Am. J. Dis. Children 63*:30–40.

Bretherton, I., and Ainsworth, M. (1974) 'Responses of one-year-olds to a stranger in a strange situation'. In *The Origins of Behaviour: The Origins of Fear,* M. Lewis and L.A. Rosenblum, (Eds.) Wiley, New York.

Coleman, R.W. and Provence, S. (1957) 'Environmental retardation (Hospitalism) in infants living in families'. *Pediatrics 19:* 285–91.

Cytryn, L. (1968) 'Methodological issues in psychiatric evaluation of infants'. *J. Amer. Acad. Child Psychiatry 7:*510–21.

Elmer, E. (1967) *Children in jeopardy.* University of Pittsburgh Press, Pittsburgh.

Elmer, E. and Gregg, G. (1967) 'Developmental characteristics of abused children'. *Pediatrics 40:*596–602.

Emde, R.N., Gaensbauer, T.J., and Harmon, R.J. (1976) 'Emotional expression in infancy: A biobehavioural study'. *Psychological Issues,* Monograph 37, International Universities Press, New York.

Emde, R.N., and Robinson, J. (1976) 'The first two months: recent research in developmental psychobiology and the changing view of the newborn'. *In Basic Handbook of Child Psychiatry,* J. Noshpitz and J. Call, (Eds.) Basic Books, Inc., New York.

Gaensbauer, T.J., Emde, R.N., and Campos, J. (1976) ' "Stranger" distress: confirmation of a developmental shift in a longitudinal sample'. *Perceptual and Motor Skills 43:*99–106.

Gaensbauer, T.J. and Sands, K. (1979) 'Distorted affect communication in abused and/or neglected infants'. *J. Am. Acad. Child Psychiatry, 18,* pp. 236–250.

Galdston, R. (1965) 'Observations on children who have been physically abused and their parents'. *Am: J. Psychiatry 122:* 440–43.

Gil, D.G. (1969) 'Physical abuse of children: 'Findings and implications of a nationwide survey'. *Pediatrics 44:* (Suppl.) 857–64.

Harmon, R.J., Durfee, J.T., and Klein, R.P. (1976) 'Infant's preferential response to mother versus an unfamiliar adult: relationship to attachment'. Presented at the Annual Meeting of the American Academy of Child Psychiatry, Toronto, Canada.

Kempe, C.H., Silverman, F., Steele, B., Droegmueller, W., and Silver, H. (1962) 'The battered child syndrome'. *J. Am. Med. Assn. 181:*17–24.

Kempe, C.H. and Helfer, R. (1974) *Helping the Battered Child and his Family.* J.B. Lippincott Co., Philadelphia.

Klein, R. and Durfee, J. (1976) 'Infants' reactions to unfamiliar adults versus mothers'. *Child Devel. 47:* 1194–96.

Klein, M., and Stern, L. (1971) 'Low birthweight and the battered child syndrome'. *Am. J. Diseases of children, 122,* pp. 15–18.

Lewis, M. and Rosenblum, L.A. (1974) (Eds.) 'The effect of the infant on its caregiver'. *The Origins of Behaviour,* Volume I, Wiley New York.

Lieshout, C.F.M. von (1975) 'Young children's reactions to barriers placed by their mothers'. *Child Devel. 46:*879–86.

Martin, H.P. (1972) 'The child and his development'. In *Helping the Battered Child and His Family,* C.H. Kempe and R. Helfer, (Eds.) J.B. Lippincott Co., Philadelphia.

Martin, H.P., Beezley, P., Conway, E., and Kempe, C.H. (1974) 'The development of abused children'. In I. Schulman, (Ed.) *Advances in Pediatrics*, Volume 21, Year Book Medical Publishers, Chicago.

Martin, H.P. (1976a) *The Abused Child: A Multidisciplinary Approach to Developmental Issues and Treatment*. Ballinger Publishing Co., Cambridge, Massachusetts.

Martin, H.P. (1976b) 'Which children get abused: High risk factors in the child'. In *The Abused Child: A Multidisciplinary Approach to Developmental Issues and Treatment*. Ballinger Publishing Co, Cambridge, Massachusetts.

Martin, H.P. and Rodeheffer, M. (1976) 'The psychological impact of abuse on children'. *J. Ped. Psychology 1*:12–16.

Milowe, I.D. and Lourie, R.S. (1964). 'The child's role in the battered child syndrome'. *J. Pediatrics 65*:1079–81.

Morse, C., Sahler, O.J.Z., and Friedman, S.B. (1970) 'A three year follow-up study of abused and neglected children'. *Amer J. Dis. Child 120*:439–46.

Parke, R.D. and Collmer, C.W. (1975) 'Child abuse: An interdisciplinary analysis'. In E.M. Hetherington, (Ed.) *Review of Child Development Research*, Volume 5, University of Chicago, Chicago, Illinois.

Provence, S. and Lipton, R.C. (1962) *Infants in institutions*. International Universities Press, New York.

Prugh, D. and Harlow, R.G. (1962) ' "Masked deprivation" in infants and young children'. In *Deprivation of Maternal Care: A Reassessment of its Effects*. World Health Organization Public Health Papers 14: Geneva.

Rheingold, H. and Eckerman, C. (1970) 'The infant separates himself from his mother'. *Science 168*:78–83.

Rodeheffer, M. and Martin, H.P. (1976) Special problems in developmental assessment of abused children. In *The Abused Child: A Multidisciplinary Approach to Developmental Issues and Treatment*, H.P. Martin (Ed.), Ballinger Publishing Co, Cambridge, Massachusetts.

Rutter, M. (1972) *Maternal Deprivation Reassessed*. Penguin.

Sameroff, A. and Chandler, M. (1975) 'Reproductive risk and the continuum of caretaking casualty'. F. Horowitz, M. Hetherington, S. Scarr- Salapatek, and G. Siegel, (Eds.) In: *Review of Child Development Research*, Volume 4, University of Chicago Press, Chicago.

Sander, L.W. (1964) 'Adaptive relationships in early mother-child interaction'. *J. Amer. Acad. Child Psychiatry*, *3*:231–64.

Silver, L. (1968) 'The psychological aspects of the battered child and his parents'. *Clinical Proceedings of Children's Hospital 24*:355–70.

Spitz, R.A. (1945) 'Hospitalism: An inquiry into the genesis of psychiatric conditions in early childhood'. *The Psychoanalytic Study of the Child 1*:53–74.

Spitz, R.A. and Wolf, K. (1946) 'Anaclitic depression: An inquiry into the genesis of psychiatric conditions in early childhood'. II. *The Psychoanalytic Study of the Child 2*:313–42.

Steele, B. and Pollock, C. (1974) 'A psychiatric study of parents who abuse infants and small children'. In: R.E. Helfer and C.H. Kempe, (Eds.) *The Battered Child*, The University of Chicago Press, Chicago Illinois.

Terr, L. (1970) 'A family study of child abuse'. *Am. J. Psychiatry 127*:125–31.

Thomas, A., Birch, H.G., Chess, S., Hertzig, M.D., and Korn, S. (1963) *Behavioural Individuality in Early Childhood*. New York University Press, New York.

Weston, J. (1968) 'The pathology of child abuse'. In: R. Helfer and C.H. Kempe, (Eds.) *The Battered Child*, University of Chicago Press, Chicago, Illinois.

9   **Child abuse as aggression.**

Neil Frude

A number of widely differing theoretical formulations have been put forward to account for child abuse. So far none has been successful in providing a means of explaining comprehensively individual cases and population parameters and the aim of this chapter is to show that the diverse nature of the 'phenomenon' demands a wider 'framework' for explanation rather than a set formula approach. It is suggested that the framework of aggression theory might be especially useful in this regard. So far there has been little consideration in the abuse literature of the potentially highly relevant work on the psychology of aggression. It is also likely that a good deal can be learnt about aggression in general from a careful reading of the voluminous clinical case material on abuse. It will be argued that some alignment of these separate areas of knowledge is feasible and appropriate and would be mutually profitable.

A major problem to be faced in looking for a suitable explanation of abuse is the prodigious variability of the phenomenon on almost all of the dimensions studied. There is no single pattern in the personality of the parents, for example, or in any aspect of their lives. Some are generally neglectful but many look after the child carefully, some have general aggressiveness problems but many do not; and such is the pattern with all of the variables which have been studied. So it is, also, if we consider the population of abused children, the nature of the parent-child relationships involved and, it seems, perinatal, demographic and all other factors. Typically the *range* of any variable for abusing parents or abused children is precisely that found among controls. Of course, the distributions do differ on many of the dimensions and a large number of variables are significantly over- or under-represented in the abusing or abused population. There is a relative excess, for example, of young parents, of lower social class families, of children with behavioural problems and handicap, of unwanted pregnancies, difficult and premature births, strict standards of discipline, harsh and frequent punishment and of unskilled child-care. However, for most of these, as for parental psychopathology and early mother-child separation, the 'abnormal' condition or level is found only in a minority of the abuse population and cannot be described as 'typical'. And we certainly cannot string together such factors and describe the resulting composite as a picture of 'the abusing parent' or 'the abused child'. Even a harsh background in the abusing parent's early life, a fairly common factor, is not universal, and of course many parents with harsh backgrounds do not abuse their children, so even this is very far from being a necessary and sufficient condition for abuse.

A causal factor which is highly salient in a particular case may be totally overlooked when the characteristics of a larger population are examined. For example, parental tumours do not play a significant part as a 'cause of child abuse' although there have been single case reports in which such an organic involvement was indicated and clearly of prime importance (Birrell & Birrell, 1968; Lord & Weisfeld, 1974).

All this points to the difficulty of basing an explanation of a highly variable phenomenon on general population characteristics. Determining the average value has some uses (for example as an aid in formulating social policy) but where there is a wide range then the average value may be a poor pointer to any explanation of why things happen.

The individual abuse case is not the 'population writ small' and a case-based approach would seem to be required. A single set explanatory formula cannot be adequate and what is needed is either a range of explanations or a framework which is flexible enough to accommodate the variability of the phenomenon. Ideally such a formulation would also be able to throw light on (and make predictions about) general population parameters and it should also be capable of generating prevention and treatment strategies, again both for individual cases and for wider populations. It will be suggested that aggression theory is such a framework and that a fairly clear account of abuse can be provided if the principal focus is the abuse *incident* within the individual *case*.

To focus on the incident is to select as the principal phenomenon to be explained something which all abuse cases have in common (that is, specific actions of parents which result in physical injury) and which has a limited time-course. These characteristics sharply distinguish incident analysis from many alternative models. For example, a model which tries to explain abuse principally in terms of bond-failure, parental psychopathology or impoverished social conditions has a limited range (since it is very easy to find cases which do not possess the key characteristic) and also has an extended time-base, so that further explanation is then required of why the abuse occurred at a particular time. It is clear from the available data that the pattern of incidents is not random and that incidents often relate to specific immediate conditions, suggesting therefore that a close examination of these must play at least some part in the account of why the event occurred.

The idea that the explanatory focus should be the incident is not currently a popular one, and a good deal of recent research and theorizing has concentrated on general features of the parental personality, social background or family dynamics. The NSPCC group, for example, in their report *At Risk* (Baher et al, 1976), quote approvingly the statement by Oliver et al., (1974) that 'it is a mistake to place too much emphasis on the immediate precipitants of abuse' and this theme is echoed in a number of other accounts. However, as a result of this orientation some studies report the demographic and personality characteristics of the families in great detail and all but ignore salient aspects of the incident itself. It could now be argued that we have amassed a great deal of data about background characteristics and that the result is a bewildering array of several hundred 'correlates of abuse' without an adequate theory to link these findings. The need for theory in this area is acute and the most urgent requirement is perhaps to integrate what is already known rather than to merely continue adding to the number of elements of knowledge. It is a familiar pattern in this research that workers study a single aspect of the phenomenon, find some significant effect, and then go on to argue that this is the vital, central or fundamental element for understanding the whole phenomenon. When there are several such contenders a very confused picture emerges.

Where studies have made a special point of looking at the incidents leading to injury then the results have generally been very illuminating. For example, the studies by Gil (1970) in the United States and Smith (1975) and Scott (1973a) in the UK indicate quite clearly that abuse is often a reaction to the immediate situation and very often to perceived behaviour of the child (this was the case in two-thirds of the large number of incidents studied by Gil). Situational factors are hardly ever to be seen as 'sufficient conditions' for attack, and may well be only a final straw after mounting stress and within the context of a poor parent–child relationship. On the other hand aspects of the immediate situation *do* commonly instigate abuse incidents and it might be that such variables as personality, mood and child-handling styles are best viewed as factors contributing to what is basically a 'violent reaction'. Even distant variables such as social class and early parental experience can be incorporated quite satisfactorily into such a model.

It is interesting to note that in fields outside that of child abuse there seems to be an increasing use of the detailed examination of incidents and of specific events and situations. This is apparent within the area of aggression and violence, for example, in Clarke's recent 'criminal event' model (Clarke, 1977), in Hans Toch's book *Violent Men*, (1972) in which there is a chapter entitled 'The Violent Incident as a Unit of Study', and in the ethogenic work concerned with violence on football terraces and in classrooms (Marsh, Rosser & Harré, 1977).

The usefulness of the 'abuse as aggression incident' framework can be demonstrated by taking a basic paradigm of the aggression incident and then mapping on to it research findings and case studies from the abuse literature.

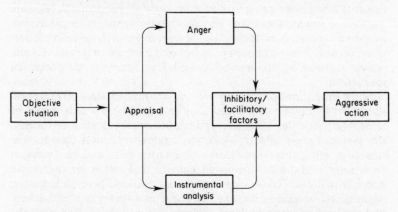

The incident paradigm is illustrated in this simple diagram (Fig. 1). The distinction made between the 'anger aggression' pathway and the 'instrumental' pathway is certainly an oversimplification but is nevertheless useful and is one which is commonly made in the general aggression literature. Tracing through the 'anger aggression' path the first element is that of the real situation in the external world. Clearly some situations 'out there' produce aggression far more readily than do others. The inclusion of the next element, a separate 'appraisal' stage, emphasizes the interpretive and judgemental processes which mediate between the objective situation and any reaction to it. Recent work has stressed the importance of the perceived 'meaning' of a situation in the elicitation of emotional reactions, particularly in the area of fear and anxiety (Lazarus, 1966) but also for aggression (Berkowitz & Alioto, 1973). Most human anger is elicited in the course of social processes and provocation often involves a very subtle interpretation of another person's actions as implying some insult or snub or as constituting some rule infringement.

The 'anger' stage is the centre of a number of important and relevant controversies, particularly those concerning the role of non-specific arousal, the relationship between cognitive, physiological and behavioural elements and the nature of (or the existence of) the phenomenon of 'catharsis'. Inhibitory and facilitatory factors then mediate between the instigation to aggression and behavioural expression. A distinction is commonly made between internal and external inhibitors and the development of internal inhibition has been the subject of a good deal of research.

Aggressive acts themselves – the behavioural 'output' of the system – vary in type, intensity and target, and the choice of target is of particular interest. It has been clearly demonstrated that anger felt towards one object or person may in some circumstances generate aggression towards another, and this phenomenon of displacement may be of special importance for the particular area under consideration, since the target chosen for displaced aggression is typically one which is immediately available and has little or no power of retaliation.

Some limitations of such an account are immediately obvious and there are a number of elaborations and qualifiers which might be added. In particular, there are well established feedback loops within the system (anger affects appraisal, aggressive action changes the situation, etc.), there are clearly alternative exits and entrances at each point, and the dichotomy of instrumental and anger aggression is not a real one. The incident pathway outlined here includes the 'immediate' variables, but each of these can be further 'unpacked' and can be shown to be related to more distant factors. For example, looking at one of the elements, appraisal, it has been shown in various studies that appraisal is related to culture, social class and personality, and that it is influenced by psychopathology, recent experiences, early learning and current physiological state. Reversing this procedure it can be considered how one of the more distant variables, say early learning or psychopathology – may influence each of the elements along the pathway. Taking as an example the influence of alcohol, it can be seen that there are particular ways in which use of this might change aspects of the situation, the appraisal process, the anger dynamics, inhibitory patterns and the nature of the aggressive act itself. A good deal is understood about interrelationships between immediate and distant variables and so the involvement in abuse incidents of factors such as bonding failure, social class, personality and so on are by no means ignored in a reorientation to the aggression incident paradigm.

Certain population predictions follow from a treatment of abuse as aggression and these can be tested against the existing literature. Often, however, failure to find a significant relationship for the population as a whole will merely reflect the non-uniformity of the phenomenon under study, and uniformity is something which must emerge from empirical studies – it cannot be assumed. It has already been suggested that in fact the abuse literature seems to point rather clearly to a marked *non*-uniformity. There are two different and complementary ways in which the paradigm of the aggression incident pathway will now be used to bring together some of the abuse literature. On the one hand population studies will be referred to (typically, in these, a group of abusing parents or abused children are compared with controls on a number of variables) and on the other hand specific illustrative examples will be quoted from the case material published.

Using these two approaches, then, the pathway elements can be considered in turn. First, the *situation*: whatever the time-base involved there is population evidence suggesting that the objective situation surrounding the abusing parent is frequently difficult, stressful, socially impoverished and frustrating. Longer term measures, using for example the Holmes and Rahe (1967) type of life-stress inventory, show that there are more frequent events of high stress potential in the life of the abusing parent, particularly in the areas of marital relationship, accommodation and difficulties with the child (Elmer, 1971; Justice & Justice, 1976). It has also been shown that 'on average' the abused child is in fact more difficult to handle (Friedrich & Boriskin, 1976). When the shorter time-perspective is considered (i.e. using the more immediate 'incident' time-base) then it becomes clear that many abuse episodes are reactions to situational stresses, and particularly to those stresses which arise in child-handling. In the Smith study, for example, the single item 'screaming or crying' seemed to have triggered the incident in a full quarter of the cases (Smith, 1975, p. 125) and in Scott's study of 29 fathers who had fatally injured their children each case was said to have been precipitated by some behaviour of the child (Scott, 1973b). At the single-case level reports abound in which a violent outburst was apparently elicited by persistent screaming or by an act of naughtiness such as rubbing scouring powder into a carpet (DeCourcy & DeCourcy, 1973), or defecating into a laundry basket (Terr, 1970).

Thus there is good population evidence pointing to the fact that often, though not in all cases, some feature of the external situation bears, as it were, some responsibility for the incident. Furthermore, when single case accounts are examined it is often possible to identify incidents in which a particular situational factor has played a major part. The implications for treatment and prevention are obvious. If, in a population or within a single case, there is an identifiable *recurring* situation which appears to trigger an extreme and dangerous reaction then the 'situation' element involved may be a highly appropriate focus for effective intervention. Examples of this include practical aid with acute environmental stressors, training the parent to behave in a way which will not precipitate excessive trigger behaviour in the child, or direct modification of the behaviour of the child itself.

Moving to the next element in the pathway – *appraisal* – there is again evidence in the literature suggesting that processes at this stage markedly influence abusive behaviour. There is relevant literature from both population studies and case material, and again the evidence relates both to the longer time perspective (focussing on parents' general style of appraisal) and the shorter (focussing on appraisal at the time of the incident). Thus it has been shown in various studies that some abusing parents are highly sensitive to screams and irritant aspects of the child's appearance and behaviour, and inaccurate in interpreting the 'meaning' of the child's signals (Melnick & Hurley, 1969). Many (but not all and possibly not most) are influenced in their appraisal by high standards and expectations about cleanliness, tidiness and obedience, and by unrealistic judgements about how children generally behave and what they are capable of at particular ages.

Case examples of an influential appraisal in a particular incident include many in which the behaviour of a tiny baby is seen as calculating and Machiavellian. Two examples of this come from Brandon (1976). Mothers reported of their young babies, 'He looks at me as if to say "Just you try to feed me" '; 'She waits till I'm enjoying something, then she starts' (p. 6). A refusal to eat, a chance turning away of the head or a cry may be interpreted as a critical statement by the child. In a case cited by Steele and Pollock (1968, p. 96) a mother reported '. . . when he cried all the time, it meant he didn't love me, so I hit him'.

Also at this level there are the cases in which the situation itself plays little part, so that what is involved is not merely distorted perception or interpretation but rather total imagination or, in certain psychotic cases, hallucination. Young (1964) quotes the case of a mother who, when her child was away from home, imagined that he might be getting into all sorts of mischief, and then beat him up on account of this when he returned. The DeCourcys quote a mother saying of her daughter 'I won't permit sin or sinful clothes or music in my house. If I have to beat her to death, I'm going to keep her on the right path, God's path'. (DeCourcy & DeCourcy, op. cit., p. 105).

Considering the next stage, that of *anger*, one might have predicted that as a population abusing parents would have identifiable emotion-linked personality characteristics which would differentiate them from others. In fact, remarkably little has come out of the relevant research to give support to this view. There is so far nothing to suggest that on the whole abusing parents over-react emotionally to a 'standard appraised situation' or that their anger follows a different time-course or is less susceptible to any catharsis effect. There is also no evidence to suggest that a significant number of abusing parents are of the 'chronic over-controlled' type described by Megargee (1966).

If, however, the time-base is narrowed and the focus is on the incident, where 'mood' becomes more salient than 'personality', then the important fact emerges that prior to the abuse incident the parent is very often in a highly aroused state. The accumulation of anger is a well documented general phenomenon and the high arousal prior to abuse often reflects indentifiable incidents earlier in the day. Population studies which have made relevant enquiries report increased frequencies of marital rows, difficulties with the child, and also of certain emotional states and physiological conditions which we know to be related to aggression. These include pain (particularly headache) and premenstrual tension, tiredness and certain drug effects. There is little evidence to suggest that alcohol plays a major role but it has been suggested that in some cases certain minor tranquillizers have paradoxical anger-arousing effects (Ounsted & Lynch, 1976).

There are a number of case accounts which illustrate well the 'conspiracy of events' which often seems to precede an incident. An example of such a build-up of emotional reaction culminating in injury to the child is that of the case of 'Larry' from the classic paper by Steele and Pollock (1968). Larry lost his job one day, and when he told his wife she walked out on him leaving him alone with the baby. The baby cried, she was hungry, and although Larry tried to comfort her he was unsuccessful. He then started to search for a bottle for her feed, unsuccessfully and frantically, while the baby continued to yell. Finally, he reported, he was overcome by intense frustration and a feeling of helplessness and he shook the baby severely and hit her head. Thus, generally, high levels of anger are commonly involved in abuse incidents and residual anger from recent events often appears to be implicated.

The next stage along the theoretical pathway is that of *inhibition and facilitation*. Most people have strong inbuilt inhibitions against hitting children severely and this high threshold is overcome only under extreme provocation. Using such a model it might be suggested that abusing parents either have lower initial thresholds or that for various reasons there is more provocation which overcomes normal thresholds. In line with the general position taken here regarding the complexity of the phenomenon and the variability of salient ante-

143

cedent factors, it would seem likely that both of these effects might be present, and there does in fact seem to be evidence in the literature to support this.

As far as low thresholds for hitting the child are concerned, it is known that abusing parents often believe in the use of strong physical methods of discipline. Some authors have linked this to social class patterns (further evidence is cited by Newson & Newson in Chapter 5) and Gil (1970) and others claim that the general permissive attitude to physical discipline in Western society makes it likely that there will be some who take the generally approved pattern of behaviour to an injurious extreme. The other relevant effect, the overcoming of 'normal' thresholds by high provocation, was indicated when evidence concerning prior stages in the pathway was considered. Inhibitions are also overcome by justificatory self-statements referring to the just deserts of the child and by a progressive lowering of anxieties about consequences of mistreatment as it continues over a period without negative consequences for the parent.

Although the presence of others and other social factors may be powerful inhibitors of attack, in certain cases others may actually encourage or support aggressive behaviour and the apparent facilitation and encouragement of abusing actions by the parent's spouse has been noted in a number of reports. The research on 'obedience' by Milgram (1963) demonstrated that in especially facilitating conditions neither anger nor obvious high instrumental gain was necessary to produce extreme injurious actions. Inhibitions may, however, return if pain or damage to the victim becomes apparent. This is a well established finding in the relevant experimental literature, and it is frequently remarked upon in parents' own reports of incidents. In a case cited by Fontana (1973), for example, it was reported that a mother who had beaten her son 'had a terrible feeling that she had come close to killing him, and that she would have killed him if the blood hadn't brought her to her senses' (p. 80). In other cases further attack is inhibited when the child is seen to be unconscious.

The pathway ends with the behavioural output, the *aggressive action* itself. Parents often have set routines of threat, punishment and aggressive action and strong physical methods are more frequently habitual in the abusing population. The parent's repertoire may be a fair copy of aggressive routines played out repeatedly in his or her own childhood.

It appears from the literature that certain patterns are common in activating injurious behaviours. There is the tendency, for example, for behaviours to escalate until they achieve a particular desired aim, this often being the child's obedience. Since severe punishment will typically produce more compliance than lenient treatment the parents' behaviour may be shaped by the child's reactions in such a way that the frequency of dangerous action is increased. Another familiar pattern is that in which an extreme (and originally perhaps quite unintended) verbal threat is eventually carried out. However bizarre or extreme a parent's warning to the child that if he doesn't behave he will be put in the oven (Renvoize, 1974) or cooked in the frying pan (D'Ambrosio, 1970), such threats seem to increase the likelihood that the promised action will be put into effect. For this reason we should perhaps be wary of the idea that verbal aggression is necessarily safer than initial low level physical aggression in terms of its likelihood of leading to serious physical attack.

Punishing acts are sometimes symbolic. A child who has been swearing, for example, may be punished by washing his mouth with soap, and in one reported case, pepper was rubbed into the genitals of a little girl who had been 'touching herself' (Young, 1964). More often, however, dangerous actions are exaggerated forms of instrumental acts, like smothering the child *in order to* keep him quiet, or forcefeeding *in order to* make him eat.

The target for aggression is not always the person who has given rise to the anger, and there are several accounts of abuse in which it is clear that the anger with the spouse is displaced onto the young child (for example Bennie & Sclare, 1969). Use of the child as a general 'whipping boy' is indicated in other reports. A mother in one case said of her daughter: 'Since she was born, I let out all the anger and frustration that I had in myself on her. Whenever she came to me, I sent her away with a beating' (Green, Gaines & Sandgrund, 1974, p. 884).

Fear of the consequences of attack may inhibit all aggression, or it may shape the particular response so that it is relatively 'safe' from detection. In one case a child was deliberately hit again on old bruises so that the effects would not show up as separate and recent injuries (Renvoize, 1974) and it has become apparent that some parents, knowing that the child's physical health is being closely monitored by agencies, switch to a psychological mode of attack. It is impossible to estimate, also, the extent to which children may be being damaged by parents who use methods such as smothering and administration of drugs which, while highly dangerous, may also be opaque to medical detection.

The alternative pathway in the diagram, in which the aggression takes its principal impetus not from anger but from instrumental concerns, has not been considered. Such cases are certainly in the minority and are probably rare, though there are recent cases in which it did appear that the child had been injured *in order to* get him

145

taken into care (Lukianowicz, 1971) or because the parents believed that they would stand a better chance of being given improved accommodation if they had an injured baby (Skinner & Castle, 1969). In 18th-century Britain the practice of paying large insurances on the death of children in what were ostensibly 'Burial Clubs' was stopped by Parliament because it was recognized that this presented a positive threat to the lives of the children. Instrumental considerations, though not usually the major impetus to action or inaction in potential abuse incidents, are nonetheless of considerable importance in attenuating the actions of an angry parent.

Thus there is existing evidence about child abuse relevant to each point in the aggression incident paradigm. The aim here has been to present a framework within which known facts can be accommodated and integrated. There are several implications, however, for treatment and prevention. If child abuse is viewed less as a single 'syndrome' and more as the common result of all sorts of different antecedent patterns leading to the violent attack, then this suggests that treatment should be carefully tailored to the individual case. In some cases, effecting a situational change may be the most useful therapeutic intervention, while in other cases the most appropriate focus might be on attitudes towards the particular child, general expectations about children or beliefs about the value of harsh training. Several effective techniques for anger control are available (for example, Novaco, 1975) and information about damage which might result from such notions as shaking the child may be sufficient to modify behaviour significantly and increase specific inhibitions. Thus there are established strategies for effectively changing processes at each point along the pathway and, in addition, many of those factors which are less directly concerned can be seen as feeding into this system and a broad-gauge intervention is likely to optimize effect. It is possible, of course, to analyze currently used intervention strategies in terms of how they serve to modify the relevant elements along the pathway.

The aggression incident paradigm does seem to offer the means for a fuller understanding of child abuse, providing a flexible framework which can accommodate both the population characteristics and features of the individual case and the specific incident. Because of the variable nature of the phenomenon the detailed consideration of case-specific material is essential for the adequate understanding of why children are injured by their parents, though the same explanation must also extend to those incidents in which injury was likely but did not in fact occur. Aggressive actions towards children which end in injury will in many cases require precisely the same psychological explanation as aggressive actions which do not.

REFERENCES

Baher, E., Hyman, C., Jones, C., Jones, R., Kerr, A. and Mitchell, R. (1976) *At Risk: An Account of the Work of the Battered Child Research Department, N.S.P.C.C.*, Routledge and Kegan Paul, London.

Bennie, E.H. and Sclare, A.B. (1969) 'The battered child syndrome'. *Am. J. Psychiat.*, *125*, pp. 975–79.

Berkowitz, L. and Alioto, J.T. (1973) 'The meaning of an observed event as a determinant of its aggressive consequences'. *J. Pers. Soc. Psychol.*, *28*, pp. 206–17.

Birrell, R.G. and Birrell, J.H.W., (1968), 'The maltreatment syndrome in children: a hospital survey'. *Med. J. Aust., II*, pp. 1023–29.

Brandon, S. (1976) 'Physical Violence in the Family: an overview', in Borland, M. (ed.) *Violence in the Family*, Manchester University Press, Manchester.

Clarke, R.V.G. (1977) 'Psychology and crime'. *Bull. B.P.S. 30,*|pp. 280–83.

D'Ambrosio, R. (1970). *No Language but a Cry*, Doubleday, New York.

DeCourcy, P. and DeCourcy, J. (1973) *A Silent Tragedy: Child Abuse in the Community*. Alfred Publishing Company.

Elmer, E. (1971) 'Child abuse: a symptom of family crisis', in Pavenstedt, E. and Bernard, V.W., *Crises in Family Disorganisation*. Human Science Press, New York.

Fontana, V.J. (1973) *Somewhere a Child is Crying: Maltreatment, Causes and Prevention*. Macmillan Publishing, New York.

Friedrich, W.N. and Boriskin, J.A. (1976) 'The role of the child in abuse'. *Amer. J. Orthopsychiatr.*, *46*, pp. 580–90.

Gil, D.G. (1970) *Violence against Children: Physical abuse in the United States*. Harvard University Press, Cambridge, Mass.

Green, A.H., Gaines, R.W. and Sandgrund, A. (1974) 'Child abuse: Pathological syndrome of family interaction'. *Amer. J. Psychiatry, 131*, pp. 882–86.

Holmes, T. and Rahe, R.H. (1967) 'The social readjustment rating scale'. *J. Psychosom. Res.*, *11*, pp. 213–18.

Justice, B. and Justice, R. (1976) *The Abusing Family*. Human Science Press, New York.

Lazarus, R.S. (1966) *Psychological Stress and the Coping Process*. McGraw Hill, New York.

Lord, E. and Weisfeld, D. (1974). The abused child. Chapter in A.R. Roberts (ed.). *Childhood Deprivation*. Charles C. Thomas, Springfield Illinois.

Lukianowicz, N. (1971). 'Battered children'. *Psychiat. Clinica, 4*, pp. 257–80.

Marsh, P., Rosser, E., and Harré, R. (1977) *Rules of Disorder*. Routledge and Kegan Paul.

Megargee, E.I. (1966) 'Undercontrolled and overcontrolled personality types in extreme antisocial aggression'. *Psychol. Monogr.* No. 611, 1.

Melnick, B. and Hurley, J.R. (1969) 'Distinctive personality attributes of child-abusing mothers'. *J. Consult, Clinical Psychol.*, *33*, pp. 746–49.

Milgram, S. (1963) 'Behavioural study of obedience'. *J. Abnorm, and Soc. Psychol, 67*. pp. 371–78.

Novaco, R. (1975) *Anger Control: The Development and Evaluation of an Experimental Treatment*. Heath and Co., Lexington, Mass.

Oliver, J.E., Cox, J., Taylor, A., and Baldwin, J. (1974) *Severely Ill-treated Young Children in North East Wiltshire*, Oxford Regional Health Authority.

Ounsted, C. and Lynch, M.A. (1976) 'Family Pathology as seen in England', in R.B. Helfer and C.A. Kempe, (Eds.) *Child Abuse and Neglect – the Family and the Community*. Ballinger, Cambridge, Mass.

Renvoize, J. (1974) *Children in Danger*, Routledge and Kegan Paul.

Scott, P. (1973a) 'Parents who kill their children'. *Med., Sci. Law, 13*. pp. 120–26.

Scott, O. (1973b) 'Fatal battered baby cases'. *Med., Sci. Law, 13*. pp. 197–206.

Skinner, A.E. and Castle, R.L. (1969) *Seventy-eight Battered Children; a Retrospective*

Study. National Society for the Prevention of Cruelty to Children, London.

Smith, S.M. (1975) *The Battered Child Syndrome*. Butterworths.

Steele, B.F. and Pollock, C.B. (1968) 'A psychiatric study of parents who abuse infants and small children'. Chapter in R.E. Helfer and C.H. Kempe (Eds.) *The Battered Child*, University of Chicago Press, Chicago.

Terr, L.C. (1970) 'A family study of child abuse'. *Amer. J. Psychiat.*, *127*, pp. 665–71.

Toch, H. (1972) *Violent Men*. Penguin.

Young, L. (1964) *Wednesday's Children*. McGraw-Hill, New York.

Treatment Studies

Carolyn Okell Jones.

While detailed experience with the diagnosis and treatment of physically abused children is a recent development, it is already clear that the needs of these children are enormous; that these needs represent a developmental emergency; and their diagnosis and treatment by encouraging emotional growth and development and providing a safe and supportive curative environment must be initiated at once when the diagnosis of physical abuse has been made (Kempe, 1976).

Introduction.

Since the early sixties, when Kempe and his colleagues in Denver, Colorado alerted the world to the nature and prevalence of the battered-child syndrome (Kempe et al., 1962), intense interest and activity have been generated in the field of child abuse. There has been a rapid extension and strengthening of the services to protect children from inflicted injuries in many different countries. Much professional effort has been channelled into understanding abusive parents and developing a variety of intervention strategies to meet their needs, in the hope that the children would indirectly benefit from the attention and support offered to their parents.

At first glance it seems somewhat ironic that both in the literature and in practice comparatively little attention has been focused on the children themselves, in terms of their developmental and psychotherapeutic needs. Yet, on reflection, it is understandable that professionals who were preoccupied with developing measures to save children's lives, to prevent severe handicaps and the recommencement of serious abuse, tended to concentrate on their physical injuries and problems, and on their immediate physical safety.

During the seventies many new approaches to the problem of child abuse have been developed, with concomitant changes in professional attitudes and emphasis. The publication of data from available follow-up studies indicating serious *sequelae* among abused children (including those whose families have received intensive, supportive intervention – e.g. Martin and Beezley, 1976; Baher et al.,

151

1976) have begun to make an impact. Professionals are becoming more aware of the necessity of looking at the rights, treatment and placement needs of abused children separately from the rights and needs of their parents or caretakers, and in a broader context than that of physical safety. Moreover, it is becoming increasingly apparent that 'therapeutic optimism' is simply not justified in some cases, and that children should not be left in limbo while long drawn-out efforts are made to change or modify their parents' attitudes and behaviour (see, for example, Adcock, 1979; Speight, Bridson & Cooper, 1979).

Making Sense of the Data on Abused Children.

Lynch (1978a) has aptly described the task of making sense of the data on abused children, and the area of study generally, as a researcher's nightmare. When surveying the literature on children diagnosed as abused, it soon becomes clear that researchers conduct-ing follow-up studies have adopted a variety of approaches and encountered many methodological problems which place limitations on the reliability and validity of their data. For example, sampling problems are common. Initial samples of abused children have been obtained from many different settings, e.g. casualty departments, juvenile courts and social welfare agencies, and each of these may limit the type of abuse studied and influence the outcome. Abusive families have often proved difficult to trace because of their frequent high mobility, some parents have resisted subsequent evaluation of their children, and some children are found to have died or have been placed far away from their family of origin in institutions or adoptive or foster homes.

Other methodological problems arise from the use of differing definitions of abuse (these have ranged from the 'all embracing' to definitions based on strict criteria – e.g. children who have suffered multiple skeletal injuries), from the failure to employ matched comparison groups so that findings may be skewed by uncontrolled variables such as social class, and from failure to document the type, if any, of intervention which the families have received. Also, methods of assessing the children vary considerably from study to study. Some researchers have employed a range of formal psycholo-gical and developmental tests whereas others have relied predomin-antly on clinical impressionistic data.

In addition to documenting common consequences of abuse, pioneer researchers have been wrestling with the issue of assessing the extent to which identified difficulties are the consequences of abuse *per se* and to what extent they are the result of the other adverse environmental influences frequently associated with physical abuse.

These include emotional neglect or rejection, lack of stimulation, social and/or economic disadvantage, emotional disturbance in the parents and treatment planning (e.g. prolonged hospitalization, frequent changes of foster home placements, etc.). Such factors are known to have the potential to impair the growing child's development, but our understanding of the issue is far from complete. We need to know much more about *how* abuse affects children's development and *what* can be done to set growth and development back on a normal course. Furthermore, in addition to focussing on pathology, we need to explore further the question of the variation in the inherent differences between children in their capacity to escape developmental delays, to adapt to the stresses of the abusive environment and to surmount the damaging results of earlier developmental insults when placed in more favourable environments (Kadushin, 1970; Koluchova, 1972; 1976; Clarke & Clarke, 1976).

Recently Martin (1979), who himself has made an outstanding contribution to the literature, has urged that future research should take the form of more discerning and microscopic investigations of the effects of both abuse and neglect, because so much of our current knowledge relates to the most gross and obvious consequences of maltreatment. There is also a need for more controlled follow-up studies of the kind recently conducted by Elmer (1977) in order to correct conclusions based on the study of abused children alone. Her findings are surprising and controversial and require replication since they have important implications for social policy. Elmer followed up a group of traumatized infants referred to the Children's Hospital, Pittsburgh. She compared them, some eight years after abuse, with controls matched for age, sex, race and socio-economic status. Looking at multiple variables in their development she unexpectedly found few differences. Children in each group were equally 'behind' in their development and equally 'disturbed' in personality terms. Hence Elmer (1978) concludes 'the results of child abuse are less potent for the child's development than class membership. The effects of poverty or lower class membership on children are devastating'.

Lastly, more resources should be allocated to longitudinal studies of abused children as most work to date has been relatively short-term. Such an approach would help us discover more about what happens to abused children when they start school, during latency and adolescence, and during the period when they find marital partners and embark on parenthood themselves. It is only by obtaining more insights into the mechanisms underlying abnormal intergenerational patterns of parenting that we can hope to break the cycle of violence so often detectable in these families.

In spite of the difficulties and limitations alluded to, and the

153

dangers inherent in making generalizations from small samples or methodologically flawed research, there is a growing body of information about the characteristics of abused children on which practitioners can usefully draw. Some of this information will now be summarized and discussed.

Developmental Disabilities of Abused Children.

Reviews of findings from a variety of follow-up studies conducted in different countries indicate that abused children are at high risk of damage to the central nervous system and of maldevelopment of ego function (Martin et al., 1974; Jones, 1977a; Lynch, 1978b; Solomons, 1979). Neurological damage, visual impairment, mental retardation, cerebral palsy, perceptual motor dysfunction, impaired speech and language, learning disorders, growth failure and emotional disturbance have all been documented, some with depressing frequency (Elmer, 1967; Elmer & Gregg, 1967; Birrell & Birrell, 1968; Johnson & Morse, 1968; Terr, 1970; Morse et al., 1970; Harcourt & Hopkins, 1971; Mushin, 1971; Martin, 1972, 1974, 1976, 1977; Baldwin Oliver, 1975; Sandgrund et al., 1974; Smith & Hanson, 1974; Straus & Girodet, 1977; Appelbaum, 1977; Kline, 1977; Eppler & Brown, 1977; Martin & Beezley, 1977; Berkeley Planning Associates, 1977; Buchanan & Oliver, 1977; Jones, 1977b; Elmer, 1978; Green, 1978a; Roberts, Lynch and Duff, 1978; Lynch, 1978a, Van Staden, 1979). However, there are conflicting findings on the extent to which such physical or developmental disabilities antedate abuse and are of a congenital nature or are the result of rearing in an abusive environment. These findings have stimulated continuing debate about the role of the child in the aetiology of child abuse (Friedrich and Boriskin, 1976), and closer examination of such factors as the significance of birth-related difficulties and illness (Goldson et al., 1978; Lynch, 1975) and the influence of different kinds of handicap on the pattern of abuse (Glaser & Bentovim, 1979).

It is beyond the scope of this chapter to consider in detail all the disabilities referred to above and so just a few will be singled out for discussion in order to highlight some of the complex issues inherent in assessment.

Neurological Damage.
Much of the hard data from follow-up studies relate to mortality and significant intellectual and neuromotor handicap. Considerable variation has been noted in the type and severity of neurological damage sustained by abused children, but the incidence of abnormality is high. Martin et al. (1974), carefully defining the degree of

154

handicap, found that 53% of the children in their sample had some neurological abnormality, and for one third of these the handicap was severe. Physical assaults to the head may be the cause of a child's neurological handicap but it is important to emphasize that a young child can suffer significant damage to the brain through violent shaking (Caffey, 1972, 1974) with no outward sign of damage to the head such as bruises or fractures to the skull. Martin et al. (1974) report that, as expected, neurological dysfunction is closely related to delayed development and a history of head trauma. However, they emphasize that some children with serious head injury do escape without retardation or neurological handicap. Furthermore, they report that significant neurological dysfunction occurred in 16 children in their sample with no obvious explanation of the cause and no documented history of head trauma.

Such evidence has led Martin, Baron et al. (1970) and others to conclude that the nervous systems of abused children may also be at risk from the psychological and environmental stresses to which they are exposed, and that neurological dysfunction may be an adaptation to the abusive environment.

It is hardly surprising that, as many abused children's problems have appeared to be so severe, professionals have suspected that they are neurologically determined. This is especially true of the clumsy, uncoordinated children, careless of personal danger in the environment, often prone to accidents, and erupting into unpredictable and uncontrollable outbursts of temper. However, many such children tend to improve rapidly if they are exposed to a calm, structured environment, and this suggests that they are in fact suffering from disorganizing anxiety and have learnt to seek pain and provoke violence as a release from chronic tension. For example, Galdston (1975), on the basis of observations of abused children recently admitted to a day-care centre, reports that some children were so retarded in their development and that their movements were so clumsy and uncoordinated that brain damage was suspected. However, after a short period of attendance at the centre, the same children demonstrated such rapid improvements in motor activity that the diagnosis of organic brain damage was precluded.

Growth Failure.

Growth retardation (including the condition 'failure to thrive') often accompanies child abuse. A number of studies (see, for example, Elmer, 1967; Birrell & Birrell, 1968; Martin, 1972; Smith & Hanson, 1974) report poor physical growth and poor nutrition in approximately 25–35% of abused children at the time of identification. In the follow-up studies reporting on growth there is a high incidence of continuing growth failure. Martin's (1972) report of 42 abused children, and Elmer's (1967) report, also indicate a significant difference in intellectual prognosis when undernourished abused children were compared with well-nourished abused children. It appears that children who are undernourished as well as physically abused have a much poorer prognosis in terms of mental function and neurologic integrity. The importance of keeping careful height and weight records on children from abusive families cannot be over-emphasized. Growth patterns tend to reflect both positive and negative interaction in families and should be regarded as vital hard data for decision making and for inclusion as evidence in juvenile court proceedings.

Psychological Damage.

Early clinical observations on abused children suggested that many were considerably damaged emotionally as well as physically by the time they came to professional attention. However, rigorously documenting the often subtle effects of the abusive environment on the children's personalities, emotional development and behaviour is no easy task. Hence the psychological damage sustained by the children has, until recent years, been the subject of speculation rather than hard facts. For example, Green (1968; 1978b) documented a link between physical abuse and subsequent self-mutilation in schizo-phrenic and other children, and postulated that early physical abuse occurring in a matrix of overall rejection and stimulus deprivation may enhance the development of pain-dependent behaviour. The children may become accident prone, indulge in self-destructive behaviour, or establish a pattern of inviting harm or 'playing the victim' (Bender, 1976).

The latter effect may explain why some children recreate the dynamics of their families of origin and get rebattered in foster homes. Other writers have highlighted the tendency of the children to identify with aggressive parents and to pattern themselves on the parents' behaviour. Galdston (1975), on the basis of considerable clinical experience, proposed that the young child physically abused at a pre-verbal stage of development is particularly prone to develop violent behaviour as a character trait.

Several recent studies of the emotional development of abused children have produced more detailed findings. Martin and Beezley (1977) studied the behaviour of 50 children $4\frac{1}{2}$ years after abuse and reported that over half had poor self concepts, were sorrowful children and exhibited types of behaviour which made peers, parents and teachers reject them. The nine characteristics noted with impressive frequency and intensity were as follows: impaired capacity

156

to relax and enjoy life, psychiatric symptoms (e.g. enuresis, tantrums, hyperactivity, bizarre behaviour), low self-esteem, school learning problems, withdrawal, opposition, hypervigilance, compulsivity and pseudomature behaviour. The last three are examples of the kind of 'precocious' survival manoeuvres into which young endangered children may invest a great deal of their energy at considerable cost to themselves in terms of learning, flexibility and so forth (Malone, 1966).

Green (1978a) ran a therapeutic programme involving intensive study and treatment of 20 abused children (age range five to 14 years) and reported the following prominent areas of disturbance: overall impairment of ego functioning, associated with intellectual and cognitive defects, traumatic reactions with acute anxiety states, pathological object relationships characterized by the failure to develop 'basic trust', excessive use of primitive defences such as denial, projection, introjection and splitting, impaired impulse control, impaired self-concept, masochistic and self-destructive behaviour, difficulties with separation and problems in school adjustment. The vast majority of these children had been subjected to recurrent abuse during the first two years of life. However, Green emphasizes that although there was evidence to indicate that psychopathology had been present in most of the children prior to latency, it was not usually recognized until day-centres or schools confronted the parents with the abnormal behaviour of the child.

A study by Roberts et al. (1978) of teacher's views of children from 'abusing families' provides further evidence of emotional and behavioural problems some time after the original abuse. By the time they first reach primary school such children are often socially isolated and identified as 'hostile' by their teachers. Some may become disruptive and violent, leading to exclusion from school and the need for special educational provision (Jones, 1978a).

There is some evidence to suggest that environmental factors correlate with emotional disturbance in abused children, while type of severity of the injury or the age at which it was inflicted do not. In their follow-up studies, Martin and Beezley (1977) have found that a number of symptoms in the children were related to the quality of parenting they experienced, whether in biologic, adoptive or foster homes. For example, they report that psychiatric symptoms were significantly correlated $4\frac{1}{2}$ years after abuse with factors such as the impermanence of the subsequent home, instability of the family with whom the child was living, and punitiveness and rejection by caretakers, as well as the emotional state of the parents or parent surrogates. Bearing this in mind, it is hardly surprising that the relatively few studies which have involved siblings of the presenting

157

children report that they often appear as deviant in their functioning as the child identified as abused. (Johnson & Morse, 1968; Skinner & Castle, 1969; Baldwin & Oliver, 1975; Smith and Hanson, 1974; Baher et al., 1976; Straus & Girodet, 1977; Roberts et al., 1978).

Familiarity with the kind of information provided above is essential for whoever is assigned the role of safeguarding the abused child's interests and monitoring his progress. It can be too easily forgotten by social workers, lawyers and others that care arrangements which are made for children in need of protection may replicate, in many important respects, the damaging features of the environment from which the child has been removed.

Future Therapeutic Intervention

Probably the most important finding about the developmental and functional delays or deficits of abused children is that they exhibit an extremely wide range of problems, and in varying combinations. There is, in short, no composite picture of *the* abused child, no specific personality or neurologic profile (Berkeley Planning Associates, 1977; Martin, 1976). Delayed or arrested development (Helfer et al., 1976; Appelbaum, 1977) and emotional disturbance (Gaensbauer & Mrazek, 1978, and Chapter 8 of this volume) can be identified even in very young infants and appear to be compounded over time by malevolent environmental factors aside from physical abuse. These findings contain positive implications as well as negative ones and provide us with a challenge. It seems that if we can develop specific therapeutic services for abused children in addition to services for parents and intervene at an early age we should be able to ameliorate many existing disabilities and forestall more permanent damage.

Some progress has already been made and existing programmes offering multi-faceted treatment services for both parents and childen under the same roof have been shown to be of considerable value (see Jones, 1978b; Martin, 1976, and Chapter 11 of the present volume). These have ranged from costly residential family centres to the imaginative provision of low-budget play therapy for severely abused and neglected children in an Extended Family Day-Care setting (Davoren, 1979). The need for comprehensive assessment of all abused children (and whenever possible their siblings) at the time abuse is diagnosed, cannot be over-emphasized. It should be remembered, however, that a single rapid evaluation of such children's abilities may leave us with a false impression. The validity of standardized test scores for both abused and neglected children has been seriously questioned during the past few years. Clinicians working closely with these children have observed that the residual effects of the abuse or neglect sustained, particularly an acute 'hypermonitoring' of adults, may preclude the child being able to give full attention to the test itself and may result in him or her being much more concerned with the tester. This situation appears to depress scores below potential (Berkeley Planning Associates, 1977; Rode-heffer & Martin, 1976).

Another important area for consideration in assessment is the child's view of the family and of the feelings towards him which he attributes to family members. Since much of the child abuse litera-ture concerns infants and young children, relatively little attention has been directed towards this issue. Recently, however, reports from several psychologists (Geddis et al., 1977; Mitchell, 1976; Turner & Geddis, 1979) indicate that the Family Relations Test (Bene & Anthony, 1957) can prove very helpful in uncovering distorted patterns of family relationships and can be used with very young children. It is apparent that continuous developmental monitoring should be an integral part of future treatment programmes. Although the breadth of problems described is wide, there are some recurring behavioural characteristics which are likely to influence service provision and effectiveness. These include an overly aggressive or apathetic posture, extreme anxiety and hypervigilance (which is likely to depress scores on standardized tests), an inability to relate to both adults and peers in an acceptable way and a poor relationship with the parents. This last factor may of course preclude support from the parents in the therapeutic process. In particular, consistent paediatric care, speech therapy, physical and/or occupational therapy, special educational help and various forms of therapy such as play therapy, group therapy or individual psychotherapy, are indicated for abused children.

All the evidence reviewed in this chapter suggests that any child protective service which continues to overlook the treatment needs of abused children in their own right is simply failing to do an adequate job. However, unless the parents or caretakers cooperate and the home environment can be modified to accommodate changes in the children, professionals may be exposing the children to further risk by stripping them of a variety of adaptive modes of behaviour (albeit psychopathological) which have high value in a dangerous environ-ment. Learning, competence, exploration, initiative and autonomy are not encouraged in many abusive homes and may even be the basis for assault by the parents. Therefore, any specific provisions for the children should always be offered in the context of a comprehensive, carefully devised intervention plan for the whole family.

Treatment Studies

REFERENCES

Adcock, M. (1979) 'Planning long-term care for the abused child'. *Child Abuse and Neglect, 3*, 1005–9.

Appelbaum, A. (1977) 'Developmental retardation in infants as a concomitant of physical child abuse'. *Journal of Abnormal Child Psychology, 5*, pp. 417–23.

Baher, E., Hyman, C., Jones, C., Jones, R., Kerr, A. and Mitchell, R. (1976) *At Risk: An Account of the Battered Child Research Department, NSPCC*, Routledge and Kegan Paul, London.

Baldwin, J.A. and Oliver, J.E. (1975) 'Epidemiology and family characteristics of severely abused children'. *British Journal of Preventive Social Medicine, 29*, pp. 205–21.

Baron, M.A., Bejar, R.L., and Sheaff, P.J. (1970) 'Neurologic manifestations of the battered child syndrome'. *Pediatrics, 45*, pp. 1003–7.

Bender, B. (1976) 'Self-chosen victims: scapegoating behaviour sequential to battering'. *Child Welfare, 55*, pp. 417–22.

Bene, E. and Anthony, E.J. (1957) *Manual for the Family Relations Test*, N.F.E.R., Slough.

Berkeley Planning Associates (1977) *Child Client Impact: Final Report. Evaluation of Child Abuse and Neglect. Demonstration Projects 1974 – 7. Vol. XI.* Available from U.S. Department of Commerce, National Technical Information Service.

Birrell, R.G. and Birrell, J.H.W. (1968) 'The maltreatment syndrome in children: a hospital survey'. *Medical Journal of Australia, 2*, pp. 1023–29.

Buchanan, A. and Oliver, J.E. (1977) 'Abuse and neglect as a cause of mental retardation: a study of 140 children admitted to the subnormality hospitals in Wiltshire'. *British Journal of Psychiatry, 131*, pp. 458–67.

Caffey, J. (1972) 'On the theory and practice of shaking infants: its potential residual effects of permanent brain damage and mental retardation'. *American Journal of Diseases of Children, 124*, pp. 161–69.

Caffey, J. (1974) 'The whiplash shaken infant syndrome: manual shaking by the extremities with whiplash-induced intracranial and intra-ocular bleedings, linked with residual permanent brain damage and mental retardation'. *Pediatrics, 54*, pp. 396–403.

Clarke, A.M. and Clarke, A.D.B. (1976) *Early Experience: Myth and Evidence*. Open Books, London.

Davoren, E. (1979) 'Low budget play therapy for very young children'. *Child Abuse and Neglect, 3*, pp. 199–204.

Elmer, E. (1967) *Children in Jeopardy*, University of Pittsburgh Press.

Elmer, E. and Gregg, G.S. (1967) 'Developmental characteristics of abused children'. *Pediatrics, 40*, pp. 596–602.

Elmer, E. (1977) 'A follow-up study of traumatized children'. *Pediatrics, 59*, pp. 273–79.

Elmer, E. (1978) *Fragile Families – Troubled Children: The Aftermath of Infant Trauma*. University of Pittsburgh Press.

Eppler, M. and Brown, G. (1977) 'Child abuse and neglect: preventable causes of mental retardation'. *Child Abuse and Neglect, 1*, pp. 309–13.

Friedrich, W.N. and Boriskin, J.A. (1976) 'The role of the child in abuse: a review of the literature'. *American Journal of Orthopsychiatry, 46*, pp. 580–90.

Gaensbauer, T. and Mrazek, D. (1978) 'Emotional Expression in abused/neglected infants'. Paper presented to the Second International Congress on Child Abuse and Neglect, London, September, 1978.

Galdston, R. (1975) 'Preventing the abuse of little children'. *American Journal of Orthopsychiatry, 45*, pp. 377–81.

Geddis, D.C., Turner, I.F. and Eardley, J. (1977) 'Diagnostic value of a psychological test in cases of suspected child abuse'. *Archives of Disease in Childhood, 52*, pp.

708–12.

Glaser, D. and Bentovim, A. (1979) 'Abuse and risk to handicapped and chronically ill children'. *Child Abuse and Neglect, 3*, pp. 565–75.

Goldson, E., Fitch, M.J. Wendell, A. and Knapp, G. (1978) 'Child abuse: its relationship to birthweight, Apgar score and developmental testing'. *American Journal of Diseases of Children, 132*, pp. 790–93.

Green, A.H. (1968) 'Self-destructive behaviour in physically abused schizophrenic children'. *Archives of General Psychiatry, 19*, pp. 171–79.

Green, A.H. (1978a) 'Psychopathology of abused children'. *Journal of the American Academy of Child Psychiatry*, pp. 92–103.

Green, A.H. (1978b) 'Self-destructive behaviour in battered children'. *American Journal of Psychiatry 135*, pp. 579–82.

Harcourt, B. and Hopkins, D. (1971) 'Opthalmic manifestations of the battered baby syndrome'. *British Medical Journal, 1971, iii*, pp. 398–401.

Johnson, B. and Morse, H. (1968) 'Injured children and their parents'. *Children, 15*, pp. 147–52.

Jones, Okell, C. (1977a) 'The fate of abused children'. In: A. White Franklin (Ed.) *The Challenge of Child Abuse*, Academic Press, London.

Jones, Okell, C. (1977b) 'Development of children from abusive families'. In: A. White Franklin (Ed.) *Child Abuse: Prediction, Prevention and Follow-up*. Churchill Livingstone, Edinburgh.

Jones, Okell, C. (1978a) 'Disruption and disturbance: observations on the management of a group of young children'. *Child Abuse and Neglect, 2*, pp. 123–27.

Jones, Okell, C. (1978b) 'Meeting the needs of abused children'. *Social Work Today, 9*, pp. 9-14.

Kadushin, A. (1970) *Adopting Older Children*, Columbia University Press, New York.

Kempe, C.H., Silverman, F., Steele, B., Droegmueller, W., and Silver, H. (1962) 'The battered child syndrome'. *Journal of the American Medical Assocation, 181*, pp. 17–24.

Kempe, C.H. (1976) 'Foreword'. In: H.P. Martin (Ed.) *The Abused Child: A Multidisciplinary Approach to Developmental Issues and Treatment*. Ballinger, Cambridge, Mass.

Kline, D.F. (1977) 'Educational and psychological problems of abused children', *Child Abuse and Neglect, 1*, pp. 301–7.

Koluchova, J. (1972) 'Severe deprivation in twins: a case study'. *Journal of Child Psychology and Psychiatry, 13*, pp. 103–6.

Koluchova, J. (1976) 'The further development of twins after severe and prolonged deprivation: a second report'. *Journal of Child Psychology and Psychiatry. 17*, pp. 181–88.

Lynch, M. (1975) 'Ill-health and child abuse'. *The Lancet, 1975, ii*, pp. 317–19.

Lynch, M. (1978a) 'The follow-up of abused children – a researcher's nightmare'. In J.M. Eekelaar and S.M. Katz (Eds.) *Family Violence: An International and Interdisciplinary Study*. Butterworths, Toronto and London.

Lynch, M. (1978b) 'The prognosis of child abuse'. *Journal of Child Psychology and Psychiatry, 19*, pp. 175–80.

Malone, C. (1966) 'Safety first: comments on the influence of external danger in the lives of children of disorganised families'. *American Journal of Orthopsychiatry, 36*, pp. 3–12.

Martin, H.P. (1972) 'The child and his development'. In: C.H. Kempe and R.E. Helfer, *Helping the Battered Child and his Family*, Lippincott, Philadelphia.

Martin, H.P., Beezley, P., Conway, E.S., and Kempe C.H. (1974) 'The development of abused children: I. A review of the literature, II. Physical, neurologic and intellectual outcomes'. *Advances in Paediatrics, 21*, pp. 25–73.

Martin, H.P. and Beezley, P. (1976) 'Therapy for abusive parents: its effect on the child'. In: H.P. Martin (Ed.) *The Abused Child: A Multidisciplinary Approach to Developmental Issues and Treatment*, Ballinger, Cambridge, Mass.

Martin, H.P. (1977) 'A child-oriented approach to prevention of abuse'. In: A. White Franklin. *Child Abuse: Prediction, Prevention and Follow-up*. Churchill Livingstone, Edinburgh.

Martin, H.P. and Beezley, P. (1977) 'Behavioural observations of abused children'. *Developmental Medicine and Child Neurology, 19*, pp. 373–87.

Martin, H.P. (1979) 'Child abuse and child development'. *Child Abuse and Neglect, 3*, pp. 415–21.

Mitchell, R. (1976) 'A psychological study of battered children'. In: E. Baher et al. *At Risk: An Account of the Work of the Battered Child Research Department, NSPCC*, Routledge and Kegan Paul, London.

Morse, C.W., Sahler, O.J.Z. and Friedman, S.B. (1970) 'A three-year follow-up study of abused and neglected children'. *American Journal of Diseases of Children, 120*, pp. 439–46.

Mushin, A.S. (1971) 'Ocular damage in the battered baby syndrome'. *British Medical Journal, 1971, iii*, pp. 402–4.

Roberts, J., Lynch, M.M. and Duff, P. (1978) 'Abused children and their siblings – a teacher's view'. *Therapeutic Education, 6*, pp. 25–31.

Rodeheffer, M. and Martin, H.P. (1976) 'Special problems in the developmental assessment of abused children'. In: H.P. Martin (Ed.) *The Abused Child: A Multidisciplinary Approach to Developmental Issues and Treatment*. Ballinger, Cambridge, Mass.

Sandgrund, A., Gaines, R. and Green, A.H. (1974) 'Child abuse and mental retardation: a problem of cause and effect'. *American Journal of Mental Deficiency, 79*, pp. 327–30.

Skinner, A.E. and Castle, R.L. (1969) *78 Battered Children: A Retrospective Study*. NSPCC, London.

Smith, S.M. and Hanson, R. (1974) '134 battered children: a medical and psychological study'. *British Medical Journal, 197*, *iii*, pp. 666–70.

Solomons, G. (1979) 'Child abuse and developmental disabilities'. *Developmental Medicine and Child Neurology, 21*, pp. 101–8.

Speight, A.N.P., Bridson, J.M. and Cooper, C.E. (1979) 'Follow-up cases of child abuse seen at Newcastle General Hospital 1974–5'. *Child Abuse and Neglect, 3*, pp. 555–63.

Straus, P. and Girodet, D. (1977) 'Three French follow-up studies of abused children'. *Child Abuse and Neglect, 1*, pp. 99–103.

Terr, L. (1970) 'A family study of child abuse'. *American Journal of Psychiatry, 127*, pp. 125–31.

Turner, I.F. and Geddis, D.C. (1979) 'The psychology of family relationships: an aid to diagnosis?' *Child Abuse and Neglect, 3*, pp. 899–901.

Van Staden, J.T. (1979) 'The mental development of abused children in South Africa'. *Child Abuse and Neglect, 3*, pp. 997–1000.

11   Setting up the Treatment Programme

Arnon Bentovim

Introduction

In setting up a treatment programme when a child has been abused or is felt to be seriously at risk, attention has to be paid to the fact that the abusive episode itself is often the final act of a long-running family drama extending over many years. There may well have been a number of failed attempts to intervene and change a highly dysfunctional system. An effective treatment programme therefore needs to be comprehensive and to respond to the many facets of the situation.

The findings of research on families in which abuse occurs (Bentovim, 1977a) indicate the extent of the pathological elements to be met if an effective treatment programme is to be mounted. The following family characteristics contribute to the immense problems posed for professionals who wish to help. Parents have often had considerable experiences of rejection as children themselves, and they become adults with unmet needs for dependency, nurturance and esteem. Having experienced discontinuity of care, active rejection, or having been involved in a cycle of violence, their demandingness and suspicion of professionals makes the establishment of an ordinary client-professional relationship a first step to be achieved. Unlike with other clients, then, this process cannot be taken for granted. If earlier developmental stages are unhappy and overburdened then later stages, including that of finding a partner, may be seen as representing an attempt at self-cure. As a result a sense of rejection and a burden of guilt or anger may add to the intense suspicion of the professional who tries to get close enough to use his skills to change the situation.

Previous contacts with professionals such as social workers, probation officers or medical practitioners will often have been experienced as punitive and unhelpful and there may be an initial expectation by these clients that the professional world is against them rather than offering a possible life-line and support. It is only too easy for the family to recreate original experiences of rejection and become locked with professionals in a similar cycle of suspicion and angry retaliation which confirms their view of the world as a threatening and unhelpful place.

Research with abusing families indicates that several pathological elements must be met if an effective treatment programme is to be established (Bentovim, 1977a). Frommer and O'Shea (1973) have shown that where there is a discontinuity in parenting and a lack of mothering experience, then professional 'parenting' too is often ignored. Recent research (Gray, Cutler, Dean and Kempe, 1977) seems to indicate that if families with an abuse risk are recognized at the time of the birth of the child then such anti-professional attitudes can be overcome by intensive intervention, and abuse can be prevented. Indeed Kempe (1978) has recently claimed that abuse can be eradicated if early intervention is provided. Such intervention cannot reverse poor parenting, but it can mean that the professional will be on hand at the point of crisis when the abusive act is about to be played out.

Early Stages of the Treatment Programme – The Initial Crisis

The professional's recognition that abuse may have occurred
The treatment programme begins from the first moment when a professional suspects that the injuries, failure to thrive, or rejection of a child could be a sign of abuse. This step or recognition is itself a creative leap for the professional to make, for parents rarely present themselves defining their problem in this way. They regularly present their children with 'problems', but they do not easily admit to having inflicted abuse. Pickett and Maton (1977) have noted that parents fear retribution and know only too well the stigmatization attached to the abuse of children in the current climate of publicity, so they hope that the problem – bruising, fractures or 'illness' – will be treated and cured, and the 'cause' ignored. Often the professional observer does not want to believe what he sees and unless he is *listening* with his eyes he may not pick up the subtle communications which tell the truth. Thus the perpetrator, the victim and the potential source of help may join together in collusive silence. It is no surprise that injuries often recur over a period of several months or even years, if the injury is not too severe. This implies that until the collusive silence is broken a treatment programme cannot be initiated.

The Crisis of Diagnosis
Once abuse is suspected a diagnosis has to be made. This involves medical examinations, admissions to hospital if there is a serious doubt, the confrontation of parents with the fact that the child's injuries or physical state are not consistent with the history that they have given, and the request for further explanation. The suggestion

may have to be made that injury has occurred through some possible abuse or omission of care. Medical practitioners need to explain that patterns of injuries, X-ray appearances, differences in colours of bruises, fingermarks and so on could indicate that a child has been picked up, shaken, hurt or neglected. Inevitably such a confrontation induces a crisis, which adds to the precipitating stress factors that may have swept away parental controls and triggered violent reactions. The incident itself produces consternation, fear and guilt, and it is helpful when a diagnosis of child abuse is suspected to arrange for the parents to have an immediate interview with a social worker to deal with anxiety about the hospitalization of their child. The social worker should also be present when the medical practitioner, who should preferably be of senior status, talks to the parents about the possible diagnosis so that the professional who represents care of the children and the family as a whole can be present to respond to the immediate crisis.

There is often a powerful wish to create a sense of comfort in the family by defusing the painful situation and attempting to reduce tension and imply that everything is well. This, however, is unhelpful in the long run. The presence of a helper allows re-enactment of the experience of tension which brought about the injury, and this reality needs both to be recreated in safety and met. The reality of the parents' actions and possible long-term consequences for themselves and the child have to be faced at the earliest possible moment if a treatment programme is to be initiated successfully.

It may be necessary for a place of safety to be secured legally by a social services department to preserve the child's safety, or interim care proceedings may be initiated if a child needs to be in a safe place for a longer period. Such procedures are felt to be a considerable threat by parents, yet they represent an opportunity for parents and helpers to change a 'stuck' situation. They are potentially productive and can lay the foundations for subsequent management and treatment.

A Case Example

To illustrate some of the elements involved in the work with the initial crisis, the case of a six-week old baby admitted with bruising of the right forehead and a fracture to the left side of his forehead will be described. As a result of his fracture there was a small bleed into the base of his brain (a small subdural haematoma), but surgery was not necessary. He had been transferred to a specialist neurosurgical unit from a small paediatric unit in a peripheral hospital. The story given by his family was that the baby seemed to be unwell and not to be breathing and was given mouth-to-mouth resuscitation by his father.

165

They said they had not called a doctor at that time, but only when he had vomited some hours later.

When asked about the bruise on his forehead his parents said that he had fallen off the settee where he had been placed when his father, who was babysitting at the time, had put him down to go to the toilet. His parents also volunteered that he was a baby who screamed easily. When asked if the bruises could have been caused by him being shaken or hit, they denied it vehemently and reiterated the story of him having fallen off the settee. It is, of course, highly unlikely that a baby of six weeks could wriggle off a settee, particularly when the seat sloped backwards. As investigations were incomplete at that time the parents were not further confronted. The staff on the specialist paediatric ward, however, became anxious because the parents were becoming increasingly difficult and hostile and there was concern that they might remove the child.

A social worker was asked to see the parents, and she found them hostile and angry with the suggestion that they might have hurt their child. (I am grateful to Miss Margaret Atkin for supplying the details of this case.) The father, a young man in his early twenties, spoke very quickly, his eyes had a startled appearance and he was very much on edge. His wife had a slight twitch around her mouth and a rapid way of talking. She showed several different swings of mood and seemed quite volatile in her responses. Both parents seemed agitated, talked too freely, and started off by saying that they did not really want to see the social worker or to discuss the situation, that there was nothing to discuss and that people were making insinuations without telling them what the trouble really was. They said that only since they had come to the specialist unit had they realized that their child might have a fractured skull.

This pattern of initial responses indicates the effect of the confrontation with reality; it shows how agitated these parents were, and how confused, and the denials seemed to indicate that the true state of affairs was not as they had reported it. During a later stage of the interview the mother said on several occasions, 'I couldn't hit him, because if I did my parents would hit me. My mum comes down three times a week and she knows what I'm like'. By persistence and remaining with the distress, the social worker was able to ascertain that this young couple had married only about 10 months before the current admission and that the baby had come 'straight-away'. He was unplanned and they had not really wanted to start a family at that point. However, the father said that he really wanted the child now. Indeed, both parents felt that their son had brought them closer together and that prior to his birth, even though they had been married for such a short time, they had been drifting apart. The father indicated that he had lost touch with his own father for some years and that he had been abused as a child himself. He described how his fear of his father had led him to hide himself away in a cellar overnight to escape the father's anger over some misdemeanour that he had committed.

The mother, who was under 21, described her parents as having separated. She said that her father had been cruel to her and had beaten her and her siblings. She had had a fractured jaw herself at the age of 18 months, and had been told that she knocked her cheek on a stony surface. This might very well, of course, have been a cover story for an abusive episode. She also described her own bad tempers and her mother's threats to her if she ever 'touched the baby'.

More evidence of denial came in their statement that in the very short time they had had the baby – six weeks – they had overcome *all* their problems in management. This was, of course, quite impossible with a first baby and was rendered all the more unlikely by the parents saying that the father liked to have his meals on time and had to work at night, and that the mother found a great deal to do in the home, keeping it clean, doing the shopping and managing the baby. When the social worker indicated that most parents would find it a hard struggle and admired their ability to cope with problems despite their difficulties, they accepted this and were then able to talk of their own sense of exhaustion and go into much more detail about what had happened when their baby had become 'ill'.

During a long two-hour interview it was clear that this couple were testing out the social worker's responses. They were hoping to impress or to frighten her, to see whether she would accept their dismissal of her or confirm their suspicions of the hospital's intentions. However, at the end of the period they were very much calmer and it was possible to talk about the interventions that were necessary, the X-rays, the brain scans, and the possible operations. It was also possible, at a later stage, to spell out to them, with the paediatricians, the fact that because of concern for the child's safety and the inconsistency between their story and the medical findings, the social services department would be involved in investigating the situation further. It was also explained that the child could not be moved from hospital and that a Place of Safety Order would be served until an overall plan could be worked out for the baby's treatment and care, and for the family's needs.

Towards a treatment programme.
The sorts of communications outlined above indicate the necessity for a firm degree of control over the family situation in a way which is quite alien to the treatments of more mature and less disturbed

individuals. Places of safety, periods in care, and a highly structured situation involving social services departments and caretaking settings are often essential in this period. Where parents have to be helped with fundamental chronic personality problems, it is essential that workers do not blur the issue of the child's need for protection, even though parents often wish to deny their difficulties and to present themselves and see themselves in a totally different light. A realistic view has to be maintained at all times.

Professionals are involved with the paradoxical task of considering the child's needs as well as those of the parents. Parents' needs and feelings have to be met whilst at the same time the circumstances in which the child has been injured are assessed. An understanding of the family and its social setting in the present and in the past has to be gained, whilst at the same time the child is protected from further injury. This has to be firmly stated and firmly put into practice. Parents need to be encouraged to ventilate the feelings caused by such confrontation and it is therefore important that workers do not seek to interrogate parents or to abolish much-needed defences. Concern and caring has to be shown without collusion and the process of decision-making needs to be explained at every turn.

Parents can respond to decisions which appear to be against their avowed wishes with immense relief, while others will strongly deny the need for help and persist in this attitude long after they have begun to accept aid. Parents expect to be judged and even accused, and may see the necessity for alternative care for their children as a punishment. They may well react with anger or hostility, appear to be cooperative and submissive, but even these responses often mask fear and desperation. Even understanding and sympathy can make parents feel that this must mask the ultimate wish of the professionals to punish them. Parents expect the law to be laid down and legal proceedings can be helpful even though they can appear in the first instance to be a punishment. Again, a firm statement to the parents that they seem unable to parent can have the paradoxical effect of releasing a powerful parenting response, as if to prove the professional wrong.

Although it might seem helpful for there to be two professionals involved, one who lays down the law and the other who is sympathetic, Pickett and Maton (1977) have indicated that surprisingly few families drop out of treatment when one professional attempts to hold both these roles. The overall attitude of the professional needs to incorporate authority, protection of the child, and care and responsiveness to the parents. Through this complex role of authority and care, firmness without punitiveness, and all this combined with help, the parent is given a new opportunity to experience a parental relationship that helps him to mature, rather than perpetuating his immaturity. At the same time the child needs to recover from abuse and rejection and this too has to be recognized.

Longer Term Treatment Plans

Treatment process in child abuse – an overview.

Baher et al. (1976), in their account of the work of the Battered Child Research Department of the NSPCC, have summarized the treatment process in child abuse as progressing through the following stages:

1. *Engagement* There is often a lengthy process of engagement during which parents need to be listened to, to be actively followed even to the point of regular intensive visiting against resistance, and to be drawn to attached workers through the provision of practical help and support. During this stage, parents' lack of responsiveness to approaches has to be accepted and attempts made to make contact despite rejection. A lifeline has to be provided for the parents, particularly when a decision has been made that a child will be returned to his family and that care proceedings will not be initiated. During this phase early decisions have to be made about such issues as the necessity for care. The case conference system which is generally involved in this has been widely documented – this involves the network of professionals who have responsibility for different aspects of the needs of both the children and the parents (Desborough & Stevenson, 1977).

2. *Attachment* In the creation of an attachment relationship for parents a measure of basic trust between the professionals and the parents must be established. Practical help with, for example, housing and encouragement of parents to assert their own needs are helpful in this respect and the process here is one of 'parenting the parents' and encouraging maturation in a setting of trust. This implies that professionals need to be available, and to show the general therapeutic elements of uncritical acceptance, non-possessive warmth and empathy. At the same time firm boundaries of time, presence, availability and preparation for any and every move or absence has to be made with a repeated working through of changes. When families have previously had severe disruption of attachment experiences, then powerful emotional responses to disruption of professional relationships and losses have to be expected.

3. *Early developmental maturation* Once attachment and a dependent relationship have been fostered the next stage in the therapeutic process is concerned with change and the maturation of parents through identification with therapists, and family members

169

are also helped to develop a more appropriate caring attitude with fewer punitive elements in their model of care. During this phase it becomes easier to interpret family members' behaviour and confront them with the necessity of finding a different model of behaviour. During this phase the extent of possible change can also be assessed and this process is often facilitated by the use of settings where parents' and children's day-to-day interaction can be observed in more detail.

4. *Later maturation.* In the next stage a more ordinary therapeutic contract can be made, involving insight – promoting psychotherapy, behavioural and developmental programmes or treatment focused on the marriage, or on the family as a whole. Therapy may involve individuals, the family unit, or groups. Parallel to that work, primarily focused on parents and their development, is the work with the children. This may proceed at the same pace or may be more rapid, particularly if the child is in a separate setting.

Some treatment principles

1. *No one specific treatment modality suffices.* The one overriding principle in working with families in which abuse has taken place is that there is no one therapeutic modality or fixed treatment plan which can meet the overall needs of the family. When the overall aim is the development and emotional maturity of all members of the family, then a therapeutic modality which merely focuses on one aspect of the problem cannot be sufficient. The results of the NSPCC battered-child research team approach (Baher *et al.*, 1976) indicated that although 'parenting the parents' can help their maturation, this method of treatment may not in itself change the pattern of relationships between the parent and the abused child. Although abuse itself could be prevented, parent-child interaction still remained hostile and aversive. There is a need for specific work focused on the parent-child relationship if a more thorough-going change is to be achieved, affecting all the sub-systems of the family – parent to parent, parent to child, and child to child.

2. *'Pseudo-maturity' has to be dealt with.* Another general principle for consideration concerns the fact that although individuals who have had serious deficits in parenting often appear to be surprisingly mature despite the lack of care, this maturity is often a 'pseudo' or 'thin' maturity, so that they present as grown-up children rather than mature adults. This often requires much painful re-education. It may show itself through disruption of carefully worked out plans, failed appointments, insatiable demands for time and attention, and rejection of professionals in the guise of the demand for the immediate return of children who may be in care. Parents who have

had to grow up rapidly in the face of privation are used to the language of coercion and emotional bullying.

Working towards independence of the family as a unit with parents being parents and parenting their own children means that adults need to be helped to relate to each other both as a parental and as a marital couple, rather than as the parent-child duo that may have inspired the marriage or partnership in the first place.

3. *Other families and a therapeutic team can help the maturation process.* A setting which provides parents with models of interaction and the possibility of observing others dealing with children in a cooperative way without competition and punitiveness often helps to create a milieu in which parents can find a more adult part of themselves in identification with others.

This implies that for the satisfactory treatment of child abuse a variety of different therapeutic modalities needs to be available, and this is most appropriately supplied by a team in an appropriate therapeutic setting. Such a team should ideally include:

(i)   workers to provide the basic attachment and parenting relationship for the parents;

(ii)   workers skilled in dyadic and family group treatments;

(iii)   workers who can work therapeutically with children either individually or in groups, and

(iv)   workers able to provide behavioural and developmental programmes to deal with specific needs.

This implies integration and careful treatment planning and a team approach. The team has to take responsibility for planning, monitoring, consultation and decision-making, and for containing the anxieties of the professionals themselves.

Although certain professionals would suggest that they are more appropriate for some of the functions described, e.g., psychologists for planning behavioural and developmental programmes, such specificity is not absolutely necessary and the majority of the functions can be carried out as well by any of the professionals involved. Specific roles will depend on experience, interest and training. Although social workers usually provide the parenting and attachment work, and have this role of necessity through their statutory function in the community, other professionals can provide it. And although child psychotherapists would ordinarily work with the children, social workers and psychologists are becoming increasingly interested in direct work with children and so with help may undertake these functions. All disciplines working in this area can usefully work with parents and children conjointly and with marital problems, either separately or in the family as a group. Although psychiatrists are often asked to consult over the psychiatric status of

171

parents and children, therapeutic roles can be taken by those from other disciplines, including psychiatric nurses. Perhaps more important than the disciplines of the professionals involved are the tasks that have to be carried out and the necessity for communication and clarification of role and function.

4. *Progress is slow and mutual professional support is necessary.* Another function of the team is to provide support through the often discouraging experience of working with families with limited potential for change. Workers do not always see the changes in the clients, just as parents fail to observe their own children gradually growing up. The team's less direct observations of family members can often help workers to see the small changes which do occur. Changes often occur paradoxically after a crisis in management, a failed appointment, or parents acting out against the therapeutic plan. Such actions induce new crises, and crises in turn can produce a creative leap and a change which neither worker nor family could have envisaged. Team members have to provide through each other and through other families the relationships that they may miss with particular clients. There can be no substitute, however, and professionals need to be aware of their own need for clients, and a rigid system can result when the professional and the family are locked in an enmeshed and perverted state of dependency.

Working in a team can help professionals to stop acting and reacting, rather than thinking, reflecting and facilitating change. Clients need to be responsible in choosing, acting and testing out the viability of the running of their own lives without being hampered, and then accepting inevitable failure. Goals should be set towards which families are motivated and which are within their potential to achieve. Pleasure needs to be shown when some achievements are gained, no matter how slight, when photographs are shown or when wine or cakes are brought for a party. Success is reached when parents want children not as a source of comfort for themselves but as a focus for their comforting. The desire to succeed without the capacity to do so will add to the burden rather than lighten it.

Bentovim (1977b) has provided a description of the therapeutic setting in the treatment of families in which abuse has occurred. This account describes the setting in which a therapeutic intervention can occur, and in which the family, the treatment agency and the professionals who work there come together and create an inter-relating and inter-communicating matrix (Britton, 1978). This facilitates the family's development and provides opportunities for growth in a secure environment. A variety of such settings has been described.

1. *Residential settings for the family and children.*

Residential facilities for the whole family, such as those described by Lynch and Ounsted (1976), provide the most comprehensive setting both for the accurate assessment of the family during the initial crisis of diagnosis and the initial formulation of a treatment plan. The combination of medical treatment, practical help and various forms of therapy makes it possible to achieve rapid change in both children and parents without the need for prolonged separation with all its attendant problems.

A paediatric hospital setting with residential facilities provides many of the features of the whole-family unit, particularly as far as assessment is concerned, but lacks amenities for parents' groups and the wider range of therapeutic modalities, and rehabilitation has to take place elsewhere. The Richmond Fellowship organization can also admit the whole family for a lengthy period of care and provide a setting for the child which is socially acceptable. Folkart (1967) has described the family unit of the Cassell Hospital and this provides a milieu for a variety of psychodynamic approaches involving individual members of the family and the family as a living group.

2. *Day settings*

The most commonly provided setting for the families of abused children when they are to remain together is some form of day setting. Here the children's needs can be met in the form of a therapeutic nursery or day care provision while parents either receive intensive case work, individually or in groups, or receive direct help in gaining parenting skills and learn different ways of responding to children. Baher *et al.* (1976), and Pickett and Maton (1977) described the NSPCC Special Unit model. Bentovim (1977c) described the use of a Psychiatric Day Centre to meet the needs of abused or 'at risk' pre-school children and their families. This centre organized one day a week in which parents and children were treated conjointly, and it provided a therapeutic milieu in which a variety of treatment was given, including individual work with parents, parent groups, and parent-child work, as well as individual and group work with the children. Britton (1978) has described the way in which the Day Care Centre can be transformed into a 'young family centre' providing both for children's and parents' individual needs.

A quite different day setting is one which focuses on the parents rather than the child. Here the setting is a psychiatric day hospital for parents but a nursery is provided for the children (West and West, 1978). Again a variety of therapeutic procedures focused on the parents can be provided although, without a child-based focus, the children's needs may be less well met. By the same token day settings which are focused on children's needs, e.g., day nurseries, may not provide adequately for a parent's needs even though parents are being seen for individual casework. The need for children to have individual attention in day care, and for parents to be involved in the care of the children cannot be emphasized too strongly (Roberts 1978). care of the children cannot be emphasized too strongly (Roberts, 1978).

3. *Settings which enhance the family's home*

The facilities considered so far involve either the whole family or various members attending a setting outside the home. These may be more or less therapeutic but in common to all approaches they involve family members being with other parents and professionals. As an alternative, people from outside the family may be introduced into the family home. Family aides who can share parenting tasks on a regular basis come under this heading but intensive regular visiting by social workers, health visitors or other professionals may also serve to provide a model of sharing and parenting and thus improve the quality of care given to the child. Such home visiting patterns are often associated with visits to clinics, social service departments or a day setting and treatment modes such as those outlined earlier often lead to a graduated process of moving from such a treatment setting to one representing a lesser degree of monitoring and supervision. The regular presence of someone in the home acts as both a support and also a lifeline – the parent may in a time of stress be able to hold on until that person comes or be able to call them. The idea of the drop-in setting that can be used in times of crisis is also important in the longer-term treatment plan for such families.

4. *Separation settings.*

In any situation in which there is moderate or severe abuse a period of separation may become necessary. Admission of the child to the hospital may be essential for safety and for the initial diagnosis to be made. Such a separation may of course prolong the problem with relationships, but by observing the parents' and child's response to the separation important information can be gained which may play a part in later decisions regarding longer-term separation. Too often children are left for long periods in a paediatric hospital setting which is quite inappropriate to their normal developmental needs because of the multiplicity of caretakers, the confusing mix of children coming in and out of hospital, and the severity of the physical illness that other children may well have. Nursing care methods are not aimed at long-term care, unless special arrangements have been made to provide for one-to-one management of the child.

However, a hospital place does provide the family and professional

174

with a setting in which to deal with the current crisis. If longer term separation is necessary, then decisions have to be made as to the possibility of the child being placed in a small children's home or in a fostering setting. Such issues are too often determined by constraints regarding the resources which are available. Foster families may be a considerable distance from the family and a children's home may even be in quite another part of the country. Fostering or placement of young children should of course be near to the family if possible to make regular visiting feasible.

An added complication with the placement of children away from their families is the necessity to break attachment relationships made with alternative caretakers when children are gradually reintroduced to their own families. There may be a complicated series of angry responses on the children's part. Anxiety transforming into anger can be expected from both the caretakers, who may well have become attached to the children, and the parents, who have to re-establish an attachment relationship with their children. Treatments in separation are too often complicated by breakdown of fostering or children's home care, changes of caretakers, and the danger of privation and inadequate care (Martin & Beezley, 1976). For these reasons treatment of the whole family in a residential setting is preferable.

5. *Permanent Separation.*
Permanent separation of parents and children may be necessary as a result of parental inability to change or if a child has been for some time in a setting which has provided continuity of care and now seems to represent the 'least detrimental setting' for his future development and care. Kempe (1978) has advocated that children be freed for adoption rather than remaining in long-term fostering settings with the attendant lack of security and attachment. If such a decision is made then the parents need to work through the sadness, grief and loss involved in accepting that they cannot provide for the care of a particular child, and work still remains necessary to help them grow. The arrangement of such a 'divorce' between parents and children as part of a treatment plan may be necessary when there is little or no likelihood of parent-child relationships being able to resume with the child's safety and adequate development being ensured.

Some Further Treatment Modalities

The general approach of 'parenting the parent' has been described. A number of other methods are also discussed in the literature.

Treatment Studies

1. *Family therapy*

Recent developments in family therapy (Bentovim, 1979; Gorell-Barnes, 1979) suggest that when violence occurs in the family it may be useful to treat that family as a group. The interactive pattern is the focus of treatment, and changing interactions leads to changes in individuals. Although the family as a group should have the task of socializing and caring for its members, this task can be overtaken by emotional responses which are then contained by a process in which individuals find alliances with each other by rejecting a third member.

Negative responses justify rejection, and violent interaction can become the normal language of family transactions. Transaction between parents and children can also be impoverished and there may be neglect and lack of response, indicating a rigid parent-child barrier. Alternatively there may be over-responsiveness and too easy anger for perceived wrong-doing, this indicating an over-permeable boundary between parent and child (Minuchin, 1974). Through consistent reinforcement, involving all members of a family, such patterns of relating become institutionalized.

The therapist's interventions have to alter the pattern in the here and now of therapy. He has to persuade, cajole or support a different response and help a parent to use firmness without threat. He must encourage the use of warmth and praise instead of coldness and rejection, point out the way parents and children are sharing and experiencing the same feeling, and help both parents and children to find unused aspects of themselves in their relationships with each other. The use of video-recording to show families their ways of relating, confronts the parent full of righteous indignation with aspects of the interaction of which he had not been aware, and through this he may come to share the therapist's real response to the danger of violence to the child.

Such work is often highly repetitive and requires a constant reiteration of the changes in the family structure that are essential in order to defuse conflict rather than to increase it.

The work of Minuchin *et al.* (1967) is a model of the way in which disorganized families can be changed, and his emphasis is basically on 'traffic control' rather than on the elucidation of themes and feelings. The scenario that is constantly re-enacted is that of attack or fear of attack, followed by an 'attack to prevent attack or further attack', with an escalation of anger that the therapist must help both to induce and to defuse. The constant repetition of attacks which are defused within the family helps the development of confidence, control and autonomy rather than repression and inhibition which may eventually break down.

2. *Group Therapy – following identification of abuse and risk, e.g. in day and residential settings.*

Group therapy is a frequently used modality of treatment for both parents and children where abuse has occurred or where risk is felt to be present. Group therapy can achieve a number of different therapeutic goals, including relief by parents and children when they meet others experiencing the same stresses and anxieties. Communication and expression of feelings can help in general maturation and the control that comes about as a result of feeling oneself to be the actor in a situation rather than one who is acted upon by external and unique forces. Individuals with complementary problems can help each other and act together as a support group extending the family network for each other.

The group goes through a cycle of development, at times behaving as a family group which feels intensely threatened from the outside, at other times acting as a source of sibling rivalry, anger and mutual rejection, and at other times functioning as a far more mature supportive whole. The therapeutic style of the group leaders depends on the stage the group is at and on the maturation of its members. In the early stages, where the aim is attachment, group members need to be actively engaged in the group and the leader needs to be far more active, involving and revealing his own feelings and experiences and thus acting as a model, than he will expect to be at a later stage. He will inevitably be the centre of a good many expectations both of punishment and of caring and he needs to shift this expectation onto the group itself, although this may take time.

The group can also serve as a resource for family members in between group meetings and, unlike classical group therapy in which contact between members tends to be discouraged, the creation of a network of support in the community can be an important goal of regular groups. Groups can be useful as a preventive aid during the stages of pregnancy and early childhood, when they can function as parent-toddler groups. Such innovations help to enlarge the extended family and community network for an isolated family.

Children's groups tend to be focused on care and stimulation, but Lynch's recent review of the development of children who have been abused (Lynch 1978) indicates how much specific professional help may also have to deal with emotional consequences of the atmosphere of violence and rejection that they have grown up in, and with the pattern of poor self esteem, pseudo-mature obsessive and difficult behaviour which makes peers, parents and teachers reject them. Placement of a child in a setting with a therapeutic group component (e.g., Bentovim, 1977; Lynch & Ounsted, 1976; Folkart 1967, and Britton, 1978), can begin to meet those needs through an approach

177

that is focused on the child's needs as well as those of the parents.

3. *Individual therapy for children.*
The most extensive discussion of the issues in relationship to individual child therapy is contained in Martin (1976). Beezley, Martin and Kempe (1976) described a study of psychotherapy with abused children and the characteristics of their behaviour and response to individual dynamically orientated psychotherapy. The therapy in this study was non-directive and supportive and encouraged children to express their feelings and conflicts through play and verbalization. Although the focus was one of exploration it was hoped that through this experience the child could enjoy a more positive relationship with an adult through the therapist's attention and attempt to understand him. It was hoped that through this the child would be able to identify, acknowledge and share feelings, enjoy play, and find pleasure in age-appropriate behaviour, so increasing his esteem and self-confidence. These authors found that the children did have a capacity to change in these directions despite the rejection they had experienced.

Boston *et al.* (1978) presented an account of psychotherapy with severely deprived children which focusses more on an examination of the transference relationship to the therapist than on the expectation of repetition of aggression. Therapists found that in attempting to make contact with these children intensely emotional experiences were communicated, and feelings were often found to be chaotic, confused and very much blocked. As a result much pain was inflicted on the therapist in the form first of criticism, then anger and finally rejection. Therapists and children required considerable support to contain the pain involved in facing feelings engendered through such experiences, but if the relationship was maintained then it could result in maturation and improved coping on the children's part.

Conclusions

Like many conditions which call for treatment, child abuse is the end result of an interacting network of personal, family and societal variables. The results of treatment (Baher et al., 1976; Martin, 1976 and Lynch, 1978) indicate how limited are the successes of attempting to change and improve the relationship of parents and children in abusive situations. A treatment plan has to be initiated from the first moment of contact with the family and the professional has of course to ensure the safety of the child and prevention of any repetition of abuse.

The studies above indicate that further abuse can be prevented and that the combination of authority and care in dealing with the family does seem to ensure both the safety of the children and the development and maturity of the parents. However, a treatment plan to achieve these ends alone is insufficient if the developmental problems of abused children are to be reversed and the relationship between parents and children are to be improved. A network of support and a variety of treatment modalities and of settings are often necessary to achieve these multiple goals. Social work intervention with a variety of community supports is often necessary to ensure the first aim, whilst more specific treatments involving the family as a whole, the parents in groups and children in settings with a therapeutic and developmental component, are often necessary for successful completion of the overall treatment plan.

Part of any treatment plan is the frequent monitoring of progress and the charting both of the overall development of the individual and of the family as a group. There needs to be a constant re-evaluation of goals, whether this means having to face the necessity for a permanent separation or the safe resumption of a family life. Parents need to find satisfaction as adults to provide adequate nurturance and control for children, including punishment when appropriate as well as rewards. Generation boundaries should be preserved with sufficient communication and responsiveness, and sharing of empathy and warmth, for the children's development to be facilitated in a reasonably anxiety-free manner – a formidable task!

REFERENCES

Baher, E., Hyman, C., Jones, C., Jones, R., Kerr, A. and Mitchell R. (1976) *At Risk: An account of the work of the Battered Child Research Dept. NSPCC*, Routledge and Kegan Paul, London.

Beezley, P., Martin, H.P., and Kempe, R. 'Psychotherapy', In: H.P. Martin (Ed.) *The Abused Child*, Ballinger, Cambridge, Mass.

Bentovim, A. (1977a) 'First steps towards a systems analysis of severe physical abuse to children in the family'. In House of Commons: *First Report from Select Committee on Violence in the Family, vol. 3*, HMSO Appendices: pp. 659–69.

Bentovim, A. (1977b) 'Therapeutic systems and settings in the treatment of child abuse' In: A. White Franklin (Ed.) *The Challenge of Child Abuse*, Academic Press, London.

Bentovim, A. (1977c) 'A Psychiatric Family Day Centre meeting the needs of abused or at risk pre-school children and their parents'. *Child Abuse and Neglect, 1*, pp. 479–85.

Bentovim, A. (1979) 'Theories of family interaction and techniques of intervention'. *Journal of Family Therapy, 1*, pp. 321–45.

Boston, M., Holmes, E., Hoxter, S., and Oliver-Bellasis, E. (1978) 'Psychotherapy with severely deprived children: a discussion paper'. *Child Abuse and Neglect, 3*, pp. 539–46.

Britton, R.S. (1978) 'Young family centres for children at risk'. Presented to 2nd International Congress on Child Abuse and Neglect, London, Sept. 1978.

Treatment Studies

Desborough C. and Stevenson, O. (1977) 'Case Conferences: A Study of Interprofessional Communication Concerning Children at Risk', Keele University.

Folkart, L. (1967) 'Some problems in treating children in the in-patient setting'. *J. Child Psychother.*, *2*, pp. 46–55.

Frommer, E.A. and O'Shea, G. (1973) 'The importance of childhood experience in relation to problems in marriage and family-building'. *Brit. J. Psychiat.*, *123*, pp. 157–60.

Gorell Barnes, G. (1979) 'Infant needs and angry responses – A look at violence in the family,' In: S. Walrond-Skinner (Ed.) *Family and Marital Psychotherapy*, Routledge and Kegan Paul, London.

Gray, I.D., Cutler, C.A., Dean, I.G., Kempe, C.H. (1977) 'Prediction and prevention of child abuse and neglect', *Child Abuse and Neglect, 1*, pp. 45–58.

Kempe, C.H. (1978) 'Recent developments in the field of child abuse,' *Child Abuse and Neglect, 2*, pp. 261–7.

Lynch, M.A. and Ounsted, C. (1976) 'A Place of Safety', In: R.E. Helfer and C.H. Kempe, (Eds.) *Child Abuse and Neglect: The family and the community*, Ballinger, Cambridge, Mass.

Martin, H.P. (1976) *The Abused Child*, Ballinger, Cambridge, Mass.

Martin, H.P. and Beezley, P. (1977) 'Behavioural observations of abused children'. *Devel. Med. Child. Neurol.*, *19*, pp. 373–87.

Minuchin, S., Montalvo, B., Guerney, B.G., Rosman, B.L. and Shumer, F. (1967) *Families of the Slums: An Exploration of their Structure and Treatment* Basic Books, New York.

Pickett J. and Maton A. (1977) 'Protective casework and child abuse', In: A. White Franklin (Ed.) *The Challenge of Child Abuse*, Academic Press, London.

Roberts, I. (1978) 'Social work and child abuse: the reasons for failure and the way to success', In: I.P. Martin (Ed.) *Violence and the Family*. Wiley, Chichester.

West, I.E. and West, D. (1978) 'Child abuse treated in a psychiatric day hospital'. *Child Abuse and Neglect, 3*, pp. 699–707.

12 The Behavioural Approach to Child Abuse

Judy Hutchings

Much of the recent behavioural work with abusing families has drawn on the growing body of literature demonstrating the value of a behavioural approach to work with non-abused children and their families, and some writers see the problems as not dissimilar. McAuley and McAuley (1977) set out a framework with which to approach child and family difficulties and they go on to suggest that abusing families are perhaps more difficult examples of child and family problems and should not be considered as having a different *sort* of problem. Hutchings and Jones (1979) also adopt this position and most behavioural approaches to child abuse have drawn on the findings of many researchers seeking to apply the approach to child and family work where child abuse itself is not the referred problem.

The excellent work of Patterson et al. (1973) in training parents of aggressive boys provides one such example. Another is the work of Phillips et al. (1973) in the 'achievement place scheme' in which adolescent offenders are helped by a teaching family to acquire new social, self help, and academic skills. Both of these groups of workers have based their approach to children and their problems on extensive theoretical knowledge and a careful behavioural analysis of the needs of the client group. Their results have been impressive. Both have seen the needs of the client group, parents of aggressive boys, or delinquent teenagers themselves, as predominantly stemming from deficits in behaviour and their therapeutic approach has therefore been constructional (see Schwartz & Goldiamond, 1975) in that it focuses on teaching new repertoires of behaviour as alternatives to the problem behaviours.

Other knowledge about teaching new behaviours and improving parents' skills as teachers has come from a somewhat different area of work – that is, from the development of services to the mentally handicapped and their families. The Portage project (Shearer & Shearer, 1972) is a good example of how parents are helped to break down tasks and teach new skills to their slow-learning child.

Against this broader background of behavioural literature concerning work with children and families, a considerable stream of work dealing more specifically with child abuse has now started to emerge. Perhaps the best theoretical paper is that of Dubanoski et al. (1978). He and his colleagues defined five areas of investigation, two of which were specific to the abuse problem and three of which concerned factors likely to underlie and provoke abuse. These were:

Lack of management skills and lack of knowledge about normal developmental processes

They suggest that some abusers lack techniques to increase children's pro-social behaviours and to reduce undesirable ones. They argue that parenting skills cannot be taken for granted and that it is easy to identify by direct observation what skills a family has. They point out that smaller families and the nuclear family model reduce opportunities to learn about child rearing from other people. This theme occurs elsewhere, and Tracey and Clarke (1974) also point to the evidence of a lack of knowledge about child development and over-high expectations on the part of many abusing parents.

Dubanoski et al. suggest several possible ways of dealing with child abuse resulting from this source. They suggest that teaching parents to become better observers of a child's behaviour would be helpful, and by this they mean both increasing parental sensitivity to the child's needs and teaching parents to recognize how their own behaviour affects the child. They also see other ways of dealing with child abuse resulting from lack of management skills and lack of knowledge about normal development, and these include teaching techniques of child management (with emphasis on extinction and positive reinforcement) and teaching parents the advantages of positive child rearing practice and the problems of punishment control. Finally, they suggest that such parents would benefit from practical teaching about normal child development.

Punitive discipline

Here they describe a distinct style of parenting based on punitive punishment practices. They point out that particular sub-cultural or broader societal factors influence discipline styles. The Newsons (1968 and Chapter 5 of this volume) have demonstrated that in Britain 95% of parents use smacking as a means of punishment at one stage or another in a child's rearing. Dubanoski et al. point out that the unique past experiences of the individual parent also contribute in an important way to the style of parenting adopted. They point out that society's sanctioning of physical punishment of children is embodied in such expressions as 'spare the rod – spoil the child'. They suggest that if punishment is a strongly established means of control then the parents may need help to be taught to punish more effectively in order to eliminate the child's undesirable behaviour more quickly, or may need to be taught alternative ways of punishing – for example using 'time out' or 'response cost' strategies.

Impulsive Aggression

An explosive act by the parent may be triggered by the child's behaviour, especially at times when the parent is tired. A common example of this is that of a child crying in the night. The authors point out that weapons are seldom used in child abuse so that it is probable that it is not, in general, planned, and they suggest the need to look at the literature on self-control for likely means of helping the parent, and also the need to look for ways of changing those aspects of the child's behaviour which provoke the abuse. They mention also the possibility of desensitizing parents. The theme of desensitization has been taken up by Sandford and Tustin (1973) and by Sanders (1978) and both of these studies will be described later.

High levels of stress

Dubanoski et al. point to the many factors that are related to abuse – for example, unemployment, poor housing and low income. They mention again, under this heading, the social isolation factor. Having argued earlier that because of such isolation parents lack models of child rearing, they now point out that it has the further effect of reducing the opportunities for help and support when a child is particularly difficult to handle. They quote Bandura's (1973) statement that 'social and verbally unskilled people having limited means of handling discord are likely to become physically aggressive on slight provocation especially in a context where violent conduct is used favourably'.

Negative attitudes towards the child or dislike of the child

From the point of view of a behavioural analysis this is perhaps the most difficult category since there are tremendous difficulties in establishing the relationship between attitudes and behaviour, and Dubanoski et al. take pains to acknowledge this problem. They point out that parents describe the abused child as a bad child, a spoiled child, a difficult child, and as a child who is a monster or is wicked. Sometimes the child-rearing pattern which has been quite successful in bringing up other children in the family does not work so well with one particular child. The child is different – he may be handicapped or very active, he may have had low birth weight or resulted from an unwanted pregnancy. The child may not be reinforcing to the parents and he or she may elicit a negative emotional response which can lead to parental avoidance. In such a situation they suggest that it may be necessary to consider an alternative home for the child.

Dubanoski et al. conclude that child abuse is a complex problem with many determinants. This theme is echoed throughout the literature, for example by Reavley and Gilbert (1978), Holmes et al. (1975) and Jeffery (1976). Hutchings and Jones (1979) argue that in order to understand child abuse we need to analyze what is happening at three levels. One level is related to the sorts of behaviours towards children that are sanctioned by society. The second level concerns the general circumstances of the home of the abused child, for example marital disharmony, single parenthood, low income and lack of educational opportunity. The third level focuses specifically on the quality of parent-child interaction.

Some other articles are more specific. They may be based on a single case study, or they look only at one possible cause of child abuse or one treatment, for example desensitization. Sandford and Tustin (1973), for example, used desensitization to gradually increase a father's tolerance of loud noises. They did this by gradually increasing the intensity and duration of noise which upset the father. This treatment followed a father's aggressive assault on his 13-month-old child when he found it difficult to stop the child from crying. In a three-phase desensitization programme they first of all assessed the level of the father's tolerance of aversive noises. They then gradually increased the frequency of the noise and linked this first to a video tape of the child playing and subsequently to a more pleasant noise. The video was introduced whilst the aversive noise was still occurring but the noise soon stopped and the reinforcing sound, in this case folk music, was then played whilst the video of the child playing continued.

In the final phase of the programme the aversive noise was increased until the father could tolerate it for 15 minutes without escape. Sandforth and Tustin considered that 15 minutes would be sufficient time for his wife to pacify the child once it had started crying. The child was returned home following this treatment but, in fact, remained at home only for a very short while before being sent for adoption because the mother had found a job. However, during this time the father was able to tolerate the crying and there were no further incidents of abuse.

Another example of desensitization is described by Sanders (1978). Sanders treated a father who had abused his child at two weeks old because it cried loudly by:

1. Four sessions of muscle relaxation,
2. asking the father to construct a hierarchy of things about the child which made him increasingly intolerant,
3. twelve sessions of muscle relaxation whilst the items from the hierarchy were discussed; and, finally,
4. muscle relaxation while the tape of his child crying was played.
On follow up there were no further incidents of abuse although on one occasion the father did get angry but was able to express it verbally.

Reavley and Gilbert (1978) also used an anxiety management approach but they focused on behavioural self-control methods and mentioned the work of Meichenbaum (1977) on self-instruction. It is interesting to note that a survey of South Wales mothers (Frude and Goss, 1979, and Chapter 4 of this volume) suggested that many mothers have times of extreme frustration and anger towards their children but that non-abusing mothers have a range of strategies for dealing with their annoyance with their child. Studying the strategies used by non-abusing families may well be useful for behaviourists. The survey mothers appeared to have developed a wide range of ways of coping that included distraction, self-instruction and other management techniques which Reavley and Gilbert (1978) and others have taught formally to abusing families.

Reavley and Gilbert also stress the importance of clients keeping detailed records both of treatment sessions and of what happens between these sessions. They argue that these records allow their clients to monitor subtle changes in their behaviour which might otherwise have been overlooked. Reavley and Gilbert emphasize that the treatment should take place where the problem occurs i.e. in the client's home. They suggest that repeated practice of new behaviours, guidance from the therapist during practice and the provision of feedback are also necessary, as are favourable conditions for practice.

Their article presents two detailed case studies:
1. A 33 year old mother had a daughter 13 months old.
She was taught an anxiety management technique and practised it between treatment sessions. A list of problem behaviours was made and ordered as to the amount of anxiety each produced, and then gradually the mother was faced with the increasingly feared situations. At the end of two weeks of daily treatment she was performing all of the tasks on her hierarchy without modelling or prompting and she was maintaining a commentary peppered with statements such as 'I will not smack Anna, I will not shout at Anna'. At this stage the therapists were only supervising the mother and were then able to hand this role over to her husband. The child responded well to the mother and the progress initially achieved was maintained.

185

2. In their second case study Reavley and Gilbert describe a 30-year-old mother who disliked her older daughter and was afraid of harming her. Reavley and Gilbert again helped the mother to construct a hierarchy of anxiety-producing situations with the child and used a participant modelling treatment approach with emphasis on the importance of the notion that behaviour change precedes attitude change.

Reavley and Gilbert conclude that a 'multi-modal behaviour therapy' approach (as propounded by Lazarus, 1973) is necessary, and if treatment is to have long lasting effect it needs to be directed towards changing 'irrational beliefs, deviant behaviours, unpleasant feelings, intrusive images, stressful relationships, negative sensations and possible biochemical imbalances.' Reavley and Gilbert's work contrasts with the work previously discussed in which desensitization was used mainly to help parents tolerate difficult child behaviour.

Much of the emphasis of other workers has been on changing the behaviour of the child as well as the behaviour of parents. One example is contained in the work of Polakow and Peabody (1975). They see abusive parental behaviour as an inappropriate response to the child's behaviour and they try to teach more effective child management skills to the parents. This approach was also employed by Tracey and Clarke (1974). Their therapeutic technique involves three stages:
1. Identifying by close observation the contingencies that are operating,
2. establishing the therapist as a social reinforcer to the parents, and
3. developing contracts between the therapist and the parent.

They followed this home-based intervention with subsequent group attendance for the mother which was also aimed at teaching social and inter-personal skills. Their intervention continued for over one year and is a good example of the recognition that child abuse is not simple and that there may be a variety of skills that require teaching. Many writers also stress the importance of teaching other inter-personal skills, perhaps particularly related to marital relationships. Examples of this may be found in reports by Hutchings and Jones (1979) and Jeffery (1976).

Another good example of a home-based intensive programme is that of Doctor and Singer (1978). Their general model is based on Tharp and Wetzel's (1969) approach in which specialist behavioural consultants advise home interventionists who are working with the family. There is other discussion about who should use a behavioural approach with abusing families within the behavioural literature. Gilbert (1977) for example, sees it as part of the developing role of the nurse therapist and Hutchings and Hughes (1979) encourage health visitors to identify the determinants of the problems in a situation where child abuse is occurring as well as identifying the risk to the child. Doctor and Singer (1978) identified two problems, one teaching effective child management skills, and the other modifying unrealistic parental expectations. They consider the problem of motivation and point out that abusive families are often not self-referred but are generally sent by the Court and other bodies, and they feel the need to indicate to the client the basis of their therapeutic relationship. They explain that it is a voluntary service and that the information is confidential. Clients are told exactly what information is subsequently sent to referring agencies and told exactly what they are required to do in order to get a good report. For example, they are told that if they attend 90% of the sessions then the therapists will report regular attendance to the Court. Doctor and Singer argue that once this is clarified most parents become actively involved. Usually these agreements are clarified in a contract.

Therapists must be separate from the other agencies who have had contact with the family and must focus on the lack of blame and the development of an appropriate and satisfying parent-child relationship. Hutchings and Jones (1979) take up this theme and point to the importance of focusing on the behaviours that need to change, behaviours of both parent and child, rather than the allocation of blame. The Open University Study Guide (Carver, 1978) reported the attitudes of professionals to abusing parents and abused children. Whilst all professionals expressed concern for the child, the attitudes of professionals towards the parent varied from the need to punish such parents for their crimes to the need to approach them with sympathy, considering them as unhappy and unfulfilled people in their own lives.

In a detailed article entitled 'Practical Ways to Change Parent Child Interaction in Families with Children at Risk' Margaret Jeffery (1976) points to the two common strands in child abuse. First, the parental handling of conflict by means of violence and, second, the problems of social isolation. She gives a number of examples of changing patterns of parenting behaviour:

1. *Simple reinforcement.* In Jeffery's example a parent was rewarded by posters to put on the wall for increased positive interaction during one hour of each day for two weeks. The tokens and social approval from the therapist followed whenever positive comments by the parent exceeded negative ones. Jeffery left a tape recorder with the family at times when the therapist was not present, to help to maintain the change. Jeffery did not see an increase of positive interaction as the end of treatment for this particular family and a social worker and a home-maker continued to teach other skills, but

the situation was considerably improved by this specific intervention and the parents no longer talked about putting the child into a home. The idea of home-makers and of teaching home management skills is stressed by a number of writers, for example Hutchings et al. (1979).

2. '*Learning to Communicate*'. Jeffery argues that care-givers often only respond to bad behaviour and that they see the child only as bad. She suggests that they have to be taught to listen to and respond to the child's needs. She quotes an example of giving a shared reward if a mother could talk for 30% of the time and the child could talk for 50% of the time during 15-minute sessions. Both child and parent had to elicit and maintain speech during the 15-minute period in order to get the reward.

3. *Learning to play*. Jeffery sees teaching parents to play with children as a good opportunity for many positive behaviours to be practised. The worker acts as a model and prompts and reinforces the parents for appropriate behaviour. Jeffery notes that play can become rapidly established and maintained by the naturally rewarding consequences, whereas asking parents to change their behaviour in response to difficult behaviour or management problems can be harder to maintain. This is because problem behaviour which may be on quite intermittent schedules of reinforcement may increase dramatically before it extinguishes.

4. *Making a house adapt to children's needs*. Jeffery says that the lack of positive interaction can relate to the physical household arrangements. There are, for example, cramped or over-tidy houses with too many things that children are prohibited to touch and nowhere for them to make a mess.

5. *Contracts*. Jeffery suggests that contracts for agreement between parents and children to avoid certain problem areas can be very valuable. Contracts are also mentioned in the writing of Doctor and Singer (1978), Hutchings and Jones (1979), and Tracey et al. (1974).

6. *Teaching alternative management strategies*. An example of this would be distraction, where a parent sets up a situation for a child to be rewarded for behaviour other than the one in which they are engaged. Jeffery's example is that of a child hanging out of the window and the parents starting to play with toys and talk about the toys in order to distract the child back to play. This is interesting, but there could be difficulties in the approach because giving attention to the child to shift from one activity to another may inadvertently reinforce the undesirable behaviour. This may already be the approach used unsuccessfully by the parents. Jeffery also discusses the benefits of reducing instructions to children and defining which rules will apply.

Important behavioural work has also been reported by Sandler et al. (1978). They demonstrate excellent procedures of baseline recording, treatment and collection of follow-up data, using the Patterson et al. (1969) coding system of 29 possible behavioural categories as a basis for defining client problems. To use this coding the clients, adult members of the family and children, are restricted to two rooms of the house with the television off and all members present. A category coding is made every six seconds. The results of the baseline recording of one family led the therapists to decide to try to increase approval and physical positive contact with the child. They approached this by setting nine sessions of reading plus weekly assignments followed by a role play in which the therapist modelled as the mother and the parent modelled as the chld. Success for the parent in taking part in this programme led to tangible reinforcers, such as free meals and movie passes. Sandler et al. demonstrated considerable increases in both approval and physical positive contact with the child. There were increases both in the pro-social behaviour which was targeted and also in non-targeted pro-social behaviour, although the latter declined at follow-up. They argue that tangible reinforcers are necessary for families who don't admit to child management problems and who do not enter treatment voluntarily.

Some writers, for example Hutchings and Jones (1979), Petts and Geddes (1978) and Appleton et al. (1978), have suggested that parent-teaching groups are one method of helping parents to acquire child-management skills. Hutchings and Jones (1979) see this as one way of fading out a home-based intervention while at the same time ensuring both the maintenance of the behaviour change that has been achieved during the intervention and the generalization of the new skills to other difficulties. Hutchings and Jones (1979) also mention the importance of dealing with other family problems. This is also discussed by Tracey and Clarke (1974) who give examples of such other problems as the need for a cot, bed or housing. This illustrates the claim of Holmes et al. (1975) who say that in the multi-problem family child abuse is often just one of the family's problems. These writers also stress the lack of interactional skills within abusing families.

Conclusion

It is apparent from the literature that some writers consider the behavioural approach to abusing families to be based on relatively simple manipulations of consequences – for example, Bedford (1978) and Sandford and Tustin (1973). It may be that some proponents of the behavioural approach have been guilty of giving the impression that it is easy to apply such techniques to complex human problems and it is therefore worthy of note that many of the writers do discuss the complexity of the determinants of child abuse problems.

The more sophisticated approaches based on applied behavioural analysis appear to have an important contribution to make to therapeutic work with abusing families. This will require careful observation and analysis of the behaviour of both parents and children to help to understand what is happening in the home in which children have been abused. It is important too that this analysis be focused on the whole range of parenting behaviours and not restricted to an attempt to understand the abusing incident in isolation. A variety of methods to change the parenting behaviours are explored in the behavioural literature and child abuse is predominantly seen as a deficit in parenting skills. A variety of therapeutic approaches have been tried, including modelling and prompting appropriate parenting behaviours, feedback and re-inforcement for parents, systematic desensitization and teaching facts about child development. As yet relatively few families in which children are identified as 'at risk' are receiving the sort of help that has been described in the behavioural literature and it remains to be seen whether these approaches will fulfil their promise of generating effective methods of helping the many families in our society who are at risk of injuring their children.

REFERENCES

Appleton, P., Ramharry, P., Durant, B., Bundy, H. and Bewick, T. (1978). 'Group treatment for families having severe handling difficulties with a pre-school child'. *Occupational Therapy*, pp. 200–6.

Bandura, A. (1973). *Aggression: A Social Learning Analysis*. Prentice-Hall, Englewood Cliffs, N.J.

Bedford, A. (1978). 'Behaviour modification in child protective social work'. *Social Work Today*, *10*, pp. 27–8.

Carver, V. (1978). 'The behavioural approach to child abuse'. In: Carver (Ed.) *Child Abuse: A Study Text*. The Open University Press, Milton Keynes.

Doctor, R.M. and Singer E.M. (1978) 'Behavioural intervention strategies with child abuse parents: a home intervention program.' *Child Abuse and Neglect*, *2*, 57–68.

Dubanoski, R.A., Evans, I.M. and Higuchi, A.A. (1978). 'Analysis and treatment of child abuse: a set of behavioural propositions'. *Child Abuse and Neglect*, *2*, pp. 153–72.

Frude, N. and Goss, A. (1979) 'Parental anger: a general population survey'. *Child Abuse and Neglect*, *3*, pp. 331–3.

Gilbert, M.T. (1977). 'The developing role of the nurse therapist: child abuse', *Nursing Mirror*, *144*, pp. 50–1.

Holmes, S.A. , Barnhart, C., Cantoni, L. and Reymer, E. (1975). 'Working with the parent in child abuse cases'. *Social Casework*, *56*, pp. 3–12.

Hutchings, J. and Hughes, N. (1979). 'Child Abuse'. *Journal of Community Nursing*, *2*, pp. 14–15.

Hutchings, J. and Jones, R. (1979). 'Child Abuse and Parenting Skills'. Paper given at the MIND Annual Conference October 1979. To be published in the 'Proceedings of the MIND 1979 Annual Conference'.

Hutchings, J., Jones, R. and Hughes, N. (1979) 'Child Abuse'. Paper given at the B.A.B.P. Annual Conference, Bangor, June.

Jeffery, M. (1976) 'Practical ways to change parent-child interaction in families of children at risk'. In R.E. Helfer and C.H. Kempe (Eds.) *Child Abuse and Neglect*, Ballinger, Cambridge, Mass.

Lazarus, A.A. (1973) 'Multimodal behaviour therapy: treating the "Basic Id"'. *Journal of Nervous & Mental Disease 156*, pp. 404–11.

McAuley, R. and McAuley, P. (1977) 'Delinquency and non-accidental injury: some aspects of aetiology and management'. In: R. McAuley and P. McAuley (Eds.) *Child Behaviour Problems: An Empirical Approach to Child Management*. Macmillan, London.

Meichenbaum, D.H. (1977) *Cognitive-Behaviour Modification*. Plenum, New York.

Newson, J. and Newson, E. (1968) *Four Years Old in an Urban Community*. Allen & Unwin, London.

Patterson, G.R., Cobb, J.A. and Ray, R.S. (1973) 'A social engineering technology for retraining the families of aggressive boys'. In: H.E. Adams, I.P. Unikel (Eds.). *Issues and Trends in Behaviour Therapy*. C.C. Thomas, Springfield, Illinois.

Patterson, G.R., Ray, R.S., Shaw, D.A. and Cobb, J.A. (1969) *A Manual for Coding Family Interactions*. Microfiche publications. New York.

Petts, A. and Geddes, R. (1978) 'Using behavioural techniques in child management'. *Social Work Today, 10*, pp. 13–16.

Phillips, E.L., Phillips, A.E., Fixen, D.L. and Wolf, M.M. (1973) *The Teaching Family Handbook*. Research Press, Champaign, Illinois.

Polakow, R.L. and Peabody, D.L. (1975) 'Behavioural treatment of child abuse'. *International Journal of Offender Therapy and Comparative Criminology, 19*, pp. 100–3.

Reavley, W. and Gilbert, M.T. (1978) 'The behavioural treatment approach to potential child abuse – two illustrative cases', *Social Work Today, 7*, pp. 166–8. Reprinted in C.M. Lee (Ed.) *Child Abuse: A Reader and Sourcebook* (1978) The Open University Press, Milton Keynes.

Sanders, R.W. (1978) 'Systematic desensitization in the treatment of child abuse'. *Am.J.Psychiat, 135*, pp. 483–4.

Sandford, D.A. and Tustin, R.D. (1973) 'Behavioural treatment of parental assault on a child'. *New Zealand Psychologist, 2*, pp. 76–82.

Sandler, J., Van Dercar, C. and Milhoan, M. (1978) 'Training child abusers in the use of positive reinforcement practices'. *Behav. Res. and Therapy, 16*, pp. 169–75.

Schwartz, A. and Goldiamond, I. (1975) *Social Casework: A Behavioural Approach*. Columbia University Press.

Shearer, M. and Shearer, D.E. (1972) 'The Portage Project; a model for early childhood education'. *Exceptional Children, 36*, pp. 210–17.

Tharp, R.G. and Wetzel, R.J. (1969) *Behaviour Modification in the Natural Environment*. Academic Press, New York.

Tracey, J.J. and Clark, E.H. (1974) 'Treatment for child abusers', *Social Work, 19*, pp. 338–42.

13   Training Social Workers to use Behaviour Therapy with Abusing Parents

William Reavley and Gary Griffiths

This chapter looks at the value of formal behaviour therapy training for Local Authority Social Workers, particularly in relation to child abuse. An outline of a particular social worker's training experience is given and this is then followed by a case history which illustrates how he was able to employ what had been learned. We conclude with some observations on the selection and training of social workers for behaviour therapy.

In recent years social workers have shown an increasing interest in behaviour therapy and this is reflected in the growing number of relevant books written with social workers in mind (Jehu, 1972; Herbert, 1978). There are probably many reasons for this growth of interest (Hudson 1976), but prominent amongst them is disillusion with the traditional casework approach with 'difficult' cases and with multi-faceted problems such as child abuse.

After the abused child has been identified social workers carry the main responsibility both for the organization and delivery of help to the abusing parent and for the protection of the abused child. Emphasis has generally been laid on protecting the child through surveillance and elaborate procedures have emerged to safeguard the interests of children deemed to be 'at risk'. While these procedures may often have helped to protect the child they have not generated strategies or ideas of how the social worker might begin to help his child-abusing clients. However, recent reports of the use of a behaviour-therapy approach with child abuse cases (Petts and Geddes, 1978; Reavley & Gilbert, 1975) have offered a new approach which does focus on providing such help, and it seems that this has attracted the interest of many social workers.

The Training Experience

Members of a hospital Psychology Department were involved in teaching a psychology component of a course leading towards the Certificate in Social Work. This included a seminar on the behavioural treatment of child abuse and one trainee (GG), having attended this, requested a placement with the department in order to learn something of the approach at first hand. A course was already provided by the department for training Registered Mental Nurses in the techniques of behaviour therapy and since the lectures and seminars associated with this coincided with the social worker's eight-week placement he was invited to attend these and also to join in weekly discussions of journal papers and case presentations. On the basis of the former experience with nurses in training it was anticipated that with the addition of directed reading and discussions with therapists about on-going cases this programme would provide adequate theoretical input.

It has been our experience that a working knowledge of the techniques of behaviour therapy and sufficient theoretical knowledge to use these effectively can be taught within a relatively short period of time. It can, however, take considerably longer for the student to acquire the ability to carry out a behavioural analysis of the patient's problems. The skills involved in the use of measurement in planning, monitoring and evaluation may also require some time for development. Traditionally social work training is of a 'dynamic' orientation, leading to a view of patients and their problems and symptoms which is quite at odds with the behaviour-therapy approach. To help re-orientate the social worker and to lay the foundations for training we asked him to read two articles on behavioural analysis before he joined us (Kanfer & Saslow, 1965; Lazarus, 1973). As the social worker was familiar with and favoured the task-centred casework approach he was readily able to understand and accept the concepts and approaches discussed in these papers.

During the placement the trainee was able to observe and take part in the treatment of a wide range of problems and he developed a familiarity with a variety of behavioural treatments including systematic desensitization, real-life exposure, participant modelling, contract therapy, behavioural rehearsal, anxiety management, self-control procedures and social skills training. At the beginning of the placement he watched several video-tapes of interviews and therapy and he then began to observe live treatment sessions and to participate in them. After three weeks he had 'graduated' to co-therapist status and then worked in this capacity with a child abuse case, a case of marital difficulties and sexual dysfunction, a complex 'family problems' case and with three patients with agoraphobic difficulties. Additional indirect opportunities for learning were provided when the trainee sat in regularly on supervision sessions with trainee Nurse Therapists. On these occasions the trainee therapists presented their behavioural analyses and the progress of their on-going cases and they discussed the measures which they were using to identify changes in their patients' problems.

Thus the social worker was exposed to a wide range of training opportunities and he was able to judge for himself the value of the experience which he gained during the various components of the programme. This will be discussed after the presentation of a case history account of how he was able, after this brief and rather limited training, to use the behavioural approach with a child abuse case within the context of his role as a Local Authority Social Worker.

Case History

The family was referred by the GP (through the Health Visitor) when an hysterical Mrs Y presented herself at the surgery demanding to be rid of her 21-month-old son, John, with whom she could no longer cope. John was the first child and following his birth Mrs Y experienced a mild puerperal depression which led to marital difficulties and a short separation from her husband. A second child was born 17 months after the birth of John. The baby had a cleft palate and presented feeding difficulties which consumed much of Mrs Y's time and energy. However, she appeared to respond well to this child and described him as fairly placid.

Following Mrs Y's request for John to be removed from her care a careful examination of the family history revealed that John had been admitted to hospital at one year with a fractured skull. The cause had not been determined. The mother described him as uncontrollable and stated that when he was upset he screamed and would hold his breath, roll his eyes and turn blue. It became clear that the problems of the new baby left Mrs Y with depleted energy reserves which led to an almost complete breakdown in her relationship with John.

The response of the GP was to place both Mrs Y and John on tranquillizers, and to refer the matter to the social services, who in turn placed John on the 'at risk' register and offered intense social work involvement. The focus was on Mrs Y's inability to cope with John, and strategies were implemented which, in retrospect, may be seen as possibly reinforcing her feelings of inadequacy. For example, a family aid was introduced into the home to offer advice and practical support and at one stage five-days-a-week care was provided for John. The problems continued and at one point Mrs Y abandoned John at the local hospital. They were reunited following immediate social work intervention. The health visitor then reported incidents of hitting. By now Mrs Y had developed a dependency upon a whole network of people including a social worker, health visitor, play-group leader, day-care minder, the GP and the family aid.

She demanded that the family aid be removed and replaced by

another. Clearly there were tensions developing with respect to the help being given. Both Mr and Mrs Y exhibited ambivalent feelings in relation to agency involvement, seeming to need the support but at the same time hating the fact that their own deficiencies were being highlighted. Mother now requested full care of John. Day care was terminated and the family aid was also withdrawn at a predetermined time but no noticeable improvements seemed to follow this strategy. Mr Y in particular now developed a marked antipathy to the attitudes of social workers and often complained about the lack of concrete help. During a period of two years from the referral date the family had had three different social workers. Each of these in turn experienced a good deal of unpredictable behaviour on the part of Mrs Y and during this period the 'risk factor' was considered to be high.

The behavioural approach to the problems of the family was first implemented when John was four years old. The difficulties of the family were identified as specifically as possible and following discussions and observations three main problems were seen to be present:
a) John's disruptive and demanding behaviour,
b) tension on the part of Mrs Y, and
c) marital conflict.

The nature of these problems was explored and it became possible to identify the conditions influencing them. The major emphasis was on the contemporary situation rather than on historical events. Mrs Y's high states of tension, for example, were seen to be a result of both physical and emotional factors. Tension could be expected during the immediate pre-menstrual period, and a link was established between Mrs Y's moods and the state of her relationship with her mother who lived locally and whom Mrs Y visited almost daily. This in turn added to the marital difficulties because Mr Y and his mother-in-law had never enjoyed a good relationship. The daily visits to mother contributed to a lack of interest in the material standards of the home on Mrs Y's part, and this in turn led to considerable criticism and conflict. Additional factors maintaining the marital problem were also identified. It emerged that Mr and Mrs Y led rather separate social lives and did not share pleasures. The various problems did, of course, overlap and Mrs Y's handling of John did itself create considerable conflict in the marriage.

As a result of this analysis specific contracts were made with the couple. These included a reduction in the frequency of Mrs Y's visits to her mother, increased involvement with household tasks both by Mr and Mrs Y, a fixed minimal degree of shared social life ('at least one evening a week') and a relaxation programme to be practised by the couple together during the pre-menstrual period. Both parents accepted that John's difficult behaviour, which provoked the situations of risk of injury, were maintained or reinforced by mishandling on the part of Mrs Y. Tantrums were seen as the method which John employed, often effectively, to achieve his aims, and the 'time out' technique of separating him for a fixed time-period was suggested. Mrs Y was later able to report that this technique had been employed with modest success.

It was felt that John needed firmer but calmer handling by his mother. Her tendency, for example, to raise her voice to combat John's was seen as introducing an element of competition into the interaction. Mrs Y consequently agreed to practice lowering her voice during disagreements. Much discussion centred on the use of the physical punishment and slapping which had become almost habitual on Mrs Y's part. Both parents held a basic belief in the value and justice of corporal punishment but Mrs Y exercised little discrimination in her use of such discipline. Every misdemeanour was seen as worthy of physical punishment and John was smacked frequently during the course of the day. Mrs Y did acknowledge that slapping frequently induced a worsening of the behaviour and both parents accepted that it seldom achieved the desired aim.

Alternative methods of punishment were considered and it was decided that 'time out' and deprivation of television viewing would be particularly effective. A programme involving these methods was therefore instituted. It appeared that two aspects of John's behaviour were particularly problematical. The first of these was that John persistently wet his trousers during the day. He would not request the toilet or potty and his trousers needed to be changed on average four times a day. The second problem was John's refusal to eat his meals. This led to tantrums and created an atmosphere in which it was impossible to have an enjoyable family meal. When the health visitor and GP had been approached on these difficulties Mrs Y had been told that the wetting was something that John would 'grow out of' in due course.

We decided to institute a system in which good behaviour was rewarded and in which bad behaviour resulted in the withdrawal of rewards. 'Good behaviour' here meant requesting the potty or toilet or eating at least a little of everything on the plate. John's parents had been in the habit of distributing vast quantities of sweets but these had not been given to John as a reward and, unfortunately, he always demanded more. It was agreed that this practice should be ended and that sweets would now be given as rewards and contingent on the performance of 'good behaviour'. The quantities of food placed on John's plate were also reduced in order to make the task less formidable. The programme was instigated for a period of two weeks and it was hoped that during this time a behavioural change would be established in respect of the two problems.

One week later dramatic improvements were reported for both problems. Mrs Y reported that whereas before John would have wet his trousers many times each day he had wet them only twice during the whole of the first week of treatment, and from refusing to eat anything he was now eating 'everything'. Similar reports of success were obtained again at the end of the second week and both parents now agreed that these two problems no longer existed. And they had not re-emerged at follow-up, six months later. This programme had been the therapist's first attempt to design and carry out a treatment by himself and, in retrospect, it can be criticized methodologically in that few objective and systematic measurements were obtained of the problem behaviours involved.

The general picture which emerged, however, is one of considerable success and, as is often the case with such treatments, there were additional benefits resulting from the reduction of the principal target problems. Mrs Y has learned new ways in which to cope with John's difficult behaviour and her degree of self confidence increased as a result. At the follow-up stage both parents reported less marital conflict, improved mutual social life and a greater general enjoyment of family life. Material and hygiene standards in the home had also noticeably improved and Mrs Y was visiting her mother no more than twice a week.

Towards a Formal Training Programme

Based on our experience as trainer and trainee we have now developed an outline training programme for training social workers in behaviour therapy. Drawing upon the syllabus of the Joint Board of Clinical Nursing Studies (JBCNS Course 650) the main skills and knowledge which a behaviour therapist needs to have available are seen to include the following:
1) Skills at interviewing patients and family members
2) Ability to carry out a detailed behavioural analysis of the patient's problems
3) Ability to formulate specific treatment goals and to discuss these with the patient
4) Knowledge of the methods of behavioural treatment
5) Ability to organize, co-ordinate and apply treatment methods, and
6) Knowledge of appropriate measurement techniques and the ability to apply these for the purposes of monitoring treatment and evaluating outcome.

Professional social workers can in fact be expected to have covered various sections of the above list in their basic training. Most social work courses today include lectures or courses about general psychology, learning theory and psychopathology and considerable attention may also have been given to the acquisition of skills involved in effective interaction with clients. These skills might include interviewing, information gathering, rapport building and the organization of therapeutic interventions. The amount and quality of such training, however, will be variable.

Thus the problem facing those involved with training for behaviour therapy is to complement the existing strengths and to increase all elements to an appropriate level of competence. In the immediate future it is perhaps likely that much training will be on an individual basis. Where this is the case then perhaps an adaptation of the behaviour therapy approach (in terms of 'building up a desirable repertoire of skills') may be useful in helping the trainer and trainee to prepare a programme to fit the training needs. Thus in the initial baseline analysis the relevant assets and deficiencies of the trainee may be assessed. Suitable measurable targets may then be agreed and, after a consideration of the resources available, strategies may be planned to help achieve these ends, and appropriate measures devised to monitor the success or otherwise of the enterprise.

Selection of trainees

In connection with the initial behavioural analysis attention needs to be paid to the selection of trainees in terms of attitudes compatible with the behaviour therapy approach. Social attitudes have been shown to be related to treatment orientation and preferences (Pallis & Stoffelmayr, 1975) and to discriminate between therapists with organic, sociotherapeutic and psychotherapeutic orientations. While training undoubtedly exerts some influence over attitudes (Caine & Smail, 1969) it is probably most efficient, in view of the likely limitations on resources available for training, to select candidates with attitudes already generally favourable to the behaviour therapy approach. Sympathy towards and familiarity with task-centred casework also seems to indicate attitudes compatible with the behavioural approach, and may well accelerate and facilitate training in behavioural analysis and therapy.

Style of training

Having identified the 'what' of training the problem remains of 'how' this can best be delivered. The training that most behaviour therapists receive is a mixture of theory and practice and this is the style of training that we favour – essentially an apprenticeship. In the training programme outlined at the beginning of this chapter a variety of procedures was used and when training had been completed the trainee was invited to rank-order the value of the various training components. This produced the following ordered list:

1) Working as co-therapist
2) Exposure to case presentations
3) Attendance at lectures and seminars
4) Directed reading
5) Viewing video-tapes of treatment sessions
6) Discussing with supervisors
7) Watching films, and
8) Discussing informally with other therapists.

The ordering here is almost identical with that of listings given by nurses at the end of their courses on behaviour therapy.

Conclusion

Behaviour therapy is not the exclusive province of any one professional group. Registered Mental Nurses are currently being trained in behaviour therapy at three centres in England (there are JBCNS approved courses at Graylingwell, the Maudsley and Moorhaven Hospitals). They can be effective therapists with a wide range of adult psychiatric problems (Marks et al., 1977) and particularly with child abuse cases (Gilbert, 1977). Social workers are in the front line with regard to child abuse and are showing an increasing interest in gaining knowledge and experience of behaviour therapy to help abusing parents and clients with other problems. They have the potential to be effective behaviour therapists, but what they lack at present are the training opportunities. Many Departments of Clinical Psychology will have the expertise to offer this training, and working with social workers in this venture will also provide the psychologists involved with opportunities for the kind of community-oriented work which many of them would very much welcome.

REFERENCES

Caine, T.M. and Smail, D.J. (1969) 'The effect of personality and training on attitudes to treatment: preliminary investigations'. *British Journal of Medical Psychology*, 42, pp. 277–82.

Gilbert, M.T. (1977) 'Behavioural approach to the treatment of child abuse'. *Nursing Times*, 72, pp. 140–3.

Herbert, M. (1978) *Conduct Disorders of Childhood and Adolescence*. Wiley, Chichester.

Hudson, B.L. (1976) 'Behavioural social work in a community psychiatric service'. In: M.R. Olsen (Ed.) *Differential Approaches in Social Work with the Mentally*

Disordered. B.A.S.W., London.

Jehu, D., Hardikers, P., Yelloly, M. and Shaw, M. (1972) *Behaviour Modification in Social Work*. Wiley, Chichester.

Kanfer, F.H. and Saslow, G. (1965) 'Behavioural analysis: an alternative to diagnostic classification'. *Archives of General Psychiatry, 12*, pp. 529–38.

Lazarus, A.A. (1973) 'Multimodal behaviour therapy treating the "Basic Id"', *Journal of Nervous and Mental Disease, 156*, pp. 404–11.

Marks, I.M., Hallam, R.S., Connelly, J. and Phillpott, R. (1977) *Nursing in Behavioural Psychotherapy*, Royal College of Nursing, London.

Pallis, D.J. and Stoffelmayr, B.E. (1973) 'Social attitudes and treatment orientation among psychiatrists'. *British Journal of Medical Psychology, 46*, pp. 75–81.

Petts, A. and Geddes, R. (1978) 'Using behavioural techniques in child management'. *Social Work Today, 10*, pp. 13–16.

Reavley, W. and Gilbert, M.T. (1976) 'The behavioural treatment approach to potential child abuse'. *Social Work Today, 7*, pp. 166–8.

Towards Prediction
and Prevention

14   Towards the Prediction of Child Abuse*

Mia Kellmer Pringle

How many children in this country are seriously ill-treated by their parents (or permanent substitutes), physically, psychologically or both? How many are permanently maimed or killed as a consequence of such abuse? That the answers to these questions are not at present known with any degree of certainty is itself quite significant because to a considerable extent it reflects common attitudes to this problem. They are a mixture of revulsion, disbelief and plain ignorance. There is repugnance or sheer disbelief, not only among the general public but some professional workers too, that a parent could kill his or her own child; for example, 'many courts in the United Kingdom have only just begun to believe that child abuse truly exists' (Kempe, 1978). Ignorance extends even to doctors, who are either unaware of the syndrome or avoid confrontation by ascribing death to an associated existing clinical entity (Howells, 1975).

Another reason why the extent of the problem is not known is because parents (and others) do not always kill their children in easily ascertainable ways which can be identified by pathologists and classified into accidental and non-accidental categories. Thus some of the causes of death given in the Registrar General's statistics for England and Wales may not be as innocent as the designation implies. Examples are deaths from pneumonia or bronchitis in infants who have failed to thrive because of physical or emotional neglect; poisonings (Rogers et al. 1976); suffocation caused by pressing a hand or pillow against a baby's face; deaths following intracerebal and subdural haemorrhages after shaking; and deaths from a multiplicity of causes among severely sub-normal children whose handicap itself originated from a battering months or years previously (Oliver, 1975; Buchanan and Oliver, 1977).

There are two common misconceptions. One is that we are all potential batterers and that the main causes are depression and poverty. In fact, most parents who violently assault their children are young, immature, ill-educated, disorganized and aggressive; many of

---

* This and the following chapter reflect the author's views and do not necessarily represent those of the National Children's Bureau.

the fathers involved have criminal records. Their incomes are similar to those of non-battering families, but they organize their finances badly (Smith, 1975).

The other misconception is that child abuse is very rare. In fact, at a conservative estimate some 8,000 children suffer 'non-accidental injuries' every year and about 110 babies are battered to death; in addition, every day one infant under a year old is brain-damaged as a result of parental violence, some becoming blind or paralyzed for the rest of their lives. Moreover, all those who have made a special study of the problem are now agreed that these are only the tip of an iceberg since reported cases represent only a fraction of the total (Cooper, 1978; Kempe, 1978). Thousands more grow up maladjusted and severely disturbed because they have been emotionally neglected, rejected and abused.

Psychological Consequences of Abuse

Remarkably little attention has so far been paid to the likely psychological consequences of child abuse compared with the considerable and still expanding literature on the problems and needs of their parents. The same discrepancy is evident between the emphasis on supporting and treating the violent and abusing adult on the one hand and, on the other hand, the almost total lack of support and treatment services for the child victim – except for the physical injuries.

Similarly, there is a great volume of research on the parents' socio-economic background, health, personality, marital and personal history (Jobling, 1976). In contrast, scant attention has been given to the emotional, social and intellectual effects on children of being subjected to parental violence, or of growing up rejected and ill-treated, even though not to the point of maiming or death. This apparent lack of concern for the psychological consequences is mirrored too in all the official reports of Committees of Inquiry into fatal cases, starting with Maria Colwell in 1974 right to the present day. None of them even refer to likely emotional damage arising from physical abuse. Yet this must surely have been evident in most cases long before the final tragedy? (DHSS, 1974; DHSS, 1975a; 1975b; Lambeth et al. 1975; Norfolk, 1976).

It was undoubtedly so in the case of six-year-old Maria Colwell. Within a period of 15 months she changed from being a happy, responsive, well-behaved, attractive little girl, who was making good progress at school and getting on well with other children, to becoming withdrawn, solitary, depressed, unable to communicate, sitting for hours staring into space, and not responding to children or adults. She began wetting and soiling her bed, shunned other children and her school work deteriorated markedly. Indeed, the descriptions of her behaviour shortly before she was killed by her step-father indicated clearly that she was in a state of severe shock, depression and deep mourning for the 'parents' she had lost – namely, the foster parents with whom she had lived practically all her life.

But it was not only that her appearance and behaviour deteriorated rapidly after she was made to leave her foster home. When in preparation for the move she was taken to spend days and then weekends in her mother's home, Maria clearly showed her dislike and fear of these visits by the most strenuous protests, both verbally and physically. She began to show stress symptoms, such as biting her nails, being unable to go to sleep and was, in fact, prescribed a 'nerve tonic' by her doctor. When made to stay overnight at her mother's home, she ran away half-dressed and barefoot on several occasions.

Thus from the outset, Maria displayed unmistakable signs of great psychological strain and unhappiness – signs which required hardly any psychological or psychiatric skill to interpret. And a minimal knowledge of normal child development is sufficient to appreciate that running away in the middle of the night is a sign of real desperation and terror in a six-year-old.

The treatment subsequently meted out to her by both her mother and stepfather – exploitation, under-nourishment, imprisonment and violence – destroyed her not only physically but emotionally too. Yet apparently none of those professionally concerned – teachers, social workers, health visitors and doctors – considered her to be in need of psychological support or treatment, and even during the enquiry into her death no reference was made to the psychological warning signs which should have been heeded as much as the physical symptoms of her suffering (DHSS, 1974).

Among abused infants, behavioural indicators may not be as dramatic or clear cut as physical injury, and hence are more difficult to explore. Nevertheless, experienced paediatricians and psychologists can determine whether developmental progress is normal or gives cause for concern, calling for closer enquiry. Unless there is a recognized, diagnosed physical cause, all 'non-thriving' children should be given a comprehensive psycho-social assessment which should include an elucidation of how the child himself sees his family. It is possible to obtain this picture at a very much younger age than is sometimes realized, even by some professionals. In addition to systematically observing the infant's behaviour, play and capacity for making relationships with friendly adults, a range of more structured instruments for assessing personality is available (Bene & Anthony, 1957; Geddis et al., 1977; Howells & Lickorish, 1962; Jackson,

1952; Pickford, 1963).

It remains a matter for conjecture and disquiet why the importance and relevance of the psychological consequences of abuse should have remained a largely ignored issue, not only as early warning signals but also later on as criteria indicating whether or not a child should be returned to its previously abusing home. Similarly overlooked have been the likely psychological effects on the siblings of observing and living with the daily reality of a brother or sister being neglected, rejected or abused, whether physically, emotionally, or both. One would suspect these to be deeply disturbing and hence at least as deserving of treatment as the adult perpetrators.

Another largely unexplored area is that of the long-term consequences of child abuse. The few available follow-up studies indicate severe and lasting disturbance and malfunctioning, even when there is no further physical ill-treatment (Oliver & Cox, 1973; Martin & Beezley, 1977; Strauss & Girodet, 1977; Jones, 1978). Hence even from the point of view of cost effectiveness – let alone the equally if not more important humane considerations – it is vital to work towards developing more adequate methods of prediction and prevention.

The possibility of prediction

Prediction will require complex, multi-dimensional and in-depth methods since abusing parents are unlikely to be a homogeneous group, either regarding their personalities or their social background; nor is there likely to be one set of common causal factors or predisposing conditions which bring about their behaviour. Failure to differentiate between all these may well account for the rather confused body of research findings. There are at least four different approaches to prediction which are not mutually exclusive: the first is to distinguish, as far as present knowledge permits, between the different motives of parents who violently assault their children; the second is to consider the likely long-term psychological effects of abuse on children which in turn will make them more liable as adults to become abusing parents themselves; the third approach is to explore how early it is possible to detect danger signals that a baby's future safety and well-being may be 'at risk'; and the fourth is to examine the availability of check lists systematizing the insight and knowledge obtained from the first three approaches.

Patterns of parental violence

As I see it, there are several sets of circumstances which may lead to a child being seriously abused. There is the isolated incident which is unlikely to be repeated. In this category is the mother or father who has no previous history of violence, who has coped adequately with the stresses and strains of everyday life, and who may have brought up other children quite well. Then some disaster strikes or there is an accumulation of stressful events which lead to a sudden outburst of anger in which a hitherto well-cared for and loved child is injured, followed by shame and remorse. Such a violent incident could not have been predicted, nor is its recurrence likely since it is quite out of character.

Another pattern represents a persisting and potentially dangerous parental attitude, namely where one child is singled out for ill-treatment. Reasons for such 'scapegoating' include the child who is a pre-marital or extra-marital 'mistake', or who reminds the mother of a despised husband or a hated relative, or the child who is felt to be in some way 'different' from the other children. This difference may be due to a difficult delivery or to prematurity or to early 'bonding failure'; or the baby may have some physical or mental handicap with which the parent cannot come to terms. The rejection and ill-treatment in such cases are child-specific, and hence none of the siblings are at a similar risk. Recurrence is likely unless the mother is able and willing to work through her hostility with psychiatric help. If instead she chooses to relinquish the child, she should be supported through this course of action.

Probably a more numerous group liable to neglect and ill-treat their children are inadequate parents. They include teenage couples who additionally may be immature even for their ages; those of limited abilities who themselves have often been neglected, if not ill-treated, in childhood; and those who have grown up in institutional care. Such parents often lack knowledge of normal child development. For example, they do not understand that a baby is unable to stop soiling or wetting until he has reached the necessary stage of physical maturity, or that a terrified infant may fail to acquire sphincter and bowel control just because he is terrified.

Environmental pressures, such as inadequate housing, poverty, and too many or too closely spaced pregnancies, may further add to the parents' inability to cope. Often too the child has been neither planned nor wanted and, even more crucial, may remain unwanted. All these features are chronic and so neither quick nor profound change can realistically be expected. Therefore the children inevitably remain at risk unless frequent, continuous and long-term support services can be given, including intensive training in home-making and child-rearing skills. The outlook even then is not always hopeful.

Violence as a way of life characterizes a group of parents who can

207

be predicted to constitute the greatest risk to their children's safety. Their habitually violent behaviour is directed not only towards their offspring but also towards each other, as well as their neighbours, relatives and workmates. Among them are found the psychopath who lashes out indiscriminately; the mentally ill, including the delusional schizophrenic; the pathologically authoritarian parent, more often male, who continually punishes a child for failing to come up to his unrealistically high demands; and the sadistic pervert who gains satisfaction from the suffering of the weak and helpless.

Probably most, if not all such parents, were themselves damaged in childhood through an uncaring or violent upbringing. So parental hostility perpetuates itself from one generation to another in what is quite literally a very vicious circle. Thus, to allow a child to remain or return to such a home perpetuates the pattern of violence in the long term. In the short term it puts even the child's physical welfare at risk. There is no reliable way to ensure his safety since there is no known effective and quick enough treatment which will modify the behaviour of adults for whom violence is a way of life.

Predicting the long-term effects of abuse as being self-perpetuating

Since there is as yet inadequate research evidence, I shall consider the likely effects of child abuse on long-term development in the light of what is known about the needs of children (Pringle, 1975 and 1978). To begin with, an abused child's sense of security and of being valued is bound to become undermined, if indeed it has ever been established. When rejection and ill-treatment are intermittent, then he or she lives in a state of constant uncertainty, never knowing what to expect; these may be the children whose attitude has been described as one of 'frozen watchfulness'. When abuse is continuous, then either submission or anger will become the typical reaction.

The child who submits is likely to develop a 'victim' mentality, attempting to appease, to ingratiate himself, even clinging to the abusing parent; or he may withdraw, trying to become inconspicuous, but remaining chronically apprehensive. On the other hand, the child who responds with anger and defiance is liable to provoke a battle of wills, making the abusing adult determined 'to show who is master'. Since a child cannot be 'made' to do anything – be it to keep down food, stop crying or go to sleep – and since the immature, violent parent finds his own impotence unacceptable, a headlong clash is as inevitable as its tragic outcome.

The ill-treated baby is in an even more desperate plight than the young child because he is as yet physically incapable of responding to force and pain in one or other of the natural ways, namely, either fight or flight: he can no more hit back than run away. Hence, ill-treatment may well arouse helpless rage and hate, which will then be carried into adult life to become the smouldering anger of the wife or child batterer (Pizzey, 1974); or the equivalent of Harlow's (1969) female monkeys, 'hopeless, helpless and heartless mothers' who either ignore or brutally abuse their offspring.

A preliminary study of wife battering concludes that 'fear must be expressed for the 315 children of the 100 women reported, as many males are developing the prodromal signs of violence while the older age groups manifest a disturbing picture of uncontrolled violence and conflict with the law. Unless an urgent retraining programme can be undertaken with these children a future generation will be subjected to family violence' (Gayford, 1975). This vicious circle of inter-generational neglect and violence has been confirmed by other evidence, which also shows that children from violent families not only tend to marry early but to have large families (Martin, 1976; Frommer & O'Shea, 1973b; Rutter & Madge, 1976). Then they in turn fail to provide love and security for their offspring, having been unloved and rejected in their own childhood.

Next, when the need for new experiences remains inadequately met, then intellectual potentialities as well as personal growth remain to some extent unrealized. In the infant, insufficient sensory stimulation can retard or even impair development, including later on the ability to think, reason and communicate. Since the great majority of neglected and ill-treated children come from socially and culturally deprived families, they would in any case be adversely affected by the relative lack of stimulation in such homes. However, their plight is likely to be worse. To begin with, the abused baby has to spend much of his time lying in his cot, lonely, uncomfortable and probably in pain; such conditions stifle exploration and curiosity and hence 'learning'.

Next, while trying to cope with new demands – such as to feed less messily, or to become dry and clean – he is bound to be slow and to make 'mistakes' just because he is immature and a beginner. He will then be meted out punishment for what is seen by the inadequate or violent parent as defiance or lack of love. The resulting anxiety and fear will inevitably retard or inhibit adequate learning. And so the infant is caught in an unending spiral of unrealistic demands, failure to improve and consequent punishment.

If brain damage results, then, of course, improvement becomes even less possible, the more so the more severe the impairment. Once he becomes a mobile toddler, who naturally wants to explore his surroundings, his 'being into everything' is also likely to arouse parental anger, as will his normal attempts to assert his own will.

Thus his striving towards knowledge and independence will be stifled through fear and punishment. Hence it is not unexpected that follow-up studies of abused children report their development to be retarded, both in the neuro-motor and intellectual fields, as well as in the acquisition of language skills (Martin & Beezley, 1977; Strauss & Girodet, 1977).

Turning now to the need for praise and recognition, when this is inadequately met, then in the long term the effects are destructive of self-respect and of confidence in tackling new situations, tasks and relationships. There can be little doubt that the abused child will be among the most serious under-achievers since – almost by definition – he is under-valued and rejected. Even ability and talent well above average may never declare themselves if adequate nurture and emotional support are lacking (Pringle, 1970). Rather than calling out compassion, his backwardness and under-functioning themselves compound his plight by apparently justifying parental punishment. Thus their rejection carries the seeds of his continued failure to come up to their expectations and so it becomes inexorably a self-fulfilling prophecy.

Lastly, with regard to the need for responsiblity, the abused child is likely all too often to suffer simultaneously from being given both too little and too much responsibility. On the one hand, he may be deprived of toys over which he can exercise exclusive rights; he may be denied sufficient practice to learn to feed and dress himself because he is considered to be too slow and clumsy; and he may also lack opportunities of acquiring the responsibility of give-and-take in the company of other children. On the other hand, he may far too early be left to fend for himself; also he, or perhaps more often she, may be made into a household drudge. In any case, the child will all too often be punished for what is seen as unhelpful or irresponsible behaviour. Yet he has little chance to improve upon past performance because of being denied the relaxed and unhurried practice of those very skills which would enable him in time to act responsibly. So the basis is laid for later avoidance of responsibility.

In summary, a consideration of the likely long-term psychological effects of abuse strongly suggests that it will to a greater or lesser extent impair emotional, social and intellectual development because a violent upbringing makes it impossible to meet a child's basic psychological needs. Hence, as an adult, he or she will be more liable to become an inadequate and probably abusing parent in turn.

How early is prediction possible?

Recent evidence suggests that prediction is possible before or soon after a baby's birth (Frommer & O'Shea, 1973a and 1973b; Lynch & Roberts, 1977; Wolkind, 1977; Cooper, 1978; Kempe, 1978). Several screening procedures have been developed which take into account such factors as the parents' own childhood experiences, their marital relationship, feelings about the pregnancy and expectations about their unborn child. For example, a series of danger signals has been identified in the delivery room, the most significant of which seemed to be a mother responding passively to her baby (i.e. not touching, holding or examining it); either parent reacting to it with hostility; neither of them looking into the baby's eyes; and not being affectionate towards each other. The observations made in the labour wards and delivery rooms were found to make over 76% correct predictions regarding successful or unsuccessful parenting (Kempe, 1978).

Another series of studies has been concerned with the development of the reciprocal relationship between mother and baby immediately after its birth and with the factors which promote mother-infant bonding (Ainsworth et al., 1974; Brazelton et al., 1974; Ringler et al., 1975; Klaus and Kennel, 1976; de Chateau and Wiberg, 1977 and 1978). These too provide persuasive evidence of the diagnostic importance of observing the earliest interactions between adult and child.

Check lists of characteristics common to abusing parents and to abused children

A wide range of early warning signals that a child may be at high risk of being abused is now available. However, there is no agreed range of predictors and the number suggested varies from study to study (from half a dozen to over 70). Preparing and using check lists, as well as keeping 'at risk' registers, are useful aids for professional workers in alerting them to those features which tend to characterize abusing parents and abused children. None can be regarded, however, as a substitute for a comprehensive and detailed assessment of each family and for an equally comprehensive developmental examination of each child.

Below some examples are given of check lists which set out a series of characteristics common to abusive parents and abused children.

I. *Characteristics Common to Abusive Parents (Steele, 1975)*
  1. Immature and dependent
  2. Social isolation
  3. Poor self-esteem
  4. Difficulty seeking or obtaining pleasure

     5. Distorted perceptions of the child, and often role-reversal
     6. Fear of spoiling the child
     7. Belief in the value of punishment
     8. Impaired ability to empathize with the child's needs and respond appropriately

II. *Factors Clearly Differentiating an Abused Group from a Control Group (Lynch & Roberts, 1978)*

     1. More abusing mothers were under 20 years when they had their first children: 50% compared with 16%.
     2. Abusing mothers were more likely to have signs of emotional disturbance recorded in the maternity notes: 46% compared with 14%.
     3. More abusing parents were referred to the maternity hospital social worker; 58% compared with 6%.
     4. The abused babies were more likely to have been admitted to the special care baby nursery: 42% compared with 10%.
     5. The abusing mothers more often evoked concern over their mothering capacity: 44% compared with 6%.

III. *Key Characteristics of Child Abuse (Hanson, McCulloch & Hartley, 1978)*

     1. *Parental characteristics*
     Mother under 20 years old at birth of first child
     Mother has psychiatric diagnosis of neuroticism
     Mother has high neuroticism score on Eysenck Personality Inventory
     Mother has psychiatric diagnosis of personality disorder
     Father has psychiatric diagnosis of personality disorder
     Mother has borderline or subnormal intelligence on a short form of the Wechsler Adult Intelligence Scale
     Father has a manual occupation
     Mother has criminal record
     Father has a criminal record
     Mother has a high General Health Questionnaire score
     Mother has an abnormal EEG
     Father has an abnormal EEG

     2. *Social characteristics of the families*
     Child's natural father absent from the home

Mother unmarried
Parents acquainted less than six months before marriage
Mother conceived pre-maritally
Mother considers the marriage unsatisfactory
Battered child illegitimate
Mother thinks her partner rejects the child
Mother says there is no discussion about child-rearing
Mother considers herself the decision-maker in the house
Child lacks his own room
Accommodation lacks one or more basic amenities
Mother rarely sees her parents
Mother rarely sees any relatives
Mother has no opportunities for breaks from child
Mother has no social activities
Mother has no friends
Mother considers her allowance inadequate
Mother is generally dissatisfied with her situation

3. *Interpersonal relations*
Mother was unhappy in childhood
Mother recalls two or more childhood neurotic symptoms
Mother thinks she was a poor scholar
Mother got on badly with her parents as a child
Mother's mother scolded her as a chief means of punishment
Mother gets on badly with her parents now
Mother had bad relations with siblings as a child
Mother gets on badly with siblings now
Father's mother was unreasonable in discipline
Father's father was unreasonable in discipline
Mother's mother was unreasonable in discipline
Mother's father was unreasonable in discipline
Mother has a high 'lie' score in the Eysenck Personality Inventory
Mother scores high on criticism of others, paranoid hostility and guilt on the hostility and direction of hostility questionnaire
Father scores high on guilt

213

4. *Child-rearing practices*

Mother is abnormal (very quick or very slow) in responsiveness to the child's crying

Mother becomes emotional over feeding problems

Mother is now very demonstrative towards the child

Mother is abnormal in her enjoyment of the child (says she finds no pleasure in him or he is 'her life')

Infrequent surveillance of child's well-being or whereabouts

Obedience expected at second or third request

Mother physically punishes frequently

Father physically punishes frequently

Mother withholds love as a punishment

Mother uses tangible rewards (pacifiers) for good behaviour

Crying in baby or clinging and whining in toddler a problem

Partner does not help mother with child as she would like

5. *The child*

Has a general developmental quotient of 90 or under on the Griffiths Scales of Mental Development

Physically neglected on admission to hospital

Has a history of failure to thrive

Mother says he is not wakeful (half hour plus) at night

Mother says he is not excitable or lively by day

Mother says he is not tired during the day

There is delay in bringing the child to hospital for attention to the injury

Had low birth weight

IV. *Factors in the Parents' History which Predict Risk Extremely Accurately (Kempe, 1978)*

1. As a child was the parent repeatedly beaten or deprived?
2. Does the parent have a record of mental illness or criminal activities?
3. Is the parent suspected of physical abuse in the past?
4. Is the parent suffering lost self-esteem, social isolation, or depression?

5. Has the parent experienced multiple stresses, such as marital discord, divorce, debt, frequent moves, significant losses?
6. Does the parent have violent outbursts of temper?
7. Does the parent have rigid, unrealistic expectations of the child's behaviour?
8. Does the parent punish the child harshly?
9. Does the parent see the child as difficult and provocative (whether or not the child is)?
10. Does the parent reject the child or have difficulty forming a bond with the child?

V. *Untreatable Families where Early Termination of Parental Rights is Indicated (Kempe, 1978)*
1. Cruel abusers who might torture their children slowly and repetitively
2. Psychotics whose children form part of their delusional systems or borderline psychotic patients not amenable to treatment
3. Aggressive sociopaths who might unpredictably and lethally strike out when angered
4. Fanatics, outwardly reasonable, respectable people with an encapsulated psychosis that could kill their children (such as a couple who believed their baby should live only on carrot juice, since all other food was poisonous)
5. Parents so addicted to alcohol or drugs that they cannot provide even minimal care for their babies
6. Parents too retarded or mothers simply too young to raise children
7. Families where other children have already been seriously injured, and where there may have been one or more unexplained deaths

VI. *High Risk Rating Check List (Greenland, 1979)*

Parents	*Child*
Previously having abused, neglected a child	Was previously abused or neglected
Age 24 years or less at birth of first child	Under five years of age at the time of abuse or neglect
Single-parent or	Premature or low birth-

215

separated
Partner not biological parent
History of abuse, neglect or deprivation
Socially isolated, frequent moves, poor housing
Poverty, unemployed or unskilled worker. Inadequate education
Abuses alcohol and/or drugs
History of criminal assaultive behaviour and/or suicide attempts
Pregnancy, post partum or chronic illness

weight
Now under-weight
Birth defect, chronic illness, developmental lag
Prolonged separation from mother
Cries frequently, difficult to comfort
Difficulties in feeding and elimination
Adopted, foster or step child

VII.   *Clinical Features in the Abused Child (Cooper, 1978)*

1. Physical injuries – non-accidental

   Bruises, weals, lacerations and scars
   Burns and scalds
   Bone and joint injuries
   Brain and eye injuries
   Internal injuries

2. Other clinical disorders

   Poisoning
   Drowning
   Cot deaths
   'Funny turns'
   Repeated problems with crying and feeding
   Overactivity and demanding behaviour
   Hysterical moods (in older children)

3. Failure to thrive without organic cause

4. Disordered behaviour (observed)

5. Sexual abuse

6. Abuse while in care

VIII. *Characteristics Commonly noted in Abused Children in addition to Developmental Delay (Martin & Beezley, 1977)*
1. Impaired capacity for enjoyment
2. Psychiatric symptoms, e.g. enuresis, restlessness and tantrums
3. Low self esteem
4. School learning problems
5. Withdrawal
6. Rebelliousness
7. Compulsivity
8. Hypervigilance
9. Pseudo-mature behaviour or role reversal

An examination of these various check lists shows a number of recurring features which appear to characterize families in which child abuse is more likely to occur. Ten of these seem to be most common, thus indicating that children in such circumstances are at a potentially greater risk than others. These can be summarized as follows:

1. One or both parents have, when young themselves, been subjected to violence
2. One or both parents have had an unhappy, disrupted and insecure childhood
3. One or both parents are addicted to drugs, alcohol, or are psychotic
4. There is a record of violence between the parents
5. Another child has already been abused, or suffered an unexplained death
6. The pregnancy was unwanted; the baby was rejected at birth or soon after
7. Failure of early bonding
8. Both parents are under 20 years of age, immature for their years and socially isolated
9. The family live in poor housing and on a low income
10. The family is suffering from multiple deprivation

REFERENCES
Ainsworth, M.D.S., Bell, S.M. and Stayton, D.J. (1974) 'Infant-mother attachment and social development: socialization as a product of reciprocal responsiveness to signals'. In: M.P.M. Richards (Ed.) *The Integration of a Child into a Social World.* Cambridge University Press.
Baher, E. *et al.* (1976) *At Risk: An Account of the Work of the Battered Child Research*

Department of the NSPCC, Routledge and Kegan Paul.

Bene, E., and Anthony, E.J. (1957) *Manual for the Family Relations Test*, Slough, National Foundation for Educational Research.

Brazelton, T.B., Koslowski, B. and Main, M. (1974) 'The origins of reciprocity in mother/infant interaction'. In: M. Lewis and A. Rosenblum (Eds.), *The Effect of the Infant on its Caregiver*, John Wiley and Sons.

Buchanan, A. and Oliver, J.E. (1977) 'Abuse and neglect as a cause of mental retardation', *B.J. Psychiatry*, 131, pp. 458–67.

Cameron, J.M. and Rae, L.J. (1975) *Atlas of the Battered Child Syndrome*, Churchill Livingstone.

Cooper, C. (1978) 'Child abuse and neglect – medical aspects'. In: Selwyn M. Smith (Ed.) *The Maltreatment of Children*, MTP Press Ltd.

De Chateau, P. and Wiberg, B. (1978) 'Long-term effects on mother-infant behaviour of extra contact during the first hour post-partum'. In: *Psychosomatic Medicine of Obstetrics and Gynaecology*, Basel, S. Karger.

De Chateau, P. and Wiberg, B. (1977) 'Long-term effects on mother-infant behaviour of extra contact during the first hour post-partum'.
1. First observation at 36 hours. *Acta Paediatr.Scand.* 66, 137.
2. A follow-up at three months. *Acta Paediatr.Scand.* 66, 145.

Department of Health and Social Security (1975a) *Report of the Committee of Inquiry into the Provision and Co-ordination of Services to the Family of John George Auckland*, HMSO.

Department of Health and Social Security (1975b) *Non-accidental Injury to Children. Proceedings of a Conference held in June 1974*, HMSO.

Department of Health and Social Security (1974) *Report of the Committee of Inquiry into the Care and Supervision provided in relation to Maria Colwell*, HMSO.

Frommer, E.A. and O'Shea, G. (1973a) 'Ante-natal identification of women liable to have problems in managing their infants', *B.J. Psychiatry*, 123, 149.

Frommer, E.A. and O'Shea, G. (1973b) 'The importance of childhood experience in relation to problems of marriage and family building', *B.J. Psychiatry*, 123, 157.

Gayford, J.J. (1975) 'Wife battering – a preliminary survey of 100 cases'. *B.M.J.* 5951.

Geddis, D.C., Turner, I.F. and Eardley, J. (1977) 'Diagnostic value of a psychological test in cases of suspected child abuse', *Archives of Disease in Childhood*, 52, 708–12.

Greenland, C. (1979) 'A checklist to recognize a possible situation for child abuse'. *Contact*, McMaster Univ. 10, 23.

Hanson, R., McCulloch, W. and Hartley, S. (1978) 'Key characteristics of child abuse'. In: A. White Franklin (Ed.), *Child Abuse*, Churchill Livingstone.

Harlow, H.F. and Harlow, M.K. (1969) 'Effects of various mother-infant relationships on rhesus monkey behaviour'. In: B. Foss (Ed.) *Determinants of Infant Behaviour*, Methuen.

Howells, J.G. (1975) 'Deaths from non-accidental injuries in childhood'. *B.M.J.* 5984, 13 September.

Howells, J.G. and Lickorish, J.R. (1962) *Manual for the Family Relations Indicator*, National Foundation for Educational Research, Slough.

Jackson, L. (1952) *A Test of Family Attitudes*, Methuen.

Jobling, M. (1976) *The Abused Child. An Annotated Bibliography*, National Children's Bureau.

Jones, C. Okell (1978) 'Meeting the needs of abused children', *Social Work Today*, 9, 26, 9–14.

Keen, J.H., Landrum, J. and Wolman, B. (1975) 'Inflicted burns and scalds in children', *B.M.J.* 5991, 1 November.

Kempe, R.S. and Kempe C.H. (1978) *Child Abuse*, Fontana/Open Books Original.

Klaus, M.H. and Kennel, J.H. (1976) *Maternal-Infant Bonding*, St. Louis: C.V. Mosby.

Lambeth, Southwark and Lewisham Area Health Authority (Teaching); the Inner

London Probation and After Care Committee; and the London Borough of Lambeth (1975) *Report of the Joint Committee of Inquiry into Non-Accidental Injury to Children with particular reference to the Case of Lisa Godfrey*, London Borough of Lambeth.

Lynch, M.A. (1978) 'The prognosis of child abuse', *J.Child Psychol. Psychiat.*, 19, 175–80.

Lynch, M.A. and Roberts, J. (1978) 'Early alerting signs'. In: A. White Franklin (Ed.), *Child Abuse*, Churchill Livingstone.

Lynch, M.A. and Roberts, J. (1977) 'Prediction of child abuse – signs of bonding failure in the maternity hospital', *B.M.J.* 1, 624.

Martin, H.P. (Ed.) (1976) *The Abused Child: A Multi-disciplinary Approach to Development Issues and Treatment*, Ballinger, Cambridge, Mass.

Martin H.P. and Beezley, P. (1977) 'Behavioural observations of abused children', *Devl. Med. Child Neurol.*, 19, 373–87.

Norfolk County Council, and Norfolk Area Health Authority (1976) *Report of the Review Body Appointed to Enquire into the Case of Steven Meurs, 1975*, Norfolk County Council.

Oliver, J.E. (1975) 'Statistics of child abuse'. *B.M.J.* 5975, 12 July.

Oliver, J.E. and Cox, J. (1973) 'A family kindred with ill-used children', *B.J Psychiatry*, 123.

Pickford, R.W. (1963) *Pickford Projective Pictures*, Tavistock Publications.

Pizzey, E. (1974) *Scream Quietly or the Neighbours Will Hear*, Penguin.

Pringle, M. Kellmer (1978) The needs of abused children. In: Selwyn M. Smith (Ed.) *Maltreatment of Children*, MTP Press Ltd.

Pringle, M. Kellmer (1975) *The Needs of Children*, Hutchinson; New York, Schocken.

Pringle, M. Kellmer (1970) *Able Misfits*, Longman in association with National Children's Bureau.

Ringler, N.M., Kennell, J.H., Jarvella, R., Navojosky, B.J. and Klaus, M.H. (1975) 'Mother to child speech at 2 years: effects of early post-natal contact', *J. Paediatr. 86.* 141.

Roberts, J. (1978) 'Social work and child abuse'. In: J.P. Martin (Ed.) *Violence and the Family*, John Wiley, New York.

Rogers, D., Tripp, J., Bentovim, A., Robinson, A., Berry, A. and Goulding, R. (1976) 'Non-accidental poisoning: an extended syndrome of child abuse'. *B.M.J.* April 13, 793–6.

Rutter, M. and Madge, N. (Eds.) (1976) *Cycles of Disadvantage*, Heinemann Educational.

Smith, S.M. (1975) *The Battered Child Syndrome*, Butterworth.

Steele, B. (1975) *Working with Abusive Parents from a Psychiatric Point of View*, U.S. Department of Health, Education and Welfare, Office of Child Development, OHO 75-70.

Strauss, P. and Girodet, D. (1977) 'Three French follow-up studies of abused children,' *Child Abuse and Neglect*, 1. pp. 99–103.

15   Towards the Prevention of Child Abuse

Mia Kellmer Pringle

Prevention must be based on three principles. First, that early action is likely to be less damaging and more effective than crisis intervention which by its very nature places a premium on speed rather than well-considered judgment. Second, that prevention must promote the best interests of the child rather than merely remove him/her from harmful experiences. When parental care is so damaging that alternative care has to be provided, then this must not only be better in the sense of being conducive to optimal development, but also therapeutic in the sense of healing the damage done, be it emotional, social, intellectual or physical. Otherwise there is a high risk of to-day's child becoming tomorrow's abusing parent.

Third, prior to an abused child being returned to his parents it is essential to apply very rigorous criteria to prevent re-injury or continued ill-treatment. On the basis of his own work, Kempe (1978) suggests 'four objective changes' which need to have taken place: the abusive parent must have made at least one friend with whom he shares regular and enjoyable experiences; both parents must have found something attractive in their abused child and be able to show it by talking lovingly, hugging or cuddling; both parents must have learned to use lifelines in moments of crisis; and brief reunions with their child must become increasingly enjoyable. If all four criteria are not met then, Kempe warns, it is premature to allow the child's return to his parents: 'he will be attacked again, and probably much more severely. Of course, it is very important to be sure that the reason for the family's improvement is not the absence of the child because, if so, his return will obviously reverse the process.'

Some may argue that not enough is known to prevent child abuse and that the results of further research must be awaited. However, in my view a simile from the medical field illustrates more accurately the present situation. Some years ago it became possible to vaccinate successfully against whooping cough or polio without understanding why a particular child was more liable to contract the disease or how to cure it. In the same way there is now a sufficient understanding of some of the broad preventive measures which could achieve a significant reduction in the incidence of child abuse. To bring this about, a major shift in public and professional attitudes must first take place.

Then the adoption of three measures would go a long way towards preventing child abuse. The first is the introduction of developmental checks for all children and a comprehensive assessment of every suspected case. The second is the provision of an independent voice for every child who is 'at risk'. The third, preparation for parenthood, is essentially a long-term measure.

Changing professional and public attitudes

First and foremost it is essential that in all cases of abuse the balance should be tilted much more in favour of the child's interests and rights rather than those of the biological parents. This means making his/her long-term need for continuing, consistent and dependable loving care of paramount importance instead of, as at present, considering mainly the probability of future physical ill-treatment. When such care seems unlikely, then permanent separation or 'divorce' of the child from his family should become an option to be considered more frequently and earlier than is currently the case.

If psychological well-being were to be given equal weight with physical safety, then no child would be allowed to return to an environment where his all-round development would continue to be impeded or distorted. The criterion should be that a marked improvement has taken place, or can be expected with a high degree of confidence, in a previously damaging milieu. Clearly the more immature, disturbed or unstable the parents, and the more punitive or depriving their attitude to the child, the less realistic it is to expect such improvement. In these circumstances, the child's need for loving care should take precedence in law over the rights of the biological parents.

Professional attitudes need to change also in relation to the compulsory notification of child abuse; without it, the true incidence is unlikely ever to come to light. Resistance to this idea tends to be justified on the grounds of confidentiality, a breach of which, so it is argued, would damage the relationship of trust between a patient/client and his professional advisor. Yet recent evidence from New South Wales, Australia, might provide grounds for a reconsideration of this attitude. When a law was passed obliging doctors to report their suspicions, the number of known battered children tripled within 12 months.

A further change in professional attitudes relates to the need to shift the whole burden of responsibility for recognizing and dealing with abusing parents and abused children from social workers to a broadly based team drawn from many disciplines. In every case, at least a general practitioner, paediatrician, psychologist and a lawyer should be involved and often a health visitor, teacher, psychiatrist and police officer may also have to be brought in. Of course, these and other professional workers are already participating in case conferences but are less often directly responsible for the assessment, treatment and rehabilitation of every member of the family.

Both investigation and decision-making must in future become a truly shared task. Such sharing of responsibility seems essential not only because of the complex social and psychological factors underlying rejecting or violent parental behaviour, but also because no single profession can be expected either to have the necessary expertise or to bear unaided the strain involved in this work.

In addition to creating a climate of opinion which gives paramountcy to the interests of children, greater public awareness needs to be brought about regarding the likely incidence of child abuse. Few people realize that the present minimum estimate is that about 300 children in England and Wales are killed by their parents every year, about 3,000 receive serious injuries (including permanent brain damage) and another 40,000 are victims of assault. The media have an influential and responsible part to play in changing people's reluctance to 'interfere'. Getting across the realization that the sheer survival of a small child may be at stake may make neighbours, shopkeepers and tradesmen prepared to convey what they know to someone with authority to investigate the situation.

Developmental checks and comprehensive assessments

Regular developmental checks, at least for under-fives, have been shown by a large-scale French project, started 10 years ago, to be a cost-effective undertaking (Strauss & Girodet, 1977). Handicaps are detected at an early stage and hence the need for lengthy hospital treatment is reduced. Cost-benefit studies also show that the earlier intervention and treatment take place, the lower the cost and the greater the benefits (Wynn, 1976). Because the youngest age group is the most vulnerable, their need for such checks is the greatest. If introduced as a universal service, it would in no way stigmatize families where there is the highest risk of child abuse.

Those of pre-school age are at greatest risk because if ill-treated they can neither 'tell' nor even run away. Hence between birth and three years of age the checks should be at least once every six months, and then up to the age of five years at nine-monthly intervals.

To reduce costs, a first screening could be carried out by a health visitor. If there is any cause for anxiety, then a full developmental

222

assessment should follow. This must be multi-disciplinary, covering all areas of growth. Hence both a paediatrician and a psychologist will be involved to begin with, then calling on other specialists as required.

Achieving complete coverage

Only by achieving near-complete coverage of all children can it be hoped to prevent or at least reduce the incidence of child abuse. One way of doing so would be to offer a special incentive payment to mothers who seek the required screening and full assessment when needed; however, economic considerations and possibly current public attitudes too, are likely to preclude the introduction of such a new benefit at present. An alternative would be to link developmental checks to the payment of family allowances. No doubt some will reject this suggested sanction as being unwarranted state intrusion into the privacy of family life. Critics may also argue that it is unnecessary to enforce developmental checks for all children when only a minority are likely to be either handicapped, rejected or abused. However, to judge from the French experience, this minority is very sizeable, at least one in three infants.

Others may fear that parents of poor children will be penalized because they may for a number of good reasons be unable to take them for regular checks. But these could take place in their own homes or in day-care facilities in which many of the most dis-advantaged under-fives are placed. The number of health visitors would have to be considerably increased to make this possible. However, it would pay to do so since the hospital services required to treat handicapped and abused children are much more costly.

Parental right to privacy has to be balanced against another right which ought to concern society equally – the right of a child to loving care and protection both of his physical and mental health. After all, the state gives an allowance to parents in order to encourage good child care. Is it not common sense and good housekeeping to ensure that such care is in fact being provided? And if it is deficient, then to compensate for what is lacking or, if it is too damaging, then to find alternative care?

Comprehensive, multi-disciplinary assessments

Until regular and frequent developmental checks are available to all infants, it is essential that a comprehensive, multi-disciplinary assessment is undertaken in every suspected case of child abuse. Early warning signs must always be heeded to prevent more serious damage. Among these are 'failure to thrive', avoidance of eye contact and, when with adults, withdrawal, silence, lack of smiling, apparent distrust and 'frozen watchfulness'. Another sign is if a child's appearance, weight, behaviour and relationships improve on going to hospital or when placed in a foster home; then rejection or abuse should be suspected, since removing well-cared infants from familiar, secure surroundings has the opposite effect.

At present, there is a multiplicity of assessment services, located in hospitals, assessment centres of social services departments, in school psychological services and in child guidance clinics. This is not only wasteful, but not infrequently leads to expensive duplication. The manpower resources required for assessment are both highly skilled and expensive. Hence, almost by definition, they are likely to remain scarce. An amalgamation of these various services would not only be cost effective but might also be the first step in learning how to bring the various professions together in an interdependent, effective working relationship.

The child guidance service has for some years been under a cloud, with its long term future uncertain and controversial. Yet it is, and has been from the outset, a truly multi-disciplinary service where the basic team consists of a doctor, a psychologist and a social worker. This is not the place to consider why child guidance has become something of a backwater during the past 10 years or so. It could, however, provide the prototype pattern for the assessment of all children whose development is causing concern, or who are considered to be 'at risk' – the socially disadvantaged, the educationally handicapped, those failing to thrive physically, children with physical or sensory handicap, the truant and delinquent, the emotionally disturbed child and those deprived of a normal family life who have to be received into care because their own parents are unable or unwilling to look after them. Among all these groups a proportion will be found to have been neglected, rejected or even abused by their parents or parent substitutes, either physically, psychologically or both.

The role of the school

Once children go to school they come under the daily care of a trained professional person for a period of 11 years. Hence schools could potentially play a crucial role in prevention. Yet so far they have not done so in this country, unlike their American counterpart. There increasing participation has started to take place in recent years through a variety of child protection programmes involving both teachers and school children (Broadhurst, 1978). Partly as a result of this work, two-thirds of the cases of child abuse and neglect reported in 1975 were found to involve school children between the ages of five and 17 years. This finding runs counter to the commonly accepted view that it is the under-fives, and young infants in particular, who are at greatest risk of abuse.

Further work is needed to reveal whether this is yet another undiscovered iceberg which comes to light only when the spotlight is turned on to older children. After all, a mere 25 years ago child abuse and the 'battered baby syndrome' were virtually unsuspected and unknown in the United States (Woolley & Evans, 1955; Kempe et al., 1962). In this country, the fact that cases of multiple fractures of the long bones of infants and other injuries may be caused not by disease but by the violent actions of parents or other care-givers received attention even later (Griffiths & Moynihan, 1963; Cameron et al., 1966).

Stemming from an increased involvement of schools in child abuse, most have reported a significant increase in the number of identified cases. 'Where schools have taken an active role in discovering and preventing child abuse and neglect, the result has been to help hundreds of families and children at risk. Each of them is a compelling reason for school systems everywhere to become involved' (Broadhurst, 1978). Surely this applies to Britain with equal force?

In fact in the case of Maria Colwell – the first to arouse public attention – a teacher was very aware of the child's rapid physical and mental deterioration and tried to get help for her. To enable teachers to play an active part in prevention, they would benefit from some in-service training to as to become more skilled in recognizing early warning signs and to know the courses of action open to them to protect the child.

'Child abuse, even if we exclude emotional deprivation, is a very widespread problem, and the consciousness is growing that traditional child-protection agencies are simply not equal to it . . . they cannot possibly bring to bear all the skills this multi-faceted problem requires. What is needed, and what is now beginning to be created, is a new and more broadly based approach that will draw more effectively on the resources of the community' (Kempe & Kempe, 1978).

An independent voice for the child at risk

'Many judges in Great Britain still demand the sorts of proof they would demand in a criminal case even in a civil case involving simply taking a child into care. For centuries the child has been a chattel in common law, and still today for many judges the rights of children are not yet nearly so important as the rights of parents'. This is the view of the foremost experts on child abuse (Kempe & Kempe, 1978). They argue that 'one radical but effective move to improve children's safety would be to make them full citizens, entitled to all rights except the vote.'

As recently as 1977, the Official Solicitor expressed the view that 'it is only in a minority of cases that the court would benefit from representation of a child's point of view by an advocate' (House of Commons, 1977). Though the House of Commons Select Committee accepted this view, at least it did recommend that 'the supervisor of an abused child should be given legal authority to visit the child or to obtain a medical examination'. Welcome though this recommendation is, it in no way affects what seems to me a strong case for giving all abused children the right to an independent spokesman who would ensure that their views and feelings are heard and taken into account.

At present, it is only in adoption proceedings that courts are required by statute to give consideration to the child's wishes; many of them are too young to make this a reality. In contrast, the age range of children who are abused or rejected, or involved in custody cases, spans the whole period of childhood right into adolescence. Paradoxically, these are denied the right to be heard and to have an independent spokesman.

A small step forward.

The 1975 Children Act takes a small step towards changing the situation, but it still has two serious drawbacks. First, when there is a potential conflict of interest between parent and child, courts are to have discretion to appoint an 'independent social worker' or solicitor or both to act for the child. But common sense and elementary justice demand that in all such situations the child's voice should be heard as of right. Hence this provision should be mandatory.

Secondly, an 'independent social worker' in this context means that he or she will be working for a different local authority from the one concerned with the parents and child. This seems unsatisfactory for a number of reasons. To start with, would not such a worker's first loyalty be (quite understandably) to his professional colleagues and, though to a lesser extent perhaps, to the viewpoint taken by another local authority? Next, I doubt whether hard-pressed social workers could take on this additional commitment on the scale required if all children in need were to be given a voice. Equally, if not more important, child care skills have, in my view, markedly declined during the past 10 years, because of the change in social work ethos resulting from the Seebohm reorganisation.

Who then should undertake the role of spokesman? I see it as work akin to that being done by the Samaritans or Marriage Guidance Counsellors: a responsible job undertaken on behalf of the community by specially appointed lay people. In fact, a report from the Manchester Branch of the Samaritans (March, 1979) recorded that some 15% of its 35,000 phone calls during 1978 were from children, some as young as eight years. This shows that even without a service specially designed to meet their needs, unhappy children are seeking adult support.

In order to provide an independent voice, a spokesman would require firsthand experience of children; some basic training in child development would also be essential. For particularly difficult cases (especially very young infants) the spokesman would need to call on the services of someone with a systematic and thorough knowledge of children's development and of how to observe and to communicate with them, such as child psychologists, paediatricians, child psychiatrists or those social workers who have specialized in this field.

What difference might a spokesman have made to Maria Colwell?

By getting to know six-year old Maria while she was still living with her foster-parents, the spokesman would have seen a child well-loved by them and whom she loved in return; who was happy, well behaved, mixing normally with other children and making good progress at school. He would also have observed that when she was made to visit her mother's home Maria began to show clear signs of stress, and when she was made to stay overnight, she objected most strenuously and, in fact, ran away several times half-dressed and barefoot.

These signs the spokesman would have recognized as early warning signals of great strain and unhappiness. Nor would he have needed much skill to find out Maria's feelings since she was making them only too clear. But his training would have made him aware that running away, for example, is a much more serious symptom in a six than a 13-year-old, as is soiling by a child who had previously been clean.

Since the spokesman would be trying to see the situation through the child's eyes, determining what seemed in her best long-term interests, he would also have been given access to all the relevant background information. Knowing that Maria's foster parents had lovingly cared for her since babyhood would have been as relevant as knowing that of her mother's nine children, six had been taken into care because of being neglected and had remained in care since early childhood, that during a recent three-year period the mother had had

227

no fewer than 19 different addresses, that the stepfather-to-be had several aliases and a criminal record including violence, and that her three children by him were not only often unkempt and dirty, but that neighbours were alleging they were being left alone at night.

Having discovered Maria's wishes, the spokesman's second task would have been to brief a lawyer on her behalf when the question of her care was being disputed in a court of law. Even if all the evidence had nevertheless failed to persuade the court to respect Maria's wish to remain with her foster-parents, the spokesman would still have been able to offer her some protection. For the third task of the spokesman would be to keep in touch with every child who is 'transplanted' from one family to another to ensure that the transplant has 'taken'. Also he would insist that there should be some continuity of contact with former parental figures and that contingency plans are available in case the transplant fails. The spokesman could meet these tasks only if he had the right to see the child alone, even if the 'new' parents denied access to their home. Had these principles been in force at the time, Maria might well be alive today.

It would have become quite evident to the spokesman after a short time that the 'transplant' was not succeeding. The dramatic deterioration of the child's physical and mental condition would have been a clear indication that something was going seriously wrong. Moreover, the spokesman would have been able to hear of Maria's distress from several other people. At least two teachers were deeply worried; several neighbours expressed their concern to the authorities on a number of occasions; and a local shopkeeper had objected so strongly to this small child having to heave heavy sacks of coal (equal to about two-thirds of her own weight) up the road to her home that she threatened to cease selling them unless Maria was given some sort of conveyance (an outsize pram was then provided by her mother).

In fact, Maria was to remain imprisoned (on occasions quite literally locked in a room) with people she had every reason to fear. She was forcibly restrained from ever seeing again the foster-parents she had loved and trusted for most of her life. And there was no one to whom she could even talk about them or about what was being done to her.

Within a period of 15 months Maria changed from a happy, responsive, well-mannered child to being totally withdrawn, solitary, depressed, sitting for hours staring into space and not responding to children or adults. Clearly she was in a state of severe shock and deep mourning for the parents she had lost.

'Independent social workers'

Under new legislation which was enacted after Maria's death, she would have had as of right an 'independent social worker' to speak for her. But this would not necessarily have led to a different outcome because of two widely held social work tenets. One is that a child should wherever possible grow up with his or her biological family, since otherwise he or she would face an 'identity crisis' in adolescence. Yet there is little evidence that this is inevitably so. On the contrary, adoption provides vulnerable, and even damaged children with a second chance, even if they are placed with their new families long after infancy (Bohman, 1971; Kadushin, 1970; Seglow et al., 1972). What is also well-documented is that children whose early life is extremely stressful and who fail to have mutually satisfying relationships with parental figures, become emotionally very vulnerable and prone to serious behaviour difficulties in later life.

The other belief is that stressing the importance of psychological rather than biological parents is a device for providing childless middle-class couples with children from inadequate working-class homes. In fact, this is a quite unwarranted slur on working-class families. It is exposed for the nonsense it is in Maria's case: her working-class foster-parents showed her the loving care and concern typical of the great majority of such parents.

Just as the 1975 Children Act made it possible to appoint an independent advocate for children caught in a 'tug-of-love' battle, whether between divorced parents, would-be adoptive parents, foster-parents or relatives, so a lay spokesman should be introduced and become mandatory for every abused child before the decision is taken whether he or she should return to those who have abused him or her.

The official Colwell report fails to make what seems to me a most significant point. Even if Maria had survived there would have been major if not irreparable psychological scars resulting from the devastating damage to her emotional development. Actual battering is only the visible tip of the iceberg of emotional rejection and abuse, suffered daily by many thousands of children in this country. Surely a civilized society should strive to eliminate such suffering? A genuinely independent spokesman for children would be a first step in this direction.

Preparation for parenthood

This is the third measure which is not only the most basic but also inevitably more long-term than the other two discussed previously. Its aim would be to raise the level of children's emotional, social and intellectual development in a way similar to that in which their physical health has been improved during the past 40 years. The starting point would be the recognition that modern parenthood is too demanding and complex a task to be performed well merely because every adult has once been a child. Indeed it is about the only such skilled task for the performance of which no knowledge or training is expected or required. To improve the quality of family care, wide-ranging changes in the attitudes to parenthood and child rearing will have to be brought about (Pringle, 1975 and 1979).

Probably the most effective way would be to make available to all young people a programme of preparation for parenthood. What is required is neither a narrow course, seen as a branch of biology or home economics, nor a very wide general one in citizenship; the model of sex education is not appropriate either; nor should such a programme be confined to girls, and the less able ones at that, as tends to happen at present. Nor should such a programme be confined to schools.

Instead, a knowledge of human psychology would be the foundation and would include the dynamics of behaviour, the ways in which people interact and react at a great variety of levels, the role of values and the roots of prejudice. The opportunity to acquire a fairly sophisticated understanding of the sequential nature of human development, of the various stages of physical and mental growth, of motivation and of the wide variations in behaviour, including deviancy, would complement and supplement what children will have learnt already in their own homes.

Providing an effective programme

To be effective a programme of preparation for parenthood should have this broad base of human psychology and child development. Sex education, family planning, home economics and political education as well as first-hand practical experience of babies and young children would form an integral part of the programme.

Few schools do as yet provide such a broadly based scheme but the vast majority have for some time been offering their pupils sex education. With hindsight, this may have done more harm than good: an appropriate perspective on this topic is likely to be achieved only within the context of affectionate, mutually responsible relationships between the sexes rather than within the narrower biological setting of reproductive processes, childbirth, contraception and venereal diseases. Significantly enough, the need for a wider programme is well appreciated by young people themselves (Fogelman, 1976).

Developing programmes of preparation for parenthood in all

schools would be a first step towards translating into practice the belief that children are society's seedcorn for the future. Concern for improving the quality of life must start with the young of today. To begin with, they should be helped to achieve a more realistic understanding of parenthood long before they decide whether or not to become parents. This should be based on an objective appreciation of its demands, constraints, satisfactions and challenges.

Home-making and parenting, especially motherhood, are simultaneously both under- and over-valued. On the one hand, the housewife with young children is described and treated as not being gainfully employed even though her working hours are usually twice as long as those of the 35-hour-a-week worker. On the other hand, an over-romanticized picture of motherhood prevails in our society, reinforced by the media.

Instead, a more truthful, even daunting, awareness needs to be created of the arduous demands which child-rearing makes not only on the emotions, energy and time, but also on financial resources. These are most acutely felt when the first baby comes along. The inevitable constraints on personal independence, freedom of movement and, indeed, one's whole way of life, require to be spelt out. Babies should be presented as they are, warts and all, rather than as heart-warmingly attractive, invariably sunny tempered with a dimply, angelic smile.

For this realistic portrayal to be believed, it must be seen to be true – hence the importance of first-hand experience with babies and young children. There are many different ways in which this could be provided. What is vital is that it should be viewed in the same way as laboratory work in chemistry or physics – work to be done regularly for a considerable period of time. In this way, the physical care required by babies and toddlers will also come to be appreciated more realistically than by using dolls as models.

Family planning – age and size

Postponing parenthood until both partners are fully mature is in the best interest not only of their own long-term relationship but also of their future child. Similarly, family planning can be linked with the concept that responsible parenthood means having only as many children as a couple can emotionally tolerate and financially afford. This fact is demonstrated by evidence showing that in general children from large families are at a disadvantage physically, educationally and in terms of social adjustment.

Family size begins to exert an unfavourable influence right from birth onwards, high perinatal mortality being associated with high

231

parity. Nor is it solely a question of low income and thus a lower standard of living: effects of family size upon development operate irrespective of social class. When parental time, attention, and maybe also patience, have to be shared, then less is available for each child. Thus large families put a strain on both financial and psychological resources. The fact that some parents successfully rear large families does not invalidate the general picture.

Promoting and supporting good parenting

Preparation for parenthood in one sense starts at birth since a child learns about it through his own experience of family life. However, those deprived of adequate parental care have little chance of becoming in turn responsible parents themselves. In any case, it might raise both the status and the level of parenting if the total population were to receive some direct preparation for the task. The earliest, and in a sense best, opportunity to achieve this occurs with school children because they are a captive audience.

To be fully effective, subsequent opportunities must continue to be available for young people, including couples expecting their first child, to prepare themselves for parenthood. Youth organizations, centres for further and adult education, advice and counselling services for young people as well as pregnancy advisory, maternity and marriage guidance services, all have a part to play in this task (Pugh, 1979). If such opportunities became freely and readily available, then the parental life style may come to be chosen more deliberately in the fuller realization of its responsibilities and satisfactions.

Abstaining from violence against children

Perhaps child abuse and its prevention ought to be considered within the wider context of physical chastisement. In this country it is practised against children both by their parents and those standing *in loco parentis* as a means of 'disciplining' them. Teachers are most likely to use an instrument, such as the cane or tawse, for corporal punishment and it is most frequently employed in secondary schools. Some 80% do so to a greater or lesser extent (Fogelman, 1976). In contrast, parents are more likely to use a hand only and to punish younger children. However, as many as 62% of parents were found to smack their one-year-olds and 93% their four-year olds, 17% of whom were smacked at least once a day (Newson, 1970).

Yet surely it is generally accepted that the aim of discipline – if it is to be effective – must lead to self-discipline and self-control. Physical punishment is therefore ineffective in a number of ways. To begin with, it produces modified behaviour mainly while the threat of being observed or discovered is present. Next, it primarily promotes greater ingenuity so as to avoid being detected. That its effect in changing behaviour is limited, is demonstrated by the fact that all too often the same pupils are repeatedly punished; some of them may even come to be regarded as heroes by their fellows because of their ability to withstand beatings. Any deterrent effect on others – again only while the threat is present – is likely to be outweighed by the feelings of hostility, particularly in the more thoughtful and sensitive, aroused by witnessing the indignity inflicted time and again on their classmates.

Research confirms (Fogelman, 1976) that corporal punishment is disliked by children and young people, contrary to the assertions of the opposite by its supporters. Last, but by no means least, it is to some extent even counter-productive since it teaches the child an unintended but nonetheless obvious lesson that 'might is right' and hence if you are bigger you can intimidate and hit those smaller or weaker than yourself. Conversely, children are better behaved in schools where corporal punishment is not used (Rutter et al., 1979).

As a society we now disapprove of violence against the person and express particular disapproval of violent behaviour by children. Also all forms of physical punishment have now been abolished by law in the armed forces, in prisons, borstals and detention centres. So is it not illogical as well as unjust that there is such general acceptance of corporal punishment of children? Is it not hypocritical to condemn their physical aggression when we practise it on them as a matter of course and disingenuous when we profess to set children an example of how to behave by the way we ourselves do? And is such a climate of opinion not bound to reduce the threshold at which parents are prepared to use grave physical violence against even quite young babies?

Anyone training dogs or other animals knows that the infliction of pain is not a good method of bringing about desired behaviour – why then do we continue to believe it to be so in relation to the human young? Moreover, in our society people consume a vast array of medicines and drugs in an endeavour to escape discomfort and pain. Why then do we continue to cling to the belief that pain inflicted on the young is educative and morally reforming?

Maybe child abuse will only be eradicated when we determine that the time has come to condemn and abstain from all physical punishment of children as we have for so many years now abolished its use against adults.

Towards Prediction and Prevention

REFERENCES

Bohman, M. (1971) 'A comparative study of adopted children, foster children and children in their biological environment born after undesired pregnancies'. *Acta Paediatrica Scandinavica*, Supplement No. 3221.

Broadhurst, D.D. (1978) 'What schools are doing about child abuse and neglect'. *Children Today*, 7, pp. 22–36.

Cameron, J.M., Johnson, J.R.M. and Camps, F.E. (1966) 'The battered child syndrome'. *Medicine, Science and the Law*, 6, pp. 2–21.

Department of Health and Social Security (1974) *Report of the Committee of Inquiry into the Care and Supervision provided in relation to Maria Colwell*, HMSO, London.

Fogelman, K. (Ed) *Britain's Sixteen Year Olds*. National Children's Bureau, London.

Griffiths, D.L. and Moynihan, F.J. (1963) 'Multiple epiphyseal injuries in babies (battered baby syndrome)'. *British Medical Journal*, No. 5372, pp. 1558–61.

House of Commons (1977) *Violence to Children. First Report for the Select Committee on Violence in the Family.*, HMSO, London.

Jobling, M. (1976) *The Abused Child: An Annotated Bibliography*. National Children's Bureau, London.

Kadushin, A. (1971) *Adopting Older Children*. Columbia University Press, New York.

Kempe, R.S. and Kempe, C.H. (1978) *Child Abuse*. Fontana/Open books, London.

Kempe, C.H., Silverman, F., Steele, B., Droegmueller, W., and Silver, H. (1962) 'The battered child syndrome', *Journal of the American Medical Association*, 181, pp. 17–24.

Newson, J. and Newson, E. (1968) *Four Years Old in the Urban Community*. Allen and Unwin, London. Penguin, 1970.

Pringle, M. Kellmer (1975) *The Needs of Children*. Hutchinson, London.

Pringle, M. Kellmer (1979) *A Fairer Future*. Macmillan, London.

Pugh, G. (1979) *Preparation for Parenthood: Some Current Initiatives*, National Children's Bureau, London.

Rutter, M., Maughan, B., Mortimore, R. and Ouston, J. (1978) *15,000 Hours: Secondary Schools and their Effects on Children*. Open Books, London.

Seglow, J., Pringle, M. Kellmer and Wedge, P. (1972) *Growing Up Adopted*. NFER, Slough.

Strauss, P. and Girodet, D. (1977) 'Three French follow-up studies of abused children'. *Child Abuse and Neglect*, 1, pp. 99–103.

Woolley, P.V. and Evans, W.A. (1955) 'The significance of skeletal lesions in infants resembling those of traumatic origin'. *Journal of the American Medical Association*, 158, pp. 539–43.

Wynn, A. (1976) 'Health care systems for pre-school children'. *Proceedings of the Royal Society of Medicine*, 69, pp. 340–43.

NAME INDEX

236

SUBJECT INDEX

238